D1593678

DECADENT ENCHANTMENTS

CALIFORNIA STUDIES IN 19TH CENTURY MUSIC

Joseph Kerman, General Editor

DECADENT ENCHANTMENTS

The Revival of Gregorian Chant at Solesmes

KATHERINE BERGERON

UNIVERSITY OF CALIFORNIA PRESS

BERKELEY   LOS ANGELES   LONDON

University of California Press
Berkeley and Los Angeles, California

University of California Press, Ltd.
London, England

© 1998 by
The Regents of the University of California

Library of Congress Cataloging-in-Publication Data

Bergeron, Katherine, 1958–
    Decadent enchantments: the revival of Gregorian chant at
Solesmes / Katherine Bergeron.
        p.   cm.—(California studies in 19th century music ; 10)
    Includes bibliographical references and index.
    ISBN 0–520–21008–5 (alk. paper)
    1. Chants (Plain, Gregorian, etc.)—History and criticism.
    2. Abbaye Saint-Pierre de Solesmes.   I. Title.   II. Series.
    ML3082.B33   1998
    782.32'22'0094417—dc 21   97–24120
                                                                      CIP
                                                                      MN

Printed in the United States of America
9   8   7   6   5   4   3   2   1

To KFB and EHB,
    AMDG

Contents

Illustrations

Prelude

Ah! que le monde est grande à la clarté des lampes!
Aux yeux du souvenir que le monde est petit!
Charles Baudelaire

ike many first books, this one was a long time coming. Its origins could probably be traced as far back as 1978, the year I learned about Gregorian chant in a classroom at Wesleyan University. At that point in my undergraduate education (it was already the fall semester of my junior year) I had experienced a fair number of such firsts—quite enough to have had my musical mind blown several times over. I could mention, for instance, the wholly otherworldly performance of Sun Ra and his Intergalactic Arkestra (my first jazz concert); or the lessons in solkatu, solfège, and Shona song (my first class in species counterpoint); or the electronic inventions of Alvin Lucier (my first experimental music); or the autumn Navaratri festival, or the all-night *wayang* (my first non-Western musics). Not to mention other, singular events: an afternoon of sonic meditation guided by Pauline Oliveros; a chance meeting with John Cage. The unfamiliar sound of chant found its place among these experiences, a voice from history unmistakably tinged, like virtually all of the repertories in the Wesleyan curriculum, with strange and compelling otherness.

But my study of chant also stood apart from these musics, for in learning something about its theory I felt I was not just discovering another unknown musical tradition but, in effect, rediscovering my own. It was a tradition that had slipped by a whole generation of Catholics who, like me, had come of age after the Second Vatican Council, a generation raised on the flat vernacular of the suburban Church, with its plain-clothed celebrants and folksy guitar masses. For us, knowledge of the Latin liturgy had become esoteric, relegated to university curricula. The secrets of its music now lay in the hands of our professors, not our priests.

I approached this new music with an odd admixture of curiosity and piety. I remember the pleasure of copying, by hand, the mysterious medieval notations of the gradual "Justus ut palma florebit," using facsimiles that my professor had xeroxed from an equally mysterious source called *Paléographie musicale*. I remember learning to read the exotic square notation printed in the *Liber Usualis*—a fat, beribboned service book with chants for the entire liturgical year. And of course I remember listening to the chant on record, elegant performances whose languid melodies reverberated through stereo speakers as if from a remote place. Each of these sources—manuscript, score, LP—left their mark, giving the impression of a music lodged in the depths of history, an image that of course stood in stark contrast to the superficial church music I already knew. But these sources had something else in common, something that surely enhanced the mystique of the esoteric music they contained: they bore the name of an order of monks called the Benedictines of Solesmes. Who were these cloistered figures, and how did their work come to occupy such a prominent position in the modern university? Answering the question is the project of this book.

My account begins where the story of Solesmes begins: in France of the 1830s, among a generation of intellectuals preoccupied with the idea of rebuilding the past, a past they did not know but imagined lost in the political wreckage of the previous century's Revolution. Among the institutions pulled from this ideological rubble were the French Church and its broken monastic traditions. Through a perfect accident of Romantic history, it was not in Paris but in a bucolic hamlet called Solesmes that this restoration first took shape. A local seminarian named Prosper Guéranger—the first character in our story—undertook to reestablish an order of Benedictine monks within an abandoned priory known to him since childhood. This meant recovering all kinds of artifacts of the monastic life vanished in the folds of history, artifacts that Guéranger himself had obviously never seen intact—not just buildings and books but the whole collection of practices aptly summarized in the notion of habit. To be sure, the most elusive of such habits were musical: the repeated acts of singing that marked the hours in the monastery, giving shape to the monastic day. The complete restoration of the musical practice, begun under Guéranger, would require the work of at least two more generations of Benedictines over another half century. What these nineteenth-century monks eventually produced was the music still taught in university classrooms as the oldest surviving genre of European music, the repertory we know today as Gregorian chant.

The history of this revival embraces two more characters, largely forgotten figures from our musical past, who worked in the last decades of the nineteenth century to rebuild the Gregorian corpus not only in performance but in print, restoring medieval authenticity to an age of mechanical reproduction. By 1880 Solesmes's first choirmaster, Dom Joseph Pothier, had conceived a performing edition so aesthetically complete that it alone, he believed, would call forth the beautiful, ineffable history of the ancient repertory. Within a few years Pothier's younger *confrère* Dom André Mocquereau would attempt to improve on this antiquarian vision by publishing photographs of the oldest manuscripts, exposing not so much the beauty as the truth of the chant through images filled with strange and illegible signs. Two monks, two media, two very different messages about the Gregorian past. My book is organized around this double vision, a disorder whose skewed perspective allows us both to reflect on the power of musical representation and—what may amount to the same thing—to rethink the very act of writing history at the fin de siècle.

It is perhaps not surprising that, perched on a hinge between two centuries, the figures of Pothier and Mocquereau should be seen to swing in such different directions, betraying historical orientations that might be called, for convenience' sake, Romantic and Modern. For Pothier, Gregorian history appeared as the aura of time imaginatively experienced by one who, standing at the end of the historical continuum, looks back—collecting the accumulated residue of the past into a single aesthetic moment. For Mocquereau, such history reappeared as a new beginning, a field of possibilities so vast that its ultimate truth, though glimpsed in the present, could only be assigned to some distant future. In one case, then, the historian imagines himself the repository of a broken past that he would seek to rebuild whole; in the other, the historian engages in a process of accounting for that which must, by definition, remain in pieces—the particles of truth in whose collective totality the past slowly reveals itself.

These two orientations become clear not so much in manifestos as in music, that is, in the range of different Gregorian products created at Solesmes—the books and pictures and performances of chant that, as my own belated experience suggests, were to have a decisive impact on music history, or perhaps I should say on the history of music history. For the historical results of the Solesmes revival were indeed twofold: not only did the monks manage to reconstruct an ancient melodic corpus they had found in ruins, but in time they also developed a set of methods through which this very Gregorian reconstruction could again be broken down and analyzed in its smallest constituent parts. This secondary product of the chant revival—the modern analytical methodology first developed at Solesmes—eventually led to something like an alternate Gregorian performance practice, in the new positivistic science of musicology. What emerged at the beginning of the century as a Romantic dream had transformed itself, by century's end, into a discipline.

By sifting through the stages of this transformation, my book thus exposes an important archaeological layer in the history of our modern discipline. Yet my goal in such an excavation is not simply to turn up isolated shards of our musicological past for reexamination, to put a few neglected men and their works on display, like curios, in a narrative museum. It is, rather, to dig deep enough to find another *terra incognita*, the imaginary landscapes that form history's invisible core. For in exploring this original site of Gregorian musicology, what we sense above all is the irresistible pull of an ancient, unheard music on the historical imagination of an entire era. Guéranger sought to fill the space of an abandoned abbey with this unheard sound; Pothier and Mocquereau later attempted to capture its elusive forms in print, on photographic film, and on wax cylinders. These media would define the image of the repertory for many generations to come, an image of lost time that functioned, in turn, to shape the very idea of music history. If such acts of putting chant into the modern imagination constitute the origins of our discipline, then musicology comes into being, in a very literal sense, through the enchantment of history. It is this enchantment that my own historical narrative attempts to restore, listening into those places where history may not be able to speak, but only sing.

· · · · ·

A book that has taken so long to write has obviously accumulated a multitude of intellectual debts. The most outstanding of these surely belong to Jon Barlow and Richard Winslow of Wesleyan University, whose wildly different perspectives on the monks of Solesmes probably convinced me, long before I ever knew it, that the story of their music might someday be worth writing. Years later Harold Powers would help to clarify that conviction when, over coffee at an AMS meeting in Philadelphia, he casually suggested that I pursue the topic in a dissertation. My advisor Don Randel, allowing me the freedom to follow hunches in haphazard and often irresponsible ways, supported my early efforts and looked on benevolently as the project took unlikely turns into the realm of what might now be called the new musicology. Philip Bohlman and James Siegel inspired me to think about institutions and disciplines; Roger Parker disciplined my prose and put me on the trail of aesthetes like William Morris. And it was from the late Edward Morris, a mentor who taught me everything I know about French literature, that I first heard the magical name of Viollet-le-Duc.

By the time I managed to pursue this lead I had already begun the long process of turning my dissertation into a book, funded in part by a summer fellowship from the National Endowment for the Humanities, as well as by awards from the Hellman Family Faculty Fund and the Prytanean Alumni Association at the University of California, Berkeley. On two separate trips to Solesmes the current choirmaster, Dom Jean Claire, proved an endlessly kind and patient interlocutor, setting me straight on many points of history and style and allowing me access to invaluable materials from the Solesmes library. Closer to home, friends and colleagues on two coasts helped to coax the book into its present shape through their wise and compassionate criticisms. I wish to thank in particular Jane Bernstein, David Cohen, Marilyn Ivy, Timothy Hampton, Leslie Kirk, Lawrence Kramer, Celeste Langan, Michael Lucey, John Pemberton, and Ann Smock. John Emerson, who knows more about this period of chant history than any other living scholar, steered me toward several useful sources. David Hamilton supplied a copy of a much-needed article on Gregorian chant discography. Leslie Sprout and Anya Suschiszky delivered top-notch research assistance. Kathleen Karn and J. R. Challacombe provided photographic expertise. Wye Allanbrook, David Code, Susan McClary, Roger Parker, Harold Powers, Richard Taruskin, Gary Tomlinson, and Mary Ann Smart read drafts of the entire manuscript, offering inspired advice and saving me from several embarrassing errors.

I owe a special debt of thanks to Doris Kretschmer and Juliane Brand, my editors at University of California Press, who managed gracefully to nudge me toward the finish line; and to Joseph Kerman, who read and commented on so many versions of the manuscript I'd be surprised if he ever wanted to see the finished product. Finally, I could never have completed this project without the ears of Joseph Rovan, who brought what were often inchoate ideas to life by giving not just advice and encouragement but another, more musical gift: he listened.

1

Restoration and Decay

Restauration, s.f.: Le mot et la chose sont modernes.
Viollet-le-Duc, 1866

ess than a decade after the French National Assembly moved to expel all religious orders from the newly constituted republic, François Réné le Vicomte de Chateaubriand began writing his famous apologia for French Catholicism, *Génie du christianisme*. It was an enormously influential book. Reprinted in multiple editions within a few years of its publication in 1802, translated into four languages, this Bible of Romanticism restored integrity to a badly disintegrating postrevolutionary Church and reawakened popular religious sentiment through a series of proofs that were more emotional than rational, proofs intended, as Chateaubriand put it, "to summon all the charms of the imagination . . . all the interests of the heart."[1] In the awesome splendor of Christian ritual, the sublime poetry of tradition, Chateaubriand found compelling evidence for the "genius" of the Christian religion, an aesthetic truth so vast as to inspire nearly a thousand pages of swollen verse, nostalgic recollection, personal confession—an entire sentimental history.

It was an immense monument to faith erected in the face of ruins.[2] If the Church, as Chateaubriand acknowledged, had suffered damage under decades of Voltairianism, it finally toppled with the events of the Revolution. In the same year that the religious orders were abolished and the clergy refashioned into civil servants, the Church as a whole was bankrupted, its property having been placed, by decree of the Convention, "at the disposition of the nation." By the end of 1790 revolutionary legislation had effectively emptied the monasteries, convents, and cathedrals of France of their inhabitants and even of their furnishings. A new Commission on Monuments, established to supervise the transfer of property, set about moving cartloads of bronze and marble into vacant Parisian hotels and cloisters, now warehouses where they were to be inventoried, sorted, and then either sold, melted down for currency, or deposited for safekeeping.[3]

Many goods never made it that far. Citizens in the popular movements, eager to remake history with their own hands, had more expedient methods for disposing of the Church's ancient possessions. At the initiative of small groups of sans-culottes, monuments and churches literally toppled: revolutionaries stormed the evacuated buildings, looking to destroy anything that bore evidence of the glories of kings, the ages of despotic rule. In this bizarre, bloodless reign of terror the heads that rolled were made of stone. At Notre-Dame the faces of the life-sized medieval kings and bishops who loomed over the huge portals, surveying the faithful, were routinely cut off. Everywhere sacred treasuries were looted and interiors reduced to rubble. By 1794 the state of destruction was so severe that Abbé Grégoire, former bishop of Blois, issued a report to the Convention, coining the term *vandalisme* to define the nature of a new kind of criminal activity: the senseless destruction of historical monuments, of a nation's patrimony. "I created the word," the bishop recalled, "to kill the thing."[4] Vandalism was a revolutionary monster.

For Chateaubriand, whose royalist sentiments were barely disguised by his piety, the sight of a demolished Paris was devastating. More than halfway through *Génie du christianisme*, in a survey of the fine arts, he interrupts his exposition on the beauty of Christian monuments to consider "the ruins of those monuments," beginning with the obligatory Romantic confession: "All men take a secret delight in beholding ruins."[5] Of the two species of ruin Chateaubriand distinguishes, however, only "natural" ruins, those produced by the effects of time, created the so-called picturesque scene capable of inspiring such private pleasure. A view of crumbling stones softened by grass and flowers was said to stimulate introspection (a moral response) or feelings of sweet melancholy. Ruins produced through human destruction, by contrast, had little to do with time or nature.

Chateaubriand imagined the figure of Time, relieved of his scythe, looking on "astonished" as men "[laid] waste in the twinkling of an eye what it would have taken him whole ages to destroy." Far from picturesque, such ruins exhibited "nothing but the image of annihilation," an image that, to judge from this *souvenir*, seemed to provoke a complex reaction:

We were one day walking behind the palace of the Luxembourg, and were accidentally led to the very same Carthusian convent which Fontanes has celebrated. We beheld a church the roof of which had fallen in; the lead had been stripped from the windows, and the doorways blocked with upright planks. Most of the other buildings of the monastery no longer existed. Long did we stroll among the sepulchral stones of black marble scattered here and there upon the ground; some were completely dashed in pieces, others still exhibited some vestiges of inscriptions. We advanced to the inner cloister; there grew two wild plum trees amid high grass and rubbish. . . . The reflections which occurred to us in this place may be made by any of our readers. We left it with a wounded heart, and entered the contiguous suburb without knowing whither we went.[6]

The destroyed convent evidently produced an extreme disorientation ("we left . . . without knowing whither we went"), disrupting the natural continuity of things and events. Quite unlike the natural ruin, whose rounded contour and charming proliferation of flora—in short, the building's entire, organic patina— signaled the slow and inevitable passage of time, the scene of vandalism offered a dizzying image of accelerated ruin. Chateaubriand, mourning the loss, longed for the ruins of old where he imagined the past to be secure—an illusion Georg Simmel has described as the ruin's unique aspect, where the past, "with all its destinies and transformations," appears to be "gathered into an aesthetically perceptible present."[7] In man-made wreckage, one could experience no such security. The past seemed to vanish along with the very idea of the ruin, as if time itself were hammered into fragments, scattered among the remains no longer whole.

Even the pieces that had escaped immediate demolition, the monuments and tombs preserved in Parisian warehouses, remained, for Chateaubriand, poignant examples of revolutionary destruction. The *dépôt* operated by the painter Alexandre Lenoir at the former Convent of the Petits-Augustins, which housed specimens of statuary and tombs from the Middle Ages to the seventeenth century, became in effect the Republic's first museum when it opened its doors to the public in 1793.[8] In Chateaubriand's view, this makeshift museum simply failed to provide an adequate substitute for what it replaced:

> We are without a doubt under great obligation to the artist who gathered up the *débris* from our ancient sepulchres; but, as for the effects produced by the sight of these monuments, it still feels very much as though they have been destroyed. Crowded into a narrow space, divided by centuries, deprived of their harmonious ties with the antiquity of the temples and of the Christian cult, subservient only to the history of the arts, and not to that of morals or religion, *not even retaining so much as their dust,* they have ceased to speak either to the imagination or to the heart.[9]

It was dust that Chateaubriand regretted, its absence a subtle but powerful sign of the true destruction these monuments had suffered. Torn from the temples, wiped clean, they were divested of the very meaning their beclouded surfaces had apparently once conveyed: a notion of the status quo, of dead kings resting. The dusty tomb was, in this sense, akin to the moss-covered ruin whose timeworn exterior always communicated something significant about the passage of time, the "natural" order of things. What the Romantic believed lay in those powdery layers accumulated on ancient stone was something like history itself. The trace of natural decay revealed the survival of the past in the present. By shocking contrast, the sight of tidy tombs rearranged in Lenoir's protomuseum betokened a break with the past.

For the Romantic spectator, then, the violent dislocation of historic monuments offered an image not so much of decay as of debris. The sight of such fragmented remains could produce no meaningful "effects," to use Chateaubriand's word, because these broken pieces no longer possessed the aura of pastness. It was the very existence of debris, a vulgar index of revolutionary change, that seemed to enable this new, Romantic ideal of decay. Decay emerged as a countersign, a shadowy figure of not-change imagined, by necessity, as aura, to use Benjamin's word. Like the *génie* (spirit or ghost) of Christianity itself, this aura surrounding the now lamented natural ruin was a haunted sign, a ghostly specter of lost presence.[10] Decay as such, together with the idea of past plenitude it embodied, became poetic only at the moment when debris had effectively taken its place.

Restoration

Soon it was a question of picking up the pieces. By 1830 the losses that had stunned Chateaubriand into nostalgic reflection became charged with an apocalyptic sentiment that impelled a new generation of artists and intellectuals into action. In the wake of the July Revolution a sensitive child of the century such as Alfred de Musset could look on an even greater collection of demolished properties and bleakly consign his generation to a wreckage that was now, in effect, normalized: "We live on debris," he wrote, "as if the end of the world was coming."[11] Victor Hugo (and, after him, Montalembert) confronted the same spectacle with indignance rather than despair, taking up the pen ostensibly to forestall the apocalypse and to bemoan the changes being wrought almost daily on Paris's urban landscape. For the chaos witnessed by Hugo's generation belonged as much to random acts of revolutionary violence as to the more mundane whims of new landowners. As ancient properties continued to change hands, old buildings were acquiring an array of new and alarmingly unfamiliar faces. It was, in Hugo's view, a trend that had to stop.

In an essay of 1832 he ridiculed the barbaric destruction of France's historic property, declaring war on all such modern vandals, with Napoleonic urgency, and calling for legislation that would protect the nation's monuments from future damage:

> We must stop the hammer that mutilates the face of our country. One law alone would suffice. If only it would be passed. Whatever may constitute the rights accorded to property owners, the destruction of a historic and monumental edifice should never be permitted. . . . There are two things in a building: its function and its beauty. Its function

belongs properly to its owner, its beauty to everyone—to you, to me, to us all. To destroy it is thus to exceed one's rights.[12]

This call to beauty seemed to temper the apparently reactionary tone of Hugo's argument against vandalism, especially the intolerance of destruction that was, from a more liberal perspective, an essential, democratic by-product of revolution. Indeed, in order for Hugo to maintain the required liberal political stance of his generation, it became necessary, while ridiculing destruction, to displace onto the realm of aesthetics values formerly associated with wealth and privilege. A property owner could never be prevented in principle from turning a newly acquired cloister into a cotton mill; but if Hugo had his way the law would prohibit any alteration of the building's appearance. His argument sought to finesse the vexed question of ownership so as to focus exclusively on the idea of architectural "beauty"—a value Hugo now imbued with patriotic significance. Beauty belonged to everyone, "to you, to me, to us all." By this logic the aesthetic dimension of architecture became a populist value, more politically righteous, and finally more democratic, than debris.

Even Hugo's popular novel *Notre-Dame de Paris* (1831), while less overtly political than his diatribe against vandalism, attempted to "inspire a love of national architecture" by reconstructing, in prose, something of the cathedral's former beauty, the birthright of every French citizen. Hugo's text flaunted, amid quaint archaisms, an impressive lexicon of little-known architectural terms that eventually became fashionable with his bourgeois readership. (Reported among the trendier epithets in Parisian salons around 1834 were, for instance, the adjectives *gothique* and the rather more arcane *ogival*, a word referring to the decoratively pointed arch of the thirteenth century.)[13] If the novel could not restore to the edifice a sense of mystery and power by replacing actual stones—repairing, so to speak, some of the physical damage wrought by revolutionary violence— at least it provided a set of terms with which such a restoration could be imagined. The specialized discourse of Gothic architecture, through both its precision and its sheer exoticism, seemed to make available to the public a sense of what had been lost, and hence what was now at stake.

Hugo's literary efforts did in fact coincide with the establishment of several government agencies to oversee France's national treasures. Most of these offices had been founded through the efforts of the historian-turned-politician François Guizot, minister of public instruction during the 1830s. After having labored in the preceding decade alongside such historians as Lamartine, Thierry, Quinet, and Michelet to shape a new, nationalistic discipline of French history, Guizot turned to politics with the somewhat self-serving goal of putting that historical project to work: institutionalizing, in a word, the act of remembering the past.[14] From a

tangled bureaucracy of competing offices and committees (a compelling sign of
how zealously the state now took charge of supervising the nation's history), the
Commission des monuments historiques eventually emerged as the official vehicle for the preservation of France's architectural heritage.

The first and, from our perspective, unlikely candidate to be named inspector general of historic monuments for the state, serving in effect as its chief
archaeologist, was the noted writer and music critic Ludovic Vitet, perhaps best
known for the polemic he waged with Stendhal around 1828, in the pages of the
literary journal *Le Globe,* over the merits of Rossini, not to mention his extrav-
agantly public obsession with the Spanish mezzo-soprano Maria Malibran.[15]
Vitet assumed his new post in 1830, yielding it four years later to the even more
modish Prosper Mérimée. That such a position (some would say sinecure) might
suit a writer of fiction was amply demonstrated by some of the stories Mérimée
still found time to write, between official reports, during his lengthy tenure as
inspector general. Nowhere more amply, perhaps, than in his novella *Carmen,* a
petite drôlerie composed in 1845 that recounted the events of a refined archaeol-
ogist-narrator and his encounter with an outlaw and a Gypsy. The undisguisedly
autobiographical introduction to this little novel, presumably drawn from an
official document, presented the true story of Mérimée's discovery of a Roman
battlefield, then flowed, as if along a curl of smoke, into the central narrative, the
tale of Carmen. The effect was a story within a story that blurred the boundaries
between science and fantasy, history and the exotic. The skillful blending of fact
and fiction seemed to cloud the image of science, imbuing the archaeologist's
expedition with the same sort of captivating power that surrounded the story's
title character. In this tale, science itself was a *carmen*—a poem, a magic spell, a
charm. Mérimée revealed the element of fascination implicit in any quest for scientific knowledge, the irresistible attraction of archaeology revolving, like the
central narrative, around a seduction. To dig up dirt, to uncover traces of the past,
was thus to brush with the very thing that motivated fiction itself, the ever
renewable desire to imagine the unknown.[16]

In his capacity as a state official, however, Mérimée's attention was directed
toward a responsibility that exceeded the imaginative limits of fiction. His charge
was finally to oversee the restoration of the monuments he visited. The ultimate
result of this job was no doubt a little daunting, since it would be materialized
not just in words but in mortar and stone. Indeed, the task seemed to rival—in
sheer scale, at least—the huge volumes completed during the previous decades
by Guizot and the other so-called Restoration historians. These, too, were monuments, running to thousands of pages. Yet the texts could hardly match, page for
stone, the ambition of the new architectural undertakings. The most challenging
of all such projects conceived during Mérimée's leadership was also the most

prestigious: the repair of Hugo's beloved Notre-Dame, a task that virtually set the standard for architectural restoration in France for the rest of the century.

The job was awarded by competition in 1844 (just one year before *Carmen*) to a little-known architect, not quite a maverick but a figure considerably out of the mainstream, who also happened to be a friend of Mérimée's, the young Eugène-Emmanuel Viollet-le-Duc. The commission essentially made Viollet-le-Duc's reputation as one of the most important, even infamous, architects of the nineteenth century. Almost solely responsible for creating a new field of restoration architecture, he challenged the neoclassicism of the Académie des beaux-arts, whose traditionally conservative architects tended to dismiss Gothic buildings as ornamental, or at best superfluous. Viollet-le-Duc set out to prove them wrong, by insisting not on the beauty but on the extremely rational basis of Gothic architecture—the structural significance of every buttress and gargoyle. His arguments were eventually compiled in a ten-volume reference work, completed some twenty years after the Notre-Dame project, bearing the proud title *Dictionnaire raisonné de l'architecture française*. This rational account was going to prove, among other things, that the architecture he most loved was not just Gothic, but French. If Viollet-le-Duc's efforts never managed to secure him a place within the Academy, his work did have an impact. By the end of the century the neo-Gothic had eclipsed the neoclassical as the reigning idiom, a shift that formed the basis for a brief (and belated) French Gothic revival.[17]

The very idea of restoring a building like Notre-Dame was, as Viollet-le-Duc conceived it, inescapably modern, both "the word and the thing" (*le mot et la chose*) having been unthinkable before the first quarter of the nineteenth century. "No people in history," he wrote in an important and original essay on the subject for his *Dictionnaire raisonné*, "has ever carried out restorations in the sense in which we understand that term today."[18] Linguistics only helped to prove the point. Ancient languages offered no term that precisely matched the modern sense: the Romans rebuilt, the Greeks renovated, the Gauls replaced. The whole, modern concept of restoration arose, then, from a distinct set of historical conditions, unprecedented in antiquity—a *mentalité*, so to speak, that foregrounded the past as the object of self-conscious study and analysis: "Europeans of our age," wrote Viollet-le-Duc, "have arrived at a stage in the development of human intelligence where, as they accelerate their forward pace, and perhaps precisely because they are already advancing so rapidly, they also feel a deep need to re-create the entire human past, almost as one might collect an extensive library as the basis for further future labors."[19]

Re-creating the entire human past was evidently the guarantee for future progress in an accelerating age. "The entire phenomenon," Viollet-le-Duc admitted, was "exceedingly complex."[20] He found proof of his generation's heightened analytical consciousness—a predilection he himself possessed—in the development of new fields of research: comparative anatomy, philology, ethnography, archaeology. All such studies reflected, he explained, a profound, modern desire to know the past, a desire that was linked to the essential problem of modernity itself: the present appeared to be advancing, and therefore disappearing, too rapidly into the future. The same modern desire to research the past, to reclaim it through imaginative effort, served as the basis for the modern notion of restoration Viollet-le-Duc now formulated. The perspective was nowhere more strikingly evident than in the definition that began the famous essay on restoration for his *Dictionnaire*. To restore an edifice, Viollet-le-Duc argued, "means neither to maintain it, nor to repair it, nor to rebuild it; it means to reestablish it in a finished state, *which may in fact never have actually existed at any given time* [c'est rétablir dans un état complet qui peut n'avoir jamais existé à un moment donné]."[21]

The definition goes against the grain, of course, appearing to threaten the rational foundation on which the dictionary of architecture was supposedly built. Rather than concealing the paradox, however, Viollet-le-Duc gives it pride of place, as if to suggest that the real truths of science remained hidden in such inscrutable logics. His definition did, in fact, echo the official, archaeological program of restoration recommended by the Commission des monuments historiques, a program that quite understandably approached the past as a complex phenomenon constructed in layers. Since medieval buildings were never, according to this rationale, completed all at one time, it was necessary before making repairs "to ascertain," as Viollet-le-Duc advised, "exactly the age and character of each part."[22] A comprehensive restoration required the architect not only to recognize but to preserve every stage of a building's history, all its developments and transformations over time.

It meant, in other words, that the architect comprehend the building like some oddly idealized ruin. For it was precisely that idea of the past "with all its destinies and transformations," experienced as a unique though fleeting aesthetic presence in the natural ruin—as the patina or aura of decay—that the restoration architect imagined he should capture. To restore therefore meant to make that sense of the past somehow more real through analyzing, cataloguing, and finally fixing every one of its imagined layers in the present—each with its own style, its own destiny. It was in this sense that a restoration could achieve the peculiar state of hypercompleteness that Viollet-le-Duc admits "may never have actually existed." The point, he maintained, was not to return the edifice to an original condition, but rather to return it to *history*, a history that was itself a modern phenomenon. Reclaiming the fullness of time past was seen as the rem-

edy for a present that was careening recklessly toward the future. By compre-
hensively retrieving and preserving all the dimensions of a building's past, the
architect imagined himself refashioning that history, changing the course of
events that had already, shockingly, been altered by revolutionary "hammers of
destruction." The architect's task, then, involved not only reclaiming time from
debris but also preserving it—restoring it as an ideal out-of-time, a reconstituted
past forever frozen in the present.

$$\bullet \quad \bullet \quad \bullet \quad \bullet \quad \bullet$$

How completely could architecture alone pretend to fulfill the project of "re-
creating the entire human past" that Viollet-le-Duc viewed as the distinctive
mark of his age? Buildings were just one part of a more complex whole. Their
hard, material form comprehended—housed—a deeper meaning, the very idea
of human existence. As Hugo himself had claimed in 1832, a building contained
two aspects: beauty and function. The very ease with which he asserted this dual
perspective gives an indication of the extent to which the monarchical past was,
by the 1830s, perceived to be cut off from the present. Urban hotels and churches
were no longer the monolithic signs of an omnipotent aristocracy and its
Church, but properties now destined for all citizens and their various, competing enterprises. It was simply impossible to conceive of a restoration in the present day that would include a return to that former, oppressive past, with its egregious repudiations of human liberty. And yet a certain disorientation still seemed
to linger in the separation of ancient building from ancient function, a severing
of meaning that left behind something like a guillotined sign—a senseless hole
of intention that in its emptiness challenged the very idea of "complete"
restoration. What did it mean to restore a church without restoring the Church?

The logic of representation made evident through this radical split of the sign
from its referent suggested that one read the damage visible on the church's exterior—damage the architect now labored to correct—as the reflection of a larger
problem whose nature was concealed. The pockmarks on the cathedral (and the
hammering of which they were the trace) were but symptoms of a more serious
disease within. To attend only to the surface was to ignore this more pressing
internal distress, as a contemporary of Viollet-le-Duc sternly indicated around
the time of the Notre-Dame restoration:

> Now that the stones of the sanctuary have become the object of fervent study and
> admiration, now that all efforts are concentrated on producing complete restorations, or,
> at least, exact imitations of the centerings, the pointed arches, the rose windows, the
> stained glass and paneling, is it not time to remember not only that your churches have
> suffered damage to their walls, their vaults, their age-old furnishings, but that, more

importantly, they are also bereft of the ancient and venerable canticles they once held so dear? . . . Is not liturgy the soul of your cathedrals? Without it, what are they but immense cadavers in which the word of life is extinguished?[23]

Such questions force attention from the material to the immaterial aspect of the building, bringing into view, by means of a negative rhetoric, what (borrowing, perhaps anachronistically, another architectural term) we might call the cathedral's "negative space." The grand litany of Gothic curiosities demonstrates the extent to which—thanks, perhaps, to Hugo—the technical language of medieval architecture had become a commonplace of contemporary discourse; so common, in fact, that the logic of the passage easily moves beyond these merely physical characteristics toward something more ineffable, that (hidden) interior of the building's interior, the "soul of the cathedral." Without this essential element, we are forced to conclude, the building is nothing more than a huge, lifeless corpse, the restoration of which would invariably produce, like a trick of embalming, a fake of real life. What was required was somehow to make this corpse walk and talk.

The author of this passage, a fiercely religious cleric named Prosper Guéranger, was prepared to do just that. As one among a large number of Catholics concerned with the state of the contemporary Church, he imagined, like Chateaubriand before him, the restoration of the Christian religion, and particularly its ancient practices of worship, as the only means to a complete rehabilitation of contemporary life. In view of such concern, Catholicism itself was being analyzed during this period with the same kind of scientific rigor that Viollet-le-Duc brought to the study of its sites of worship. An archaeological excavation of religious practice sought, in a similar way, not only to repair damage but to reestablish the modern Church's connection to its remote past. A topical essay by Charles Louandre from the *Revue des deux mondes* of 1847 offers compelling testimony of the extent of this new study. Louandre was concerned with the dramatic growth of historical studies in the first part of the century, as reflected in over a decade of publication statistics. While the history of the Revolution was, not surprisingly, at the forefront of this new enterprise, ecclesiastical history seems to have run a close second. Louandre's statistical evidence shows a fourfold increase in publications over twelve years—from 34 titles in 1833 to 121 in 1845.[24]

If this proliferation offered clear evidence of a renewed concern for the status of the Church, the burgeoning corps of intellectuals involved in Catholic politics represented another, even more active sign. Indeed, the utopian aestheticism that had informed Chateaubriand's vision of Christianity had modulated into overt political activism by the 1830s, when the outspoken cleric Félicité de Lammenais began launching sustained attacks on the complacent Gallicanism of the Restoration monarchy. The polemic made him the natural leader of a whole new party of liberals—known as ultramontanes—who hoped to renew the relation of the historically aloof French Church to Rome.[25]

Guéranger counted himself among these oppositional Catholics. It was at the encouragement of Lammenais, in fact, that Guéranger had begun his studies of the Roman liturgy, contributing several articles on the subject to Lammenais's anti-Gallican journal *Le Mémorial catholique* between February and May 1830. These early efforts eventually led to a full-length history of liturgical institutions that was to establish his scholarly reputation.[26] To return to the Roman liturgy was, Guéranger believed, the only way to reclaim the greatness of France's ancient history. The standardizing of liturgical practice was for him (as it was, perhaps, for Charlemagne, who oversaw a similar revision a thousand years earlier) as much a matter of national as of spiritual concern: "All our national customs, our poetry, our religious and civil institutions are mingled," he wrote, "with remembrances of the ancient liturgy we now mourn."[27] If the medieval cathedral was the origin of a national architecture, the medieval liturgy became, by a similar logic, the very foundation of French culture.

Imagining Communities

Guéranger expected to recover this cultural heritage by turning to the venerable religious houses, the monasteries, that had practiced those traditions since the Middle Ages. But they, of course, had been devastated along with everything else, officially emptied of their inhabitants in the course of the Revolution. This destruction of monastic life produced a vertiginous sense of cultural dislocation not unlike that associated with the wrecked buildings themselves—a sentiment Guéranger had certainly encountered in numerous sections of Chateaubriand's *Génie*, which he, like others, studied as virtual Holy Writ. In a chapter on the "moral history" of the monastic life, for instance, Chateaubriand poses a question that the young cleric could hardly have ignored: "It has been pretended that a great service was rendered to the monks and nuns in compelling them to quit their peaceful abodes: but what was the consequence?"[28] And, as if to answer that question from the backward glance of history, Chateaubriand's final, apocalyptic chapter passionately defended the role played by these figures after the fall of Rome: without the monasteries, it concluded, "the human race would have been reduced to a few individuals wandering among the ruins."[29]

Figure 1. Romantic illustration of Solesmes from around 1830, with a view of the abandoned priory above the river, a pensive shepherd resting in front. Photo: Claude Lambert Archives, Sablé, France.

By the 1830s the pious Count Montalembert, devotedly following Chateaubriand's lead, developed this topos into a seven-volume history of monasticism that he published, finally, in 1860. Taken out of context, the striking paragraph that opens his chapter on Saint Benedict could easily have been mistaken—especially with its transparent, postrevolutionary allusion to the dismembered social body—for a passage describing, like some benumbing vision of Musset, the state of society in his own day: "Confusion, corruption, despair and death were everywhere; social dismemberment seemed complete. Authority, morals, laws, sciences, arts, religion herself, might have been supposed condemned to an irremediable ruin. The germs of a splendid and approaching revival were still hidden from all eyes under the ruins of a crumbling world."[30]

It was this specter of "a crumbling world," all the more menacing after the revolutions of 1830, that made a modern monastic revival seem especially urgent—not only for Christianity, but for the future of France. And so, as early as 1831, Guéranger, barely twenty-six years old, had the idea of purchasing an abandoned priory on the Sarthe River in Solesmes, near the place of his birth (fig. 1). There he wanted to establish a small order of the very same religious community whose historical founder had, according to Montalembert's eulogy, saved antiquity from the "irremediable ruin" of the Dark Ages. Guéranger wanted to restore to France the Benedictine way of life. A year later, having learned the priory was about to be razed, he scraped up enough to purchase the buildings and won permission from the bishop in Le Mans to start a community there, submitting the names of the three or four priests who had agreed to join him. Montalembert provided moral as well as financial support. Even the aging Chateaubriand, filled with youthful enthusiasm for the project, gave his blessing, announcing in a letter in 1832 his intention to join the new community as an honorary member.[31] Thus, with the sanction of the diocese and the goodwill of a few illustrious colleagues, Guéranger and a handful of followers reestablished, inside a dank little priory, a form of Benedictine monasticism unknown in their lifetimes.

• • • • •

This revival of monastic life at Solesmes was a thoroughly modern affair. As Viollet-le-Duc himself had insisted, the task of restoration required a careful consideration of the past in all its layers. But unlike the architect, who worked from the outside in, so to speak, Guéranger (now Dom Guéranger) began the other way round, from within the monastery, where he found little physical evidence to guide his research. Written testimonies left only a trace of the archaic forms of life that had once existed within the abbey's buildings. Beyond that, the interiors were mute. If the ultimate goal of this restoration was to return the Benedictines to history, to repair their broken ties with the past, its fulfillment must have seemed more than remote when what constituted that past was a dimly illuminated space of unanswered questions. To reanimate the interiors of this ruined monastery was, even more than Viollet-le-Duc could have imagined, to create a form of life that "may never have existed."

Current histories of the monastery all but confirm this view. According to the recent promotional literature published at Solesmes, for instance, the "real" story of the abbey began, in effect, with Dom Guéranger. A glossy picture book (the kind sold to tourists) explains that well into the seventeenth century Solesmes was "nothing but a modest priory," maintaining only a dozen or so religious. Although the monastery did experience a brief renaissance at the beginning of the eighteenth century, involving a large architectural addition in the reigning neoclassical style, the political turmoil of the intervening years cut that resurgence short, bringing Benedictine history to a close. Clearly, our guidebook informs us, Guéranger did not intend to bring the monastery back to the extreme modesty of its "original" state by "slavishly copying the past," or to repair the link with its more recent, troubled history. His goal was, very much

like that of the restoration architect, to reestablish Solesmes in some other, idealized condition: to revive the "true spirit of Saint Benedict," while also making
the "material adaptations necessary in the modern age."[32]

Guéranger was so successful in this effort that in short order his newly
restored community was recognized by Rome. In July 1837, at the urging of
Montalembert, he traveled to Rome to obtain official sanction for his new
monastery.[33] The Holy See responded favorably, raising the priory to the status
of an abbey, with Dom Guéranger presiding as abbot, and consecrating Solesmes
as the official head of the French Congregation of Benedictines. The Abbaye
Saint-Pierre de Solesmes was thereby placed in line with the former, medieval
congregation of Cluny, which had first held that honored position. Now refit-
ted with a symbolic head that could, so to speak, think through the empty space
of meaning left by revolutionary narratives, the Benedictine order reclaimed its
history.

The true spirit of Saint Benedict flowed through the space of this new history in the form of two imperatives of monastic life that Guéranger was obliged
to revive: *ora et labora*, pray and work. These two activities neatly converged during the early years of Solesmes, for the labor of this tiny community (less than
half a dozen strong) was largely devoted to restoring the texts on which their
prayer, and hence their life, would be based—in particular, the texts of the
Roman liturgy whose sacred canticles represented, for Guéranger, the very soul
of the monastery. This intellectual work, in other words, directly affected their
daily existence as monks within a community dedicated to prayer, a community
of which they were among the sole living representatives.

The monks therefore constituted an essential part of the house that was now
being rebuilt. Indeed, their situation resembled, in a queer sense, that of the face-
less figures over the portals of Notre-Dame which Viollet-le-Duc hoped,
through remodeling, to return to a state of original "naiveté." In a report to the
minister of justice and religious rites on the restoration of Notre-Dame Cathedral, Viollet-le-Duc explained the delicate problem of repairing such ruined
sculptures:

> As for the restoration of both the interior and exterior bas-reliefs of the cathedral of
> Paris, we believe that it cannot be executed in the style of the period. We are convinced
> that the state of mutilation (not so serious in other respects) in which they are found is
> very preferable to an appearance of restoration that would only be very remote from their
> original character; for where is the sculptor who could retrieve with the point of his chisel
> this naiveté of past centuries? We think, then, that the replacement of all the statues that
> embellish the portals, the gallery of kings, and the buttresses can be executed only with
> the aid of copies of existing statues in other analogous monuments, and of the same

period. Models are not lacking at Chartres, Reims, Amiens, and on so many other churches throughout France.[34]

The new Solesmes monks understood their work in much the same way. To renew the ancient monastic rituals meant to remodel *themselves* according to an informed image of the past. It required them in effect to become like so many live models—living, breathing Benedictines—who through self-styling would come to embody the truths of a forgotten religious life. The transformation at first took place slowly. It was not until 1836, for instance, that the community adopted the traditional Benedictine costume, the long black tunic with pointed hood that would become a public sign of their religious conviction. As the Solesmes historian Dom Soltner tells the story, the vestments caused something of a stir among the locals, drawing to Sunday masses for several weeks a crowd of onlookers curious to witness the newly outfitted monks in action.[35]

But the remodeling involved as much habits of speech as of dress. To be sure, the revival of Saint Benedict's twin command, *ora et labora*, required a labor that was unmistakably oral: the slow and methodical process of language acquisition that would ultimately put words into the mouths of these perfectly naive figures, causing them to speak and act the way ancient monks were supposed to speak and act. It involved, that is, decisions about how to perform the liturgical texts now being reconstituted. These performance matters naturally raised questions not only about medieval Latin and its pronunciation but also about music—namely, the tradition of chanting that had long served to animate the words of the liturgy. When the monastery opened in 1833, Guéranger and his small band of followers executed their daily worship with as much integrity as possible, using the least corrupt chant books available at the time.[36] Seven years later, in the first volume of his important *Institutions liturgiques*, Guéranger was beginning to address the problem of chant more directly, to imagine the method by which a truer, more authentic Gregorian tradition might be recovered. His unshakably sensible proposal, based on principles of modern philology, would motivate the scholarship undertaken at his monastery right into the twentieth century. "The pure Gregorian phrase" would at last be captured, he posited, "when manuscripts from several distant Churches all agreed on the same reading."[37]

Guéranger was by no means the only scholar to be concerned with redis-covering this Gregorian tradition. Already in 1811 André Choron, presumably responding to France's recently established political ties with Italy, had published a thesis on the necessity of restoring the Roman chant to "all the churches of the empire." Three decades later more than a few antiquarians, including the Belgian musicologist François Fétis, were zealously responding to the imperative.[38] By the time of the 1848 revolutions (perhaps even because of them), the idea of reforming religious practices throughout France—chant included—had become an issue of widespread concern. The archbishop of Reims, for instance, decreed in that very year to reestablish the Roman liturgy in his own diocese, forming a commission with the archbishop of Cambrai to produce a new *Graduale Romanum* based on traditional sources. The organist Jean-Louis Danjou at the Cathedral of Notre-Dame in Paris also stirred up some excitement with his unexpected discovery of the Montpellier manuscript, a unique tonary preserving a double notation system (cursive neumes accompanied by alphabetic letters). The remarkable source gave new hope to all those in search of the church's musical heritage, by providing—as many believed—a marvelous new key to the ancient chant, a kind of Rosetta stone for the Gregorian repertory.[39]

One discovery led to another. The Montpellier success story spawned a veritable craze for collecting and deciphering manuscripts, a pastime that in turn generated something like a small chant industry. Freelance scholars and clerics from all over France—such as the Jesuit Louis Lambillotte and the tireless *musiciste* Théodore Nisard—began searching for similar treasures, and possible personal fortune, in libraries and monasteries across Europe.[40] Early in the 1850s Lambillotte earned himself a certain renown by bringing out a facsimile of one of the oldest manuscripts of Gregorian chant, a source he claimed to be the antiphoner of Saint Gregory himself. At around the same time Nisard, having received approbation from no less than Ludovic Vitet for his work on musical archaeology, was commissioned by the Ministry of Cults and Public Instruction to make a facsimile of the recently discovered Montpellier manuscript. The Benedictines of Solesmes, however, were taking their time. It was not until 1860, with the establishment of the abbey's new scriptorium, that they began to produce any scholarship of this kind—to undertake the meticulous study of sources imagined by Guéranger some two decades earlier. The responsibility for this new paleographic work was assumed at first by two of the younger members of the community, the twenty-six-year-old Dom Paul Jausions, who had taken vows in 1856, and the twenty-five-year-old Dom Joseph Pothier, who took them four years later.

More significant than the scriptorium, perhaps, was the Benedictine singing itself. In 1860 this relatively private practice went public at the first Paris congress for the restoration of plainchant. It was Augustin Gontier, a deacon and close associate of Dom Guéranger from nearby Le Mans, who made the formal introduction by offering a précis of his recently published *Méthode raisonnée de plain-chant* (1859), a method book presenting rules for the proper execution of chant based on the practice at Solesmes.[41] Since Gontier had been, according to the late Solesmes historiographer Dom Pierre Combe,"one of the first witnesses to the Gregorian experiments attempted by the monks," Guéranger had encouraged him to try to theorize those experiments, to explain the curiously alluring effect of the Benedictine chant.[42] His ideas formed an important starting point for the work completed by the next generation of scholars at the monastery. After the death of Dom Jausions in 1871 the job of restoring the Gregorian corpus fell mostly to Dom Pothier, who continued to copy manuscripts for the monastery's growing scriptorium while attempting to refine a theory of authentic performance.

In 1880 the passage of an anticlerical Education Bill proposed by Jules Ferry once again transformed the status of the religious orders in France. The new legislation, which eventually made primary education compulsory and free for all citizens of the republic, also forbade religious congregations from teaching. Although the measure was directed mainly at the Jesuits, all the religious orders were required to support it by pledging unequivocal loyalty to the new republican government.[43] Refusing to comply, the Solesmes monks were forced to decongregate. The brothers had no choice but to take up residence in the homes of sympathetic citizens from the surrounding village, communing in the parish church just outside the abbey to pray the office.[44] This critical upheaval of monastic life, which was to last through the next decade, did not, however, deter the progress of the scholarly work they had begun. On the contrary, the first years of their local exile saw the completion of two of the most influential books ever produced at Solesmes—works that ultimately changed the face of the entire Gregorian repertory. They were Pothier's treatise, *Les Mélodies grégoriennes d'après la tradition* (1880), and the first authoritative edition of plainchant based on paleographic research, the *Liber Gradualis* (1883).

Precious Remains

The publication of these texts marked Dom Pothier as the premier *restaurateur* of the Gregorian tradition, a figure responsible for fulfilling, in both theory and practice, the program of restoration imagined by Dom Guéranger in the monastery's early years. In essence, Pothier's work rescued chant from the ruin into which, according to the reigning topos of the century (by 1880 surely a cliché), it had inescapably fallen. The new gradual offered a collection of carefully repaired chants, which had suffered, in his words,"all sorts of alterations and mutilations." Most conspicuously, it reinstated the traditional forms not only of notation but of the melodies themselves, especially the long melismas that, like the exotic stone arabesques struck from the façades of Gothic churches, had disappeared from contemporary books—those "rich vocalises" whose presence, as Pothier put it, "had so delighted our forefathers."[45]

But these refurbished chants also required a renewed sensibility. Pothier believed that the lamentable disintegration of the melodic corpus had been due in part to a faulty performance practice—in his words, a "hammered execution" (*exécution martelée*), still heard in his own day, that destroyed the unity of the phrase, making the complex Gregorian melody unintelligible.[46] The hammering of singers, in other words, had wrecked the traditional Gregorian repertory in much the same way that the hammering of postrevolutionary vandals had hacked up medieval monuments. It was no wonder that the next generation of chant scholars should describe Pothier, whose research sought to reverse the effects of such melodic vandalism, as the "Viollet-le-Duc of liturgical chant."[47]

In probing the conceptual foundation of Pothier's restored chant we may begin to sense the resonance of this marvelous analogy. Pothier himself admitted, at the beginning of *Les Mélodies grégoriennes*, that his ideas of Gregorian performance practice had their origins some two decades earlier in Gontier's *Méthode raisonnée de plain-chant*, the first treatise on Gregorian chant performance to be sanctioned by Dom Guéranger.[48] In this book Gontier argued for the return of a "natural" style of singing, a style he believed he could still hear in a handful of chants that had managed to weather the centuries of change and neglect— popular chants like the "Gloria," the "Credo," the "Te Deum." In the same spirit that the Romantic philologists conceived the value of so many vanishing dialects, in whose accents they longed to distinguish the sound of lost voices, Gontier imagined that these lingering melodies, like debris salvaged "from the shipwreck of true principles," contained traces of the lost Gregorian tradition. What was Gregorian in these songs had been preserved, he believed, with the kind of purity one still found "among the peoples who, from time immemorial, have sung the same songs and the same words, without the benefit of any musical education."[49]

What was Gregorian emerged, in other words, not so much from written evidence as from another, less visible source—the unconscious practices Gontier called *routine*. Routine found song in a state of utter naturalness, the site of a musical legacy worn slowly and steadily into collective memory. As its etymology suggests, routine revealed the elusive path of time as a broken road, a *via rupta* on which countless souls had trod over countless centuries. "It is this routine," Gontier argued, "that we must study, this track we must get back on, these precious remains we must gather together," for only in such hollowed-out spaces of memory could one retrieve what the past had left behind—in his words, "the feeble echo of a powerful tradition."[50]

These remembered traces of song produced an effect, then, just like that of the natural ruin: their well-worn contours offering a striking image of the persistence of time, in the security of habit, the comfort of a groove. Indeed, it was this imagined residue of routine, this echo of a tradition preserved in ruins, that Gontier and the Solesmes monks sought to capture and restore to the plainchant, just as the architectural restorations conceived by Viollet-le-Duc attempted to reify the elusive (and sublime) aura—that skin of history—that remained on a building in the form of patina. Indeed, both echo and patina, in their belatedness, suggest a similar relation to history. They stand as signs of pastness *in* the present—a pastness that is communicated, however, through the very fact of decay: the decayed surface, which embodies a sublime quality of disappearance, an evanescence, forms a striking analogy to the decayed sound. If restoring historical monuments meant realizing this pastness in a more complete state, then the task of the restorer involved not so much removing the decay as, somehow almost perversely, affecting to preserve it.

It was precisely in the restoration of Gregorian melody that the monks could hope to fulfill such an apparently impossible goal. For as Gontier himself reveals, a melody always embodies a complex ontology. Vanishing in the moment of becoming, it nevertheless remains intact in the space of memory, in the invisible habits of routine. In a phenomenological sense, then, song offers the supreme example of a substance capable of preserving itself in decay. Far more than architectural restoration, or any other aspect of the work that constituted the life of the nineteenth-century Benedictine, the restoration of chant, by realizing decay in the sublime poetry of song itself, offered the most complete expression of the aura of the medieval past.

It could also be said that by its very nature the Gregorian song reproduced, in miniature, the entire imaginary space of the Gothic cathedral, both outside and in. In its completeness, the chant embodied a double aspect: *nota* and *vox*, the notated melodic form and its animating breath, one silent, the other resonant. Like the cathedral, the restoration of the song's melodic forms required, as Guéranger had advised, excavating layers of written evidence, the traces of the Gregorian song buried in countless manuscripts from "distant churches." But what mattered even more than the external appearance of this melody was the harmony one imagined one heard resonating through those pages when they all "agreed on the same reading" (*s'accordent sur la même leçon*). Restored to its

integrity, the authentic chant thus accorded, in the very notion of musical agreement (accord), the aura of distant voices captured through a philologist's dream:
the Gregorian tradition, perfectly in tune, echoing within the manuscripts.

By securing this aura in a modern practice of singing, the monks could maintain themselves, and all who followed, in the perpetual present-past that was the
essential condition not only of melody but of restoration itself. It was a condition that found history pressed into the present as if to caulk the fissures between
past and future—rendering the present a kind of holding tank, a space of restored
memory that had the power to redeem time from its dangerous leakage into an
unstable future. Pothier alludes to this redemptive function of the Gregorian
song in the words that close the preface to *Les Mélodies grégoriennes*: "We hope to
see the following pages received with interest and goodwill by secular musicians,
by those who above all believe that modern music needs to be regenerated." His
final sentence, despite its obvious hint of Wagnerian one-upmanship, summarized the entire, modern project of Gregorian history in a single, prophetic formula: "The music of the past better understood will be greeted as the true music
of the future."[51]

· · · · ·

Through the daily singing of the plainsong at Solesmes, the feeble echo of
history, now better and better understood, could become amplified and stretch
toward the future, transforming the interior life of the monastery to such an
extent that it eventually made itself felt on the abbey's exterior. This brings us
back, like a refrain, to architecture. For the essential restoration of Benedictine
history was to be realized at Solesmes only after 1895 (two decades following the
death of Dom Guéranger), the year in which the monks took repossession of
their abbey, putting an end to fifteen years of exile in their own village. While
gendarmes looked the other way, the brothers returned to their monastery and
once again set up housekeeping. But the community had grown during the years
of separation, and so the new abbot, Dom Paul Delatte, boldly conceived a plan
to renovate the existing buildings, authorizing an architectural expansion that
would house the monks in style. One of his own monks, Dom Mellet, drew up
the plans. Construction began in 1896.

The building attracted the attention of laymen from surrounding regions,
who came in increasing numbers to monitor its progress.[52] What they witnessed
was a complete transformation: the formerly undinstinguished priory (fig. 2)
had been fitted with a new exterior that seemed designed to reflect the more
robust community that now lived inside. That this community had transformed
itself, over five decades, from a modest priory into a fully historical, and power-

Figure 2. Abbaye Saint-Pierre as seen from Sarthes River around 1860. The medieval tower at the far end of the property was an innovation of Dom Guéranger. Photo: Claude Lambert Archives, Sablé, France.

ful, Benedictine center was evident in the very magnitude of the reconstruction Dom Mellet had conceived. The addition was nothing less than a Gothic marvel (fig. 3), whose massive buildings literally towered over the restrained eighteenth-century architecture of the former priory. Dom Mellet had designed a structure grand enough to look beyond that more recent past, beyond the Revolution itself—an abbey that could finally reach into the "real" history of Benedictine life.

Thus renovated, the Abbey of Solesmes and its musical practice became medieval icons to enchant the secular world. The historical aura of this remote Gothic fortress and its restored music cast a spell on countless fin de siècle artists and intellectuals in search of religion—especially the Catholic religion, whose aesthetic riches, celebrated many years before by Chateaubriand, now enjoyed a renewed vogue among the literary elite.[53] The Solesmes spell lured illustrious visitors from all over France, among them the musician Claude Debussy and the writer and critic Joris-Karl Huysmans [54] Indeed, the effect of the Benedictine liturgy was so profound that Huysmans took time to document it in *L'Oblat*, a pious novel from his late period whose first chapter actually takes place at the

Figure 3. Abbaye Saint-Pierre after the Gothic renovation of Dom Mellet. Note how the rooftops of the former priory are now hidden from view. Photo: Claude Lambert Archives, Sablé, France.

Solesmes Abbey. Here is the protagonist, Durtal, musing: "Solesmes stands alone; there is no place like it in the whole of France; religion there has an artistic splendour to be met with nowhere else; the chant is perfect; the services are conducted with matchless pomp. Where else, too, could I ever hope to meet an Abbot as broad-minded as Dom Delatte, or experts in musical paleography more skilled or learned . . . ?" The sheer thought of such liturgical perfection, which sends Durtal into a deeper reverie, evokes a startling confession: he is addicted to Solesmes. "Yes, I am haunted as it were, by phantoms of the past; I have inoculated myself with the seductive poison of the Liturgy; it now runs through my spiritual veins and I shall never be rid of it. The church services affect me as morphine affects a drug taker."[55]

    In its perversity, this account of fin de siècle piety offers the clearest—certainly the most topical—description of the attraction the monastery exercised on the era's spiritual tourists, a pull the real Huysmans himself apparently knew all too well. For he, too, gave up the decadent life in exchange for one more pure, performing, like his own character Durtal, the single most dramatic act in his well-documented life of extremes, an act that literary history has preferred to forget: in 1901 Huysmans took vows to become a Benedictine. *The Oblate* is a thinly disguised autobiography of these mostly forgotten later years.

Nor was Huysmans the only writer to document in prose the monastery's riches. Just a few years before, in 1898, the Parisian music critic Camille Bellaigue took his own intoxicating trip to the abbey on an unlikely assignment for the *Revue des deux mondes*. The long account of his stay with the monks includes elaborate descriptions of singing that the less musically sophisticated Huysmans could never have written. Yet Bellaigue's view was hardly less enthusiastic than that of Durtal himself. He considered the chanting at the abbey so exceptional, in fact, that he judged a pilgrimage to Solesmes far more worthwhile than an equivalent excursion to Bayreuth. For potential pilgrims among his readers he offered this advice, designed to enhance their aesthetic enjoyment: "If you go to Solesmes, try to arrive on a beautiful summer evening. Don't wait for the station in Sablé; get off the train a little earlier, at Juigné. From there, following the hill-side, go slowly up the river—the Sarthe of the crawling, almost pensive waters." Bellaigue's advice quickly modulates into a more absorbing description of the abbey itself and its medieval architecture:

> Soon you will be in front of the abbey; it will appear on the other bank, strong, massive, rising up in all its height. I wouldn't know how to define the style of this architecture: it recalls all at once Mont Saint-Michel, the monastery at Assisi, the papal palace at Avignon. Above the river, too narrow to reflect it quite whole, the abbey rises to a peak . . . with gigantic buttresses and walls one hundred twenty feet high, cut in lumps of bluish granite, keeps capped in slate—an enormous, almost barbaric silhouette of a holy fortress, a religious burg. The high walls are pierced with irregular, unequal openings: bays, windows, skylights, sometimes simple and sometimes ornate. The architect of this monastery, none other than one of the Fathers, is certainly right to call his work Gregorian chant frozen in stone [*chant grégorien pétrifié*].[56]

If architecture was, to recall Schelling's adage, "frozen music," then this Gothic façade offered a striking variation on the theme. It made a certain sense to connect, as the converted Huysmans had done in *En Route*, the mysterious forms of this medieval architecture to an equally mysterious music. Plainchant was, as he imagined it, "the aerial and mobile paraphrase of the immovable structure of the cathedrals."[57] But the architect of the Solesmes Abbey proposed more than a paraphrase, indeed more than Schelling's original formula suggested. Revising the architectural equation backward into antiquity, his abbey not only froze but "petrified" the most ancient type of song. To imagine the abbey's façade in this way was certainly to believe that it had captured, for all time (without threat of melting), the evanescent quality of decay that defined the modern fascination of the ruin, of history itself.

The aura of history surrounding the restored abbey was signaled even more tellingly perhaps by still another aspect of the building: the extreme decay of meanings apparent in the restoration's lack of a single, clear architectural style, the absence of a name. This new, old façade recalled (to Bellaigue, at least) no fewer than three wildly diverse monuments of the Middle Ages. The Gothic reconstruction of the abbey served, then, to realize not a particular lost period of history but the plenitude of history itself, represented as a grand, vague medieval past, in all its glorious remoteness. The modernity of this concept of time is striking: the building's very "outness" of style petrified the outness of time that was its aura of history.

Bellaigue seemed to resume this idealized temporality, this present-past tense of the restored Benedictine life, in a phrase whose oddly contorted syntax repeats the strange logic of Gothic restoration as Viollet-le-Duc had imagined it: "L'abbaye renaît . . . mais telle qu'elle ne fut jamais aux jours lointains de sa naissance." The abbey is reborn, he writes, "but in such a way as it never was in the remote days of its birth."[58] Having captured the plainchant—the soul of the monastery, the echo of history—the modern Benedictines thus affected to fix it in stone, to preserve this modern idea of the Middle Ages for future visitors to Solesmes, visitors who, like the monks themselves, found history enchanted.

2

Bibliophilia

t the same time Gregorian song reverberated inside restored spaces of worship, it began to take silent, material form in liturgical books. An equally distinctive face of the chant revival peers back from nineteenth-century printed pages, revealing countless attempts by modern printers to rebuild the ancient musical repertory in antique note forms. The best editions, abandoning the circular notation of contemporary hymn books, rendered the ancient chant in solid medieval squares, as if to reproduce the massive stone blocks of the Gothic cathedral in precious miniature. These modern volumes of Gregorian music offer us, then, another sort of enchanted space: a whole, imagined medieval world shrunk between two covers and held in two hands—a world whose aura was frozen not in stone but in type.

The Gregorian chant revival stumbles on the history of the typographic book. It is a history that turns a sharp corner toward the end of the nineteenth century, into what could be called the era of the *édition de luxe*. The term comes from the eighteenth century, associated with luxury printing at the court of Versailles, but gains fresh significance in the nineteenth when in England and on the continent men of letters zealously turned their attentions toward the art of making and collecting beautiful books. It is useful to pause over this renewal of bibliographic arts in our investigation of chant, for the restoration of any ancient musical tradition will depend to a large extent on the status of its written records. As Dom Pothier saw it, a viable Gregorian performance practice was the logical consequence of a revitalized notation: recovering the precious *vox* of Gregorian melody meant reproducing its equally precious *notae*, which meant, in turn, printing the right sort of edition. Our story of musical restoration must include, then, a story within a story—a brief but important look at the luxurious, fin de siècle art of making books.

An unforgettable image of this art comes once more from Huysmans, this time in the figure of Des Esseintes, the decadent, aristocratic protagonist of *A rebours*, a character who, if nothing else, can be read as a composite of the more extreme tendencies of his age. One chapter finds Des Esseintes lost in a bibliophile's reverie, fondling the perfect folios from his library:

> In former days at Paris, he had certain volumes specially set up for him and printed off by specially hired workmen on hand presses. Sometimes he would go to Perrin of Lyons, whose slim, clear types were suitable for archaic reimpressions of old tracts; sometimes he would send to England or the States, for new characters to print works of the present century; sometimes he would apply to a house at Lille which had for hundreds of years possessed a complete font of Gothic letters; sometimes again he would call in the help of the long-established Enschedé press, of Haarlem, whose type-foundry preserves the stamps and matrices of the so-called "letters of civility."[1]

In an equally long passage Des Esseintes fusses over the special laid papers purchased for these exclusive editions. If the exhaustive descriptions perhaps pale in comparison to other, more celebrated chapters in the novel—the famous paeans to perfume, liqueur, digested meat—they nevertheless fulfill a similar function: they represent, through sheer narrative excess, an indulgence in the materiality of material things that defines the peculiar aesthetic sensibility not only of the protagonist but, one presumes, of his entire generation. The unique pleasures of handmade books are specifically addressed when Des Esseintes later reaches for an impeccable volume of Baudelaire, printed on Japanese felt "in the admirable episcopal character of the ancient firm of Le Clere." The typography, the paper, not to mention the overlarge format of the specimen (we are told it resembles an old missal), together serve to enhance the total effect of the poetry, making it seem, he muses, "more striking and significant than ever."[2]

The epicurean tastes of Huysmans's decadent hero serve as a surprisingly coherent place to begin a discussion of book printing in the last decades of the nineteenth century, for the single most defining characteristic of the typographic arts in this period was a kind of reactionary aestheticism, in which the forgotten art of bookmaking becomes the principal means of restoring the significance of modern printed words. In conventional histories of typography, as in Huysmans's novel, this modern attitude is usually explained through a narrative of decline associated with the effects of industrialization.[3] The inventions most often cited to explain the general lowering of standards in the trade include, not unexpectedly, the very tools that allowed for the rapid expansion of the newspaper industry at the beginning of the century: steam-powered presses, as well as machines for typecasting, papermaking, and punch-cutting. As every history points out, the egregious result of such mechanization—marking, perhaps, the aesthetic nadir of nineteenth-century printing—surfaces in the glut of cheaply produced pamphlets and the proliferation of grotesque, eye-catching "display" type for advertisements.

The shift toward faster, cheaper, and ultimately more profitable methods of printing becomes a central evil in the tragic tale of ruined books. Yet, as Robin Kinross has argued, this modernization of the printing trade was probably less immediate and encompassing than most histories would have us believe. Even in heavily industrialized nations, smaller print shops using old-fashioned methods continued to exist well into the twentieth century.[4] The story of bibliographic ruins may thus reflect less about the actual state of the art of printing than about more general conditions wrought by modernization. Certainly, it would appear to conceal a kind of anxious elitism, linking the sad loss of artistic standards to a new democracy of typographic production. When printed books, formerly the domain of the privileged, became available to a larger body of consumers, standards were bound to decline. Placed in the hands of the masses, type inevitably fell to pieces. In this familiar logic we discern, of course, some of the same turns that shaped the tales of Gothic monuments—stories of vandalism that now returned, like some repressed memory, to haunt the printed page itself. The modern book appeared to have suffered, in its own way, the same tragic defacement.

．　．　．　．　．

In the technical language of the trade, this tragedy finds expression in a new concern over the printed letter's single most important virtue—what typographers call "legibility." The term conventionally refers to the ideal interaction of eye and letter in the act of reading. The seventeenth-century philosopher Charles d'Ancillon (author of a well-known treatise on eunuchs) summarized this ideal in a classic statement: "The less the eye is fatigued in reading a book, the more at liberty the mind is to judge it . . . beauties and faults are more clearly seen when it is printed in a fair character.[5] The condition of legibility would seem to involve, in other words, a kind of readerly paradox: it places a high value on the necessary *in*visibility of printed characters, a quality that allows the reader to read without being conscious of doing so, to decipher the meaning of a text without being aware of deciphering the letters that compose it. If in the seventeenth century this value formed the rule of printed texts, by the nineteenth it came to be viewed as a lamentable exception.

The problem appeared to lie in the modern face. This was the generic name for the eighteenth-century letter designed by the Italian typographer Bodoni and developed in France by Didot, the famous family of printers who ruled over several generations of French publishing. Because of increasing standardization in the trade, "Didot modern" was to define the basic look of most European books from the late eighteenth well into the nineteenth century. Didot had sought to improve on the so-called roman letter form perfected by Renaissance printers, by thickening the vertical strokes of his type while thinning the horizontal. The hair-line serifs, which imitated the effects of engraving, were combined with more robust bodies to give the printed page a new kind of brilliance, while formal similarities among the characters made the type more pleasingly uniform. Yet already in 1800 we find objections raised against this typographic aesthetic, in an address to the Société libre des sciences, lettres et arts by one citizen Sobry, who complained of the "destructive ultraperfection" of Didot's letters.[6] In his view, the modern face inhibited easy reading by its very stylishness: the relatively weightless serifs caused the character to disappear into the page; the uniformity of the letters themselves served to diminish the overall legibility of the type. Sobry was prepared to prove the point by referring to evidence from a few modest scientific experiments.

Neither his objections nor his evidence, however, was to have any immediate effect on printing styles in the next decades. As the industry expanded, in fact, the modern typographic aesthetic he rejected would only become more exaggerated. The tendency toward emboldened letters can be seen most clearly in the fashionable display types produced with increasing frequency after 1840, designs whose unusual characters made a virtue of illegibility. With their greater capacity to arrest the eye—to interrupt the act of reading—these conspicuous types had the desired ability to make readers even more conscious of the words they read. This was a condition that fulfilled, of course, the basic purposes of advertising. In the development of all such nineteenth-century types we thus see the signs of a printing industry beginning to take notice, in a very specific sense, of the habits of its reading public.

It is surely not coincidental, then, that in this same period we also witness increased interest among scientists in the visual habits of readers. In the last few decades of the century, clinical studies of the question of legibility, such as those completed by Emile Javal around 1870,[7] gave rise to a more developed field of scientific research centered entirely on the human physiology of reading. How are we to understand the meaning of this new research? The sudden development of legibility studies at the end of the nineteenth century must have been motivated by more than mere curiosity about the qualities of modern printed letters. Indeed, such research would seem to point to another, more serious question about the "modern face" of the printing trade itself, an industry that had ultimately transformed the way people took in the written word.

It was, simply put, a question of value. For the real significance of the century's mass-produced texts lay, it could be said, in their lack of value, the very absence of *luxe* that allowed words to be cheaply produced and therefore widely distributed. Nineteenth-century newspapers and handbills were not only readily available but, perhaps even more important, readily disposable. This novel condition may serve to bring the whole question of "illegibility" into clearer focus. The very fact of disposability meant, of course, that printed words had acquired not just a new look but a new function. The display types of headlines and advertisements essentially demanded that modern readers learn to read differently, not contemplating but rapidly consuming print—retaining meanings without retaining the page itself. The principal advantage of a cheaply printed text was precisely the thing that made it, in a very literal sense, "illegible": it would *not* be read for all time. By promoting reading as a transitory act, rendering words impermanent, modern printing had succeeded in making texts more available and certainly more visible, but it had also emptied them of a sense of enduring significance.

Reforming the Face

This imagined impoverishment of writing, this loss of value, lurked behind the new concern over legibility, which by the end of the century had come to redefine the discourse on print. Haunted by the modern specter of the illegible, the very concept of legibility emerged as a kind of counteraesthetic, heralding a reform of practices—of traditions—that would reinvest modern print with the permanence it was thought to have lost. The famous twentieth-century English printer and typographic historian Stanley Morison (who in 1920 invented a monotype roman font for the *Times* of London) offers perhaps the clearest statement of this modern aesthetic stance, which—by his generation, at least—had become a fundamental principle of typography. "The printer's object is that his author's work shall be read and not for the day only," he claimed, adding the following advice: "Those who wish their books to be read tomorrow as well as today will respect tradition. This applies with peculiar force to letters and type."[8]

The "tradition" to which Morison referred was that of printers of the sixteenth century, whose legacy had yielded the perfect specimen known as the roman letter. Typographic history suggested that the printed page would be able to efface its modern shortcomings—like the ideal liturgy advocated by Dom Guéranger—only by returning to this purest of forms. By the second half of the nineteenth century this forgotten ancestral letter, tellingly referred to as "old style" or "old face," represented the very image of reformed typography. The most important aesthetic quality it offered was a consistent thickness throughout its body, which created both a blacker and more permanent—that is, more legible—impression on the printed page. The printer John Southward confirmed this common perception in an essay on typography for the 1892 edition of the *Encyclopaedia Britannica*, which summarized some of the most recent research on the qualities of good type:

> About 1882 an eminent French printer made a number of experiments to ascertain what constitutes legibility in type and found that people read with less fatigue according as the letters—(a) are rounder, (b) are more equal in thickness, (c) have shorter upstrokes, (d) are dissimilar to each other, and (e) are well-proportioned in their own body. Drawings of letters from old books were visible and legible at a distance at which modern letters could not be distinguished.[9]

The traditional roman letter, as copied from "old books," evidently had the power, among other things, to reverse one of the more distressing conditions of modern life: the "fatigue" that had come to plague the act of reading itself. Indeed, the complex of qualities embodied in this letter eventually came to stand for everything that had vanished from its less legible (and therefore less "distinguished") counterpart.

· · · · ·

The revival of these old-style roman letters originated in England. The first attempts to restore a historic typeface are usually credited to Charles Whittingham of the Chiswick Press, who in the 1840s went searching for a letter with which to print a series of texts by sixteenth- and seventeenth-century authors. The type he resurrected, which owed its origins to the eighteenth-century printer William Caslon, had the distinctly historic look of early-eighteenth-century English books, featuring irregularities such as the long *s*, as well as the tied *ct* and *st* long absent from modern fonts. The success of this venture, apparent in a growing fashion for antique prayer books (in 1844 Chiswick Press issued a *Book of Common Prayer* set in Caslon types), led Whittingham and others in England to continue the quest for ancient letters by restoring even older fonts, both roman and black letter.[10]

Within a few decades, these tentative steps had turned into an international movement running at full speed. In France the antiquarian fashion made its appearance in the seventeenth-century Elzévir types revived in 1857 by the Parisian printer Théophile Beaudoire, as well as in the chic Perrin fonts—those "slim, clear types" praised by Des Esseintes—which, having been put back into circulation by Alphonse LeMerre, were all the rage with the Parnassian poets.

English printing houses continued to lead the way in the revival, however, a fact indisputably demonstrated by the end of the century in the unique artistry of William Morris, perhaps the single most important figure associated with the renewal of the modern typographic book.

Morris learned his trade at the Chiswick Press, the house responsible in 1858 for bringing out his first volume of poetry, *The Defence of Guenevere, and Other Poems*. His preferences, evident in the themes of his own verse, tended toward a historical aesthetic considerably earlier than the Reformation-period texts that represented Whittingham's specialty. As an avid student and collector of medieval manuscripts, Morris took inspiration from more ancient practices of writing and illumination, the designs of which he eventually sought to emulate in print.[11]

Indeed, Morris's predilection for medieval archaisms caused him to judge unfavorably most of the types found even at the best presses, types that by mid-century had become rationalized into the two basic categories of "old styles" and "moderns." It seemed to him inappropriate to set the Middle English orthography he preferred in an old face from a more recent era. As the historian P. M. Handover has suggested, "archaic spellings demanded an archaic type."[12] Morris's dream, encouraged by fellow Arts and Crafts leader Emery Walker, was to fashion a letter redolent of the Middle Ages, whose face would breathe in all its dark, musty history, emitting an aura at least several centuries older—and riper—than the oldest "old face" then available in books. Morris wanted a letter that reeked.

By 1870 he had moved toward this ideal with the publication of his *Book of Verse*, a lithographed volume of his own medieval-style lyric verse. Each page featured poems carefully rendered in a calligraphic hand resembling Caroline minuscule. A profusion of entwining vignettes (reminiscent of his later wallpaper designs), illuminated capitals, and perfect, miniature illustrations surrounded the verses, charmingly recalling all the virtues of the medieval craftsman, or—in Morris's mind probably the same thing—the efforts of a man with time on his hands.[13] In the 1890s, with the first books produced at his newly founded Kelmscott Press, that medieval ethos was finally to emerge in printed editions, executed on handpresses, which reissued some of the same poems published two decades earlier.[14] Now set in types Morris had designed himself, the page took on an entirely different historical aura. The printed text had none of the quaint charm and idiosyncrasy of the earlier manuscript; it now reflected a more idealistic vision of a past perfected through the merger of two aesthetic worlds, the best of both Renaissance and Gothic print.

These typographic values were partly explained in 1895, one year before his death, in a small essay he published describing the founding of the Kelmscott

Press. Morris recounts his first experiments with designing a roman letter, a design that resulted in the celebrated Golden type of his late years: "By instinct rather than by conscious thinking it over, I began by getting myself a fount of Roman type. And here what I wanted was a letter pure in form; severe, without needless excrescences; solid, without the thickening and thinning of the line, which is the essential fault of the ordinary modern types, and which makes it difficult to read."[15] The reference to instinct in this passage creates a strange counterpoint with the more permanent values he sets out to describe. Indeed, Morris's "instinctive" impulse seems to have inclined toward a good deal of self-restraint, if we are to judge from the trinity of virtues he ascribes to his roman letter: purity, severity, solidity. Its idealized form conjures up an image of the perfect body, perhaps a bit more Spartan than Roman, meticulously groomed so as to lack all "needless excrescences"—in short, a body that displays all the beauty of discipline. The timeless value associated with such beauty comes disguised, moreover, in the plain wrapper of practical necessity: the implication is that a classic roman type simply allows for easier reading, the very quality lacking in the modern faces whose illegibility was by 1895 a printer's cliché.

In fact, by almost any standard Morris's Kelmscott books are far from easy to read. It is no wonder, then, that the admiration expressed by the twentieth-century typographers who followed Morris's example has often fallen short of praise for his concept of typographic design, usually considered more extreme than beautiful. The celebrated Kelmscott Chaucer of 1896 (fig. 4), a volume for which he designed an eponymous type, is a case in point. The book revels in typographic complexity, its pages teeming with stylized flora and illustrations that dwarf the two tiny columns of text. The result is a perverse sort of legibility that Morris must have desired. The struggle of the page causes the reader, in fact, to become aware of sheer *difficulty*, an effort that ultimately serves to illuminate the aesthetic of Middle English itself. To read Chaucer in Chaucer, the book suggests, is beautiful work.

This aesthetic of difficulty is apparent even in less opulently decorative books produced in the same period. Morris's 1894 edition of Keats, for example, set not in Chaucer but in Golden, presented a far less busy design, the pages adorned with nothing but a single, elegantly placed capital. But even in these more austere pages the heavy blackness of his letters, as always set close with minimal leading, had the ultimate effect of slowing the eye's progress through the poems, forcing the reader to appreciate Keats's rhymes one word at a time, to savor their simple perfection. It was the type itself, as Morris explains, that served to convey such perfection, modeled as it was on "the great Venetian printers of the fifteenth century, of whom Nicolas Jenson produced the completest and most Roman

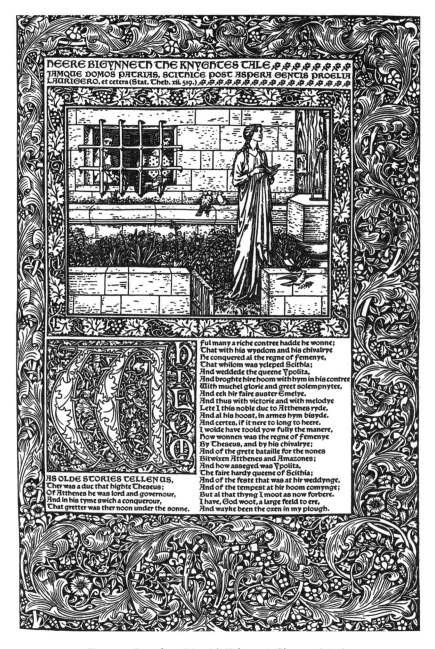

Figure 4. Page from Morris's Kelmscott Chaucer (1896).

characters from 1470 to 1476." He outlines the methodical process of discovering this Venetian secret:

> I studied [Jenson's type] with much care, getting it photographed to a big scale, and drawing it over many times before I began designing my own letter; so that though I think I mastered the essence of it I did not copy it servilely; in fact, my Roman type, especially in the lower case, tends rather more to Gothic than does Jenson's.[16]

The final sentence, which refers to the "Gothic" tendency that infects Morris's roman face, may serve to explain the strong bias toward the black letter we find in all of his type designs. More interesting, however, is the image this passage presents of Morris the student. The sense one has of the somewhat eccentric, turn-of-the-century medievalist, with his unflaggingly archaic affectations, seems slightly at odds with the deliberate use of photographic enlargements for the study of Jenson's designs. Yet it was precisely this ultramodern technology that could usher him toward his goal of mastering the type without merely copying it. By making the characters larger than life, the photographs allowed him, so to speak, to get inside the letters, to see things invisible to the naked eye. It was this insider's perspective that made it possible to extract from the type, as Morris put it, its "essence," the pungent scent of history. He might as well have called this new typographic essence *eau de Jenson*, for Morris's fin-de-siècle creation was meant to evoke a whole, heady history of letters. In its concentrated form, his modern Golden type exuded the sweet perfume of the Golden Age of the book itself, thickened by strong traces of Gothic script. The impression it left was not so much beautiful as powerful—potent enough to make the writing stick.

The Face of Saint Gregory

Morris's highly individual, even eccentric, contributions to the typographic arts at the end of the nineteenth century might at first seem like a glorious exception to the bibliographic rule—a condition that of course renders comparison difficult. Yet the unusual case of William Morris turns out to be more helpful than we might have imagined when we turn our attention to the restoration of Gregorian chant, especially at Solesmes. Like other reformers of the period, the Benedictines were searching for a musical notation that could make a suitable claim to history. An old-style Gregorian type, they believed, would confer on a book of chant the same sort of antique aura that the Caslon face had brought to *The Book of Common Prayer*.

This condition was perhaps most apparent to Dom Pothier, the young monk who shortly after his profession in 1860 had assumed responsibility not only for the monastic choir but also for the abbey's scriptorium—thereby coming into direct contact with notations from the ancient past. It was Pothier who made the first attempt to find a suitable *nota* for the rehabilitated chant, yet the idea of what a truly Gregorian face should possess escaped his grasp much as the perfect roman face had first eluded Morris. Unsatisfied with the idea of resurrecting any old type, he would also insist on a design that conveyed the full weight of history. Like Morris, Pothier wanted to recover a Gregorian face that was not just old, but ancient.

This was an issue he addressed in at least two chapters of his treatise *Les Mélodies grégoriennes*. Turning to the sources, he attempted to sketch Gregorian history through the very notational signs—the neumes—in whose collective features he believed that history resided. Far from mere archaism, the ancient neumes provided a clear vision of Gregorian tradition, an invaluable window onto the ancient song. In order to obtain the fullest view, Pothier argued, "it was necessary to study the neumes in their primitive forms, and to follow their transformations through the course of centuries—right up to the fairly recent epoch of their total destruction."[17]

This study revealed in effect two notational practices. The most ancient manuscripts preserved an elementary notation resembling diacritical marks, barely decipherable on their own terms, whose interpretation depended on an existing oral tradition. In later sources the addition of horizontal lines both extended the set of graphical conventions and increased the legibility of the notation by placing the oblique strokes in a more definite visual field. Not until the fourteenth century, however, when the neume's cursive flourishes had been absorbed into larger and more regular square forms, did the interpretation of the melodies become more or less self-evident. Indeed, by this phase the notation assumed a form legible enough for a modern singer like Pothier to decipher without difficulty.

The significance of this more legible notation, from Pothier's perspective, lay not so much in its clarity as in its pedigree. Despite transformations over several centuries, the square notes retained a formal integrity that could be traced back to primitive ancestors. The fourteenth-century notation preserved the same essential shape, and therefore the authority, of the earlier signs by subsuming them into its own forms. In these later neumes one could witness, in other words, the collected residue of at least five centuries of tradition. Pothier proved the point by offering, in a chapter on "the diverse phases of the neumes," a series of paradigmatic tables showing the chronological development of notes and ornaments in both Latin and Gothic notation (fig. 5).

The tables offer a fairly complete taxonomy of Gregorian writing, with signs separated neatly into categories bearing traditional Latin names. The fate of indi-

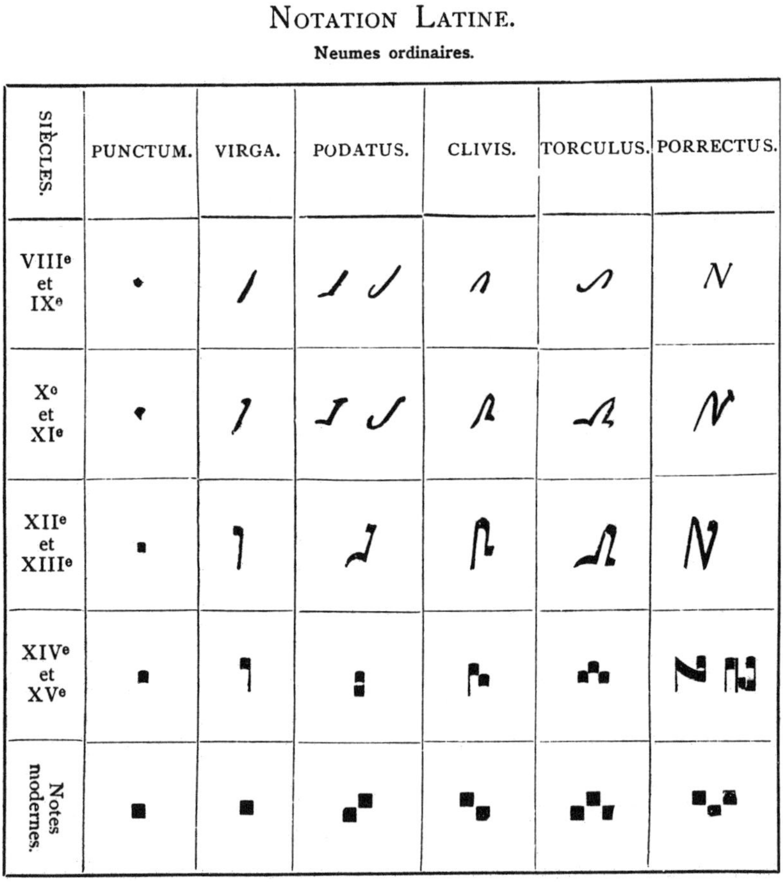

Notation Latine.

Neumes ordinaires.

SIÈCLES.	PUNCTUM.	VIRGA.	PODATUS.	CLIVIS.	TORCULUS.	PORRECTUS.
VIIIe et IXe	◆	/	⌐⌐	∧	⌒	*N*
X^o et XIe	◆	⌐	⌐⌐	∧	⌐	*N*
XIIe et XIIIe	■	⌐	⌐	⌐	⌐	*N*
XIVe et XVe	■	⌐	⫶	⌐■	⌐■⌐	⌐■ ⌐■
Notes modernes.	■	■	⌐■	■⌐	■⌐■	■⌐■

Figure 5a. Tables of neumes from Pothier's *Mélodies grégoriennes* (1880).

vidual neumes is easily glimpsed in the columns, read from top to bottom, that summarize the graphic stages in two-century intervals, beginning with the eighth century. These columns bear, in fact, a sort of formal similarity to diagrams charting the evolution of the human species. We see the signs take on increasingly definite shapes, becoming more and more heightened until they achieve, in the fourteenth century, the upright posture of a fully developed neume, a *scriptum erectum*.

Even more striking, however, is the last chronological stage, an epoch designated not by a traditional roman numeral, but by a single, ambiguous phrase, unceremoniously rotated on the table to appear completely out of place: *Notes modernes*, "modern notes." These sad squares, falling uncomfortably out of his-

NOTATION LATINE.

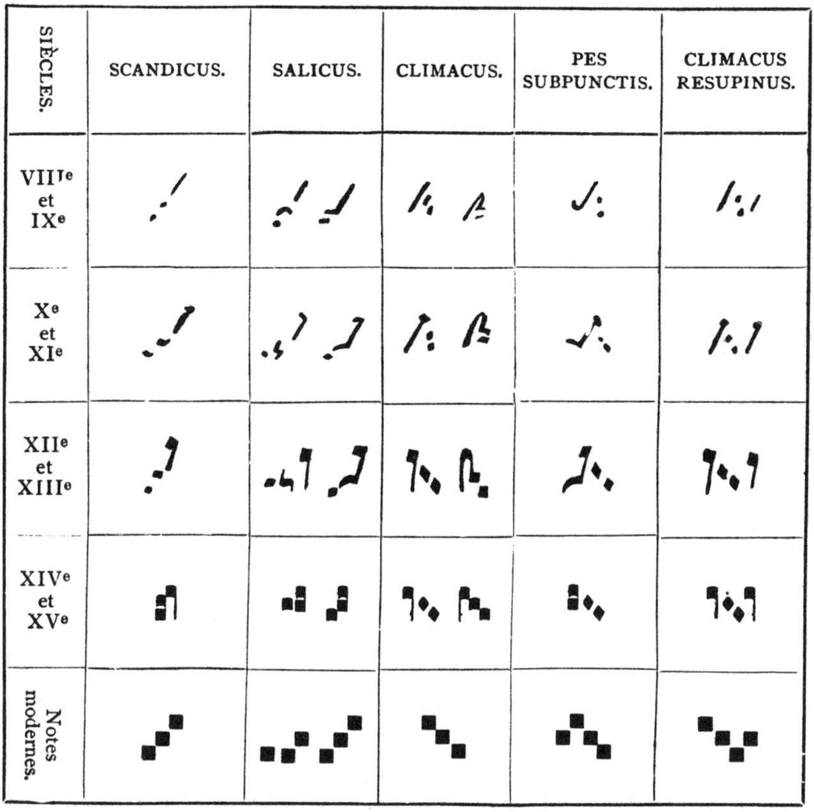

SIÈCLES.	SCANDICUS.	SALICUS.	CLIMACUS.	PES SUBPUNCTIS.	CLIMACUS RESUPINUS.
VIIIᵉ et IXᵉ					
Xᵉ et XIᵉ					
XIIᵉ et XIIIᵉ					
XIVᵉ et XVᵉ					
Notes modernes.					

Figure 5b.

torical sequence, appear to reflect the very limitations implied by their ahistorical name. They look spineless, flaccid, weak. Clumped in artless forms, no longer exhibiting the elegant postures of their primitive ancestors, these "modern notes" summarize in their blockishness all the profound losses of modernity itself. Indeed, Pothier laments the fact that such ugly notes have "come so unpropitiously to be substituted for the beautiful Gregorian neumes in contemporary chant books."[18] Far from representing the past, they herald the ruin of the ancient notation—the epoch, as Pothier saw it, "of its total destruction," the epoch of debris.

What is perhaps less obvious is that Pothier had culled these square notes from a particular contemporary source. It was the typeface used by the printing house of Friedrich Pustet II of Ratisbon (now Regensburg) for a *Graduale Romanum*

PROPRIUM MISSARUM
DE TEMPORE.
~~~~~~~~~~~~~~~~~~~~

Dominica I. Adventus.

Ad Missam.

Introitus.   Ton. VIII.

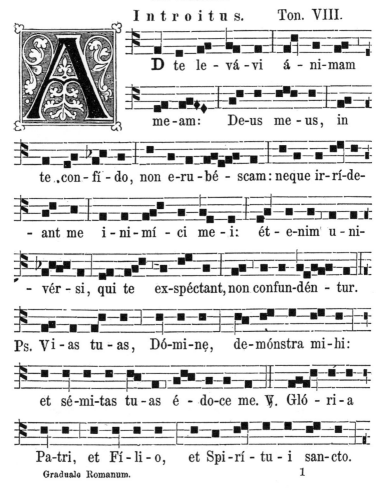

AD te le - vá - vi á - ni-mam me-am: De-us me - us, in te..con - fí - do, non e-ru - bé - scam: neque ir-rí-de- - ant me i - ni - mí - ci me - i: ét - e-nim' u - ni- - vér - si, qui te ex-spéctant, non confun-dén - tur. Ps. Ví - as tu - as, Dó-mi-nę, de-mónstra mi-hi: et sé-mi-tas tu - as é - do-ce me. ℣. Gló - ri - a Pa-tri, et Fí - li - o, et Spi-rí - tu - i san-cto.

Graduale Romanum.   1

Figure 6. Opening page from the *Graduale Romanum* published by Pustet of Ratisbon (1877 ed.).

published in 1871, an edition of chant that enjoyed substantial recognition (fig. 6). The book, which was completed under the direction of the musicologist Franz Xaver Haberl, made its reputation not as a "modern" edition but as a historical one: it claimed to have restored the seventeenth-century Medicean antiphoner (hence Pustet's edition was sometimes referred to as the "neo-Medicean" antiphoner). Haberl believed, moreover, following the Italian scholar Giuseppe Baini, that Palestrina himself had had a hand in making the edition. That story only lent greater significance to a book that already possessed a good deal of authority: Pustet was, in fact, the official printer of the Holy See, Pius IX having granted the house an exclusive fifteen-year privilege for the publication of the church's liturgical books in 1868. When less than three years later the new edition appeared, it already had Rome on its side.

Despite this papal advantage, Pothier was more than a little skeptical of the Palestrina story, and on these grounds questioned the book's claim to authority. Even more important, he objected to the chant itself, which reflected the post-Tridentine fashion of truncating the melodies and altering their rhythm. It was the potentially false pedigree of the Ratisbon edition that ultimately motivated Pothier to discredit its equally false face—to call Pustet's square notes "modern." The notation, after all, was only about as old as the so-called modern face of Didot, the impertinent font that had so bloated the classic roman form. Indeed, Pustet's font, its corpulent squares stuffed uncomfortably into staff lines, employed the same style of type that appeared in most chant books published during the century before the Revolution, books that had themselves grown so corrupt that their faces could not be trusted at all.

The vulgarity of all such modern notes defined, for Pothier, what was wrong with modern Gregorian chant performance. His dream was to produce, with Guéranger's approval, a new gradual that would unseat the Pustet edition through its own irrefutable historical authority, an authority that would trickle down to the printed page itself.

With the publication of *Les Mélodies grégoriennes*, Pothier was well on the way toward this goal, having set to work almost as soon as he had entered the order. Before that time the Solesmes monks had relied on editions printed elsewhere, such as the Reims-Cambrai *Graduel* published by Lecoffre in Paris in the 1850s. Although the monastery was beginning to oversee the publication of a modest number of texts containing chant (such as a small book of benedictions printed in 1856, and a slightly more elaborate ritual book, from 1863, describing the ceremony for the investiture of a Benedictine), little had been done toward a large-scale edition of music. For these smaller texts the monks sought the services of Henri Vatar in Rennes, a press that produced the same garden-variety pages as every other print shop of the period. In typesetting the early booklets, in fact, Vatar employed the somewhat flabby fonts Pothier would soon reject as "modern."

When later in the 1860s Pothier became more seriously involved with Dom Jausions in research on the chant manuscripts, his dream of producing a fully fledged gradual began to take more definite shape, and arrangements were made, again with Vatar, for its eventual publication. For this project, however, the press designed a new Gregorian font, boasting a larger range of neumes that reflected the evidence of the manuscripts. The font made its first appearance in 1864, in a *Directorium Chori* published by Vatar. A glance at the neumes confirms that the printer had done a respectable job. The new types were considerably smaller than the typical squares of the day—small enough, in fact, for the *puncta* to float between the lines of the staff. If the typography on the whole did not ravish (Vatar still used a modern face for the Latin text), it was indeed more legible, and displayed a kind of elegance absent from any of the pages printed by Pustet. Yet for some reason Dom Guéranger delayed the distribution of this edition. All the existing copies perished by fire in 1866. Apart from the single example reproduced in Combe's history of Solesmes,[19] the only remaining traces of Vatar's effort can be found in examples from Edmond de Coussemaker's encyclopedic *Scriptorum de Musica* (fig. 7), an impressive compilation of early music-theory treatises, using Vatar's types, whose first volume appeared in the same year as the Solesmes *Directorium*.

The disaster at the Vatar press appears in hindsight to have been something of a blessing. Indeed, it is hard to imagine that the delay in releasing the new Vatar edition had nothing to do with its still less than perfect appearance. Were Guéranger and Pothier perhaps holding out for a book that would make a stronger first impression? The conjecture is supported by a remarkable little volume produced at Solesmes almost a decade later: a handmade *Processional monastique* from 1873—what amounted to the monastery's first in-house publication of Gregorian chant (fig. 8). The ambitious text (of which only a few copies survive) featured ninety-six lithographed pages of processional chants, with Latin texts rendered by hand in imitation roman letters, beautifully illuminated capitals, full-page drawings, vignettes, and, of course, meticulously drawn melodies that employed a full range of so-called traditional neumes and ornaments, from *punctum* to *quilisma*. On the opening page of the *Proprium de Tempore*, for the first Sunday of Advent, Pothier has even taken care to include a naive little illustration of the Annunciation.

The book, designed and executed by Pothier himself, resembled nothing so much as the exquisite volumes of handwritten poetry produced by William

Exemplum de neuma et de principiis.

Primum   querite   regnum   Dei.

Ecce nomen.   Evovae.

Diffusa est.   Evovae.   *Ant.* Germinavit.

Evovae.   *Ant.* Senex.   Evovae.

Figure 7. Examples of neumes designed by the Vatar
press as they appeared in de Coussemaker's *Scriptorum
de Musica* (1864).

Morris in the same years, editions that sought to capture—completely by
hand—the aura of the past missing from modern typographic books. Pothier's
efforts apparently had the desired effect. A story related by his colleague Dom
Guépin recalls the astonishment the monks experienced on the day they
received the beautiful handmade *cahiers*, whose details seemed to imitate, as
Guépin himself recognized, "the books of hours of Simon Vostre and other
printers of the same period." It was the very resemblance that generated the
monks' delight. "What joy we felt when these books were distributed!," Guépin
remembers.[20] The antique ornaments evidently provided something more than
mere filigree; they formed a kind of graphic analogy to the music, the winding
vignettes echoing on the page the winding melismas now lovingly restored in

Figure 8a. Opening pages of the *Processional monastique* designed
and executed by Pothier in 1873. Courtesy of Abbaye Saint-Pierre,
Solesmes, France. Authorization No. 105.

PROPRIUM
DE
TEMPORE

DOMINICA PRIMA ADVENTUS.

RESPONSORIUM VII.M.

ASPICIENS a lon-ge, ecce víde-o Dei poténtiam veni-én-tem, et nébu-lam to-tam

Figure 8b.

performance. The visual aesthetic enhanced, in short, the charm of the chant, lending new significance to the act of singing itself.

Huysmans, again, reminds us most vividly of the profound impact this kind of handiwork exercised on fin de siècle antiquarians. His novel *L'Oblat* offers a few of the best examples in long speeches by the protagonist Durtal (a sort of Des Esseintes *à rebours*), whose bibliophilia now reflects an unmistakable religious fervor. We find him in the company of his neighbor, the retired collector Monsieur Lampre, who has just offered Durtal the thrill of examining an authentically medieval book of hours:

> It was a magnificent copy of *Horae Beatae Mariae Virginis*, a small quarto in sixteenth-century binding, worked in open-leaf tracery, written towards the end of the fourteenth century by a Flemish hand; it was in Gothic characters, on vellum, each page being elaborately framed by the painter; and this volume of about three hundred pages contained some fifty miniatures on gold backgrounds, amazing portraits of the Virgins of the nativity, girlish, pouting, melancholy faces.

After digressing into a long-winded account of the monastic arts of bookmaking, the collector pauses to ask the unanswerable question: "Who were these monks who were able to fascinate their contemporaries by such works of art? We don't know."[21]

Within a few short years Pothier was hoping to make his own handiwork, if not his name, known beyond the abbey by getting the chant properly into print. Like Morris, he wanted to turn his beautiful lithographic book into a beautiful typographic book. The task was not easy. Despite the steps toward typographic reform taken by Beaudoire and LeMerre in the 1850s, the standard of printing in France remained fairly constant through the century: alone among the European nations, France managed to avoid a "revival" of typographic arts comparable to that of England. In the 1870s Pothier could expect to find nothing better in his own country than the work the monastery had already seen from Vatar in the previous decade. And so he traveled to, of all places, Belgium, to begin negotiations with a new printing house in Tournai.

The decision may at first seem surprising given what we know of the rocky relationship between the printing industries in France and Belgium in the nineteenth century. The problems began, or so it was claimed, with the heavy censorship imposed by the early Napoleonic regime, causing authors in France to seek out presses beyond the border in order to escape government surveillance.[22] The literary exodus created a new market for books produced by foreign presses, a business that developed, especially among the French-language presses in Belgium, into out-and-out piracy. (It was the success of these so-called

contrafacta, which obviously threatened the financial stability of the French publishing houses, that spawned the derogatory expression "édition belge," still used
today to describe any kind of cheaply reprinted book.) But the story of French
artists taking refuge in Belgium has another, even more interesting chapter.
From around 1870 we encounter the figure of Edmond Deman, a printer from
Brussels who, by promoting the work of certain marginal French writers,
became a champion of expatriate literati at the end of the century. When,
for instance, the young Mallarmé, already rejected by the Parnassians, required
a publisher for his infamous eclogue, *L'Après-midi d'un faune*, he turned to
Deman, who in 1876 brought out the poem in a small, elegantly bound volume
featuring drawings by Edouard Manet. Deman's editions were to become
known for their *outré* typography, as well as their overlarge quarto formats, ooz-
ing display types, mauve papers, and the topical, erotic drawings of the Belgian
illustrator Félicien Rops.

Pothier's story belongs in part to this curious history. He, too, was taking
refuge in Belgium, looking for a kind of book he could not find at home.
The press he visited in 1876 had recently been founded by Jules and Henri
Desclée, two brothers already well known to the Benedictines for having
donated a sizable piece of property on which they would build the opulent
neo-Gothic Abbey of Maredsous.[23] Pothier learned that the Desclée press, dedicated in general to the monks' work of liturgical restoration, was prepared to
deal with the special problems of printing music. Better yet, it intended to produce books of impeccable quality, emulating not so much the decadent Deman
as the next best thing: the most advanced, "old-style" typographers in England.
The brothers had actually engaged the services of an English typefoundry to
help them in this work. They were ready, in short, to produce books unlike any
available in France. In a letter written from Belgium in that year Pothier relates
the exciting news to his fellow monk Dom Romary: "What do you say to that,
my good Father? We will go there, then, *to produce the purest Saint Gregory
possible*."[24]

This pure Saint Gregory—like the magnificent, pouting virgins from Durtal's
ideal book of hours—could not be imagined with anything less than a flawless
face. It was Dom Pothier himself who took the responsibility for shaping the
features, drawing on evidence from both fourteenth-century manuscripts and
fifteenth-century imprints. Not long after his consultation in Belgium he furnished the design for an entire range of Gregorian neumes and clefs to the
English typefoundry hired by Desclée to cut the punches and matrices.[25] Yet the
different Gregorian sources he consulted presented slightly different images of
the ideal neume. In the prints, such as those from the Venetian house of Giunta,

he would have seen an uncommonly skilled typeface, with geometrically perfect squares and lozenges, extremely fine ligatures, precision ornaments, and,
finally, elegant clefs in proportion with the rest of the signs on the page.[26] These
fifteenth-century neumes reflected, in other words, the same ideal of typographic perfection that Morris would ascribe to the "great Venetian printers" of
the period. Giunta was, in effect, Pothier's Jenson.

The manuscripts told another story. The Gregorian writing preserved there
issued not from the impression of a type but from the pressure of a quill.
Although such handwritten, fourteenth-century neumes formed the models for
the fine types designed in the fifteenth, there were obvious differences between
the signs, a distinction that related to the materiality of the writing itself. When
produced by hand the square was not so geometric. It showed, in fact, a gentle
curve, the unmistakable result of a pen's movement. This was an unexpected and
beautiful stroke—beautiful because it revealed the presence of the calligrapher
who produced the notation, just as Pothier's lithographed processional displayed
the unmistakable hand he had in the work.

It is no wonder that Pothier desired to keep this hand in view. The neumes
in his own handmade processional were, we could say, the "proto-type," the first
stage in the design of a new and pure Saint Gregory. The Gregorian neume he
finally furnished to Desclée both imitated a classic, fifteenth-century type and,
in the same stroke, gently massaged that form into a more remote time and
place, stretching it backward toward darker ages. The font thus reflected the
same ideology that lay behind Morris's reconceived Golden type. It was the
curve of the square that revealed Pothier's bias toward a medieval, fourteenth-
century hand, the square's subtly rounded sides repudiating everything "modern" in the contemporary chant books. It was this same, queer curve that ultimately provided the Desclée "Saint Gregory," like the idealized Kelmscott
roman, with the evocative face of a past that fell vertiginously between the
cracks of time, a face that had never before been seen in the history of Gregorian typography.

The earliest glimpse of this beautifully curved face emerged from the pages
of the very work that advocated its revival—Pothier's *Mélodies grégoriennes* (fig.
9). This was the first book from Solesmes to be published at Desclée's new
Imprimerie liturgique de Saint Jean l'Evangéliste, appearing just a few years
after Pothier began negotiations with the press. The book on the whole
reflected the high standard of typography established by the English presses
Desclée emulated. It was, in a word, opulent. Its layout anticipated the asym-
metrical, double-page format of the Kelmscott Press books, with wide outer
margins and borders to frame the printed words and a Gothic display type

Figure 9. Title page of Pothier's *Mélodies grégoriennes*.

running across the top. Each chapter began with tasteful vignettes—nothing too distracting—and featured a range of decoratively boxed initials adorned with fruits and flowers. These unique display capitals clearly took their cue from the fanciful alphabets so popular among Renaissance printers, although the letters they contained, distinctly *un*roman, seemed to invoke the more archaic whims of medieval-style illumination. Their hybrid design recalled, in other words, the same kind of aesthetic mélange—the marvelous historical confusion—that characterized Pothier's neumes and Morris's letters. Only the title page, in this respect, appeared less than felicitous. Displaying its eclecticism a bit too proudly, it showed three styles of Gothic letter and about as many species of vine enclosing a cluttered illustration of the Nativity, its chorus of dwarfed angel-musicians recalling some of the more unfortunate images recreated on the walls of Notre-Dame by Viollet-le-Duc. Neither girlish nor pouting, these musical cherubs look more like tired old men.

The misguided art did not detract, however, from the most beautiful aspect of the book: the typography of the individual words. These were the well-chosen words of Pothier, now displayed in an elegant old-style type simply never seen in the Didot-ridden books brought out by French printers of the same period. The font seemed to confer to his thoughts an easy authority, the wisdom of age, making the statements appear, as Des Esseintes had remarked of his own exquisitely printed Baudelaire, "more striking and significant than ever." Along the borders of each page, continuous glosses whispered the text's secrets in a tiny italic. What is more, a series of musical examples rendered entirely in Desclée's new Gregorian font executed the book's most brilliant aesthetic coup, gracefully interrupting the argument at irregular intervals as if to sing what no words could say. If the old-style letter supported the weight of Pothier's opinion, the restored Gregorian typeface undoubtedly clinched it.

Pothier had very astutely realized that he needed this new font to secure the authority of the historical arguments he offered in his treatise. He conceived *Les Mélodies grégoriennes*, after all, as a kind of introduction to the Gregorian chant practiced at Solesmes, and therefore intended to publish it well in advance of his projected gradual, which would not be released for another few years. The treatise formed the theoretical foundation on which the authority of the forthcoming Benedictine edition would rest. In order to forge the proper connection between theory and practice, it made sense that the Gregorian melodies discussed in Pothier's *Gregorian Melodies* should resemble those that would soon appear in the actual edition of music.[27] By employing the beautiful new Gregorian font, he believed the treatise would be able to establish—in both word and deed—the ancient pedigree of the Benedictine chant.

Indeed, he made sure of it. The flawless breeding was nowhere more clearly displayed than in those novel evolutionary tables Pothier included in his chapter on the phases of Gregorian writing (see fig. 5). There we can see, if we look closely enough, that quietly—even smugly—occupying the level of highest notational development are neumes not drawn by hand, such as those marking earlier stages, but signs printed from types. Yes, Pothier represented the glorious perfection of two entire centuries, the *XIVe and XVe siècles*, through the very types Desclée, with his help, had just manufactured. Most assuredly *not* modern, this brand-new musical notation managed, without another word, to carve a niche in history.

· · · · ·

The Benedictine *Liber Gradualis* appeared three years later, in 1883. It formed a companion volume to Pothier's explanatory treatise—a connection immediately apparent from the title page of the new work, which displayed at once the same Nativity *à la médiévale* and the same claim to Gregorian history. The weighty Latin title, rendered imposingly in red and black Gothic letters, proclaimed that this was the "Gradual Book Ordained by Saint Gregory the Great," with notation "faithfully restored from the major codices." Yet the almost too colorful title page also announced that, from an aesthetic viewpoint, this big book of chant would outshine Pothier's more modest book of words in almost every respect. The edition got right to the point, presenting over nine hundred fantasy-filled pages of print—a typographic wonderland of capitals, illustrations, and ornaments all in a medieval style, at least two kinds of Gothic display type, and, of course, the now familiar Gregorian notation, which looked even more beautiful when left on the page to speak for itself. This new book, produced explicitly for the French Congregation of Benedictines (as the title page also indicated), seemed dramatically to complete the aesthetic project Pothier had begun ten years earlier with his quaint monastic processional. The *Liber Gradualis* was a dream come true in print.

The music typography, which constituted the book's raison d'être as well as its most impressive aesthetic feature, deserves a closer look (fig. 10). From the very first page we can count the ways it distinguished itself from the standard fare of European presses, especially the chant brought out by Pustet of Ratisbon. In the opening chant of the edition, the Introit "Ad te levavi" that begins the *Proprium de Tempore*, we observe, for instance, a distinctly "old" old face for the Latin text, more archaic even than the type used for Pothier's treatise. Slightly blacker and more compact—though certainly not as dense as Morris's types—the letters fit comfortably on a page filled with heavy black notation. (Especially clever is the quadratic design of the text's punctuating colons, which, as if to match the Gregorian notes, have been designed to look like two tiny *puncta*.) The neumes themselves exhibit an impressively broad range of forms, with well over a dozen species represented on the first five lines alone. Among the most visually striking are the bold, oblique strokes of the supine *torculus* as well as the ornaments— none of which could be found, of course, on any of Pustet's pages. The very first note of this Introit proudly displays one such restored ornament: a beautifully liquescent *cephalicus*, whose sensually drooping tail calls attention to both the exoticism and the undeniable attraction of the historic face.

If all these features made the page aesthetically more pleasing, other aspects rendered it, in a word, more legible. Perhaps the most subtle—and cunning— of the notation's improvements can be seen in the form of the *pes*, whose traditionally superimposed squares always posed the biggest problem for readability. In the so-called modern chant books this neume never appeared. When Vatar attempted to reinstate it for the Solesmes Directorium chori, the resulting form constituted a sort of typographic failure: the two squares blurred on the page even when viewed at close range. The Desclée font solved the problem with an ingenious solution drawn from the Venetian manuscripts Pothier had consulted. The *pes* now featured a slightly smaller square on the top, an innovation that fostered the optical illusion of a perfectly uniform stack, thus removing the blur.

Even more fundamental, the overall impression of legibility created by the new font issued from the one aspect that also constituted its highest value: the preciously curved square. In addition to all its other attributes, this detail of the design enjoyed a highly practical function. It rendered the quadratic forms immediately distinguishable within a relentless field of parallel staff lines. Since in the layout of the printed page the staff itself now took up a good deal more space, these curved neumes had more room than ever to move about, a feature that represented perhaps the final typographic achievement. Inside the more luxurient space of this expanded staff, the chant melodies sigh, or dreamily float, on bouyant channels of white.

The opulence of these great blanks could be explained as more than mere typographic indulgence. The turn-of-the-century American scholar-printer Theodore Low DeVinne, in *The Practice of Typography*, theorized the white space on the page as a necessary element of good composition. A chapter on indention, for instance, opens with the following reflection:

> Printed words need the relief of a surrounding blank as much as figures in a landscape need background or contrast, perspective or atmosphere. Even in a book of solid

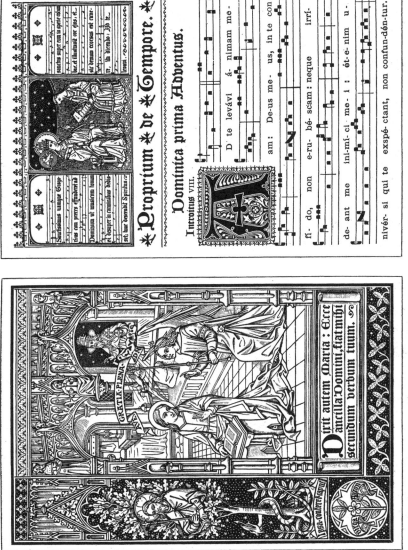

Figure 10. Opening pages of *Liber Gradualis* published by Desclée (1883).

composition, there is invariably more white than black on the page. Much of it may be in the margin, but the amount of white put between the lines and within each letter is greater than supposed. . . . White space is required to make printing comprehensible.[28]

The very features that made the print comprehensible also lent the chant itself an undeniable authority—a condition that emanated from the power of *luxe*. Indeed, the perfection of the printing seemed to signal a new kind of respect for the melodies themselves. In the Benedictine edition, the ancient music had more room to breathe, commanding a new dignity by the sheer space it occupied on the page.

∎ ∎ ∎ ∎ ∎

The same sort of bibliographic luxury was apparent even in the more popular publications released by the Solesmes monks in the 1880s. These texts were printed not by Desclée but by an entirely new printing press operating within the abbey itself. Pothier's *confrère* Dom Antonin Schmitt established the press in 1879 as a vehicle for the propagation of Benedictine ideas; from that year until his death in 1886 he served as the chief typographer. Named for the abbey, the Tipographia Sancti Petri hoped to meet the needs of the general public, by producing smaller pamphlets on popular religious subjects or little songbooks and prayer books of the type still sold at monastic gift shops. Despite the diminutive proportions of most of the work, Schmitt sought to maintain the high standard of music printing already established by Desclée. By arrangement with Belgium, in fact, the Solesmes Tipographia had access to the new Gregorian typeface for the production of its own books. The use of this font allowed the press to put the same, impressive face on every book issuing from the French Congregation of Benedictines.

It was, to be sure, a face no bibliophile could refuse. Such aesthetic appeal shone from all the pamphlets Schmitt produced at the new press, a fact made stunningly clear by a small advertisement featured on the back cover of one early pamphlet, printed in the same year as the Desclée gradual—a modest, sixteen-page book of chants for the popular feast days honoring the Blessed Sacrament and the Blessed Virgin. The advertisement, which listed items now for sale at the Solesmes press, included a few descriptions that would have made even Des Esseintes proud. The first three articles read as follows:

[1] *The Life of Saint Benedict*, extracted from the dialogues of Saint Gregory the Great. Deluxe edition on *papier chiné*, with engraving, *format in-octavo raisin* (two francs)

[2] *A List of Thanksgiving Prayers After Mass*, featuring texts extracted from the Missal following the liturgical cycle. One leaf, *format jésus*, with illuminated letters (two francs)

[3] Same list with hand-illuminated letters by the nuns of Sainte-Cécile (ten francs)

The third item for sale obviously revealed the lengths to which the monks were prepared to go in order to provide *éditions de luxe*. Luckily, they did not have to travel all that far. Sainte-Cécile was the Benedictine convent (named, of course, for the patron saint of music) less than half a mile away, a sister house to the Abbaye Saint-Pierre. The abbess of the convent, Cécile Bruyère, a lifelong spiritual companion of Dom Guéranger until his death in 1875, hoped to foster the liturgical arts of painting and illumination at her own abbey. An artist herself, she became in the 1890s a friend and confessor to none other than Huysmans, who maintained a rich correspondence with her during the entire period of his conversion to Catholicism.[29] This fact alone, together with the striking image of the nuns in their house, with brushes in hand, dipping into their palettes to make the books of their fellow monks even more beautiful, offers compelling testimony to the degree of aestheticism that surrounded the entire restoration of Benedictine life.

Such beauty came at a price. The fact was immediately apparent from the little advertisement in Schmitt's book, which indicated the fivefold increase—from two to ten francs—in the cost of the pretty, hand-decorated *feuilleton*. It was later reflected in the price of other, more substantial books printed at the Solesmes press. By the 1890s the Tipographia Sancti Petri had the financial stability, and the ambition, to bring out two formidable editions: in 1891 an enormous *Liber Antiphonarius*, containing over one thousand pages of long-awaited music for the divine offices; and, four years later, a second edition of the 1883 gradual, which had apparently sold out at the Desclée press.[30] The figure behind these two editions, whose new typographic "look" formed a matched set, was Schmitt's successor, Dom Etienne Babin, a printer who showed at least as much competence in the art as his predecessor, even if the two differed in their taste for ornaments and letters. Most significantly, Babin seemed to prefer an even whiter page than Schmitt and the Desclée typographers, a fact that might account for the size of the new books. His 1895 edition of the *Liber Gradualis*, with few new melodies added, had at least fifty more pages than that of 1883.

The price of these *Libri*, which far exceeded most books of liturgical music, soon became the object of disagreement among religious reformers. A skeptical

Jean Olive, for instance, editor of the anti-Benedictine *Revue de musique religieuse et de chant grégorien*, complained in 1896 that the "fifteenth-century characters" employed in Dom Pothier's editions, which also required the use of a wider staff, made the books "too voluminous and too expensive":

> We understand that had the edition in fifteenth-century characters not been made with a certain luxury, it would easily have become illegible. The consequence of employing such characters therefore makes it impossible ever to have cheap books. An artist, of course, would no more look at the price of a book than a millionaire. But this is not the case among the ordinary faithful. Good value [*le bon-marché*] is an important factor in the diffusion of plainchant.[31]

Olive's rather weak defense of the masses ultimately proved the aesthetic success of the Benedictine gradual. The book's luxurious typography—which he acknowledged was necessary to ensure legibility—did much more than render the music easier to read. Through the advantage of *luxe*, the music entered a different class of books altogether, lifting itself from a bibliographic ghetto to a bibliophile's estate, where, in effect, it could now look down on the poor modern books afflicted with the chronic ailment of illegibility. The expensive Gregorian melodies could no longer represent "good value" precisely because they had now attained *real* value, the sort appreciated by artists and millionaires.

We find this kind of class distinction again displayed—indeed, almost shamelessly flaunted—in a polemical essay from just a few years later representing the very opposite point of view. This time *La Revue du chant grégorien*, a journal more or less directed by Dom Pothier, featured an article coyly entitled "In Marseille This Is How They Write . . . Solesmes." The article, which was a rebuttal of another piece from Olive's *Revue*, responded not so much to the content as to the appearance of the text, and thus began by drawing attention to the printer of the rival magazine, a firm called J. Mingardon from Marseille. The author of the attack, who signed himself "A. Dabin," was probably Alfred Dabin, a *curé* from Giverville, who had published a number of essays for the Benedictine cause.

Dabin's entire rebuttal focused on a single musical example that had been cited in the contested essay, an "Alleluia" attributed to the *Liber Gradualis* of Dom Pothier. It was the attribution that most offended him, and for an obvious reason: Mingardon's notation, though accurate, looked nothing like that found in the Solesmes books. "Am I seeing things?" Dabin asked mockingly, before providing evidence that would yield an answer. On the very next page the article reproduced, alongside Mingardon's poor imitation, the "real" Solesmes

"Alleluia," offering a final judgment that testified to the monks' unquestionably superior taste:

> Nothing could be clearer, could it? Here seventy-four *signs*, well marked, distinct, easy to recognize . . . each having its particular name, *podatus, clivis, torculus, scandicus,* etc. . . . Over there, an ugly scrawl of two hundred seventeen *notes*, aligned in the old way . . . with no design, no coherence, no relief. They tell us that this is Dom Pothier's chant . . . Swindlers! . . . That's Mingardon they're serving us! Beetroot alcohol instead of *chartreuse!*[32]

The indignant analogy made the Benedictine elitism abundantly clear. Only monks, of course, knew the secret of producing a fine *chartreuse*. Next to their utterly perfect notation, the underprivileged square notes from Marseille (which looked essentially like those of Pustet) appeared exactly as they were: coarse, common, poorly bred.

It was precisely this sort of demeaning comparison that the monks believed would eventually undermine Mingardon and all the other fin-de-siècle publishers of liturgical music. Pothier's biographer Dom Lucien David confirms this view in a single sentence whose conspicuous ellipsis points, interrupting the statement like a polite cough, highlighted the indecorous issue that should never cross the lips of a tasteful Benedictine: "In truth, the work of Pothier, despite its completely pacifist appearance, represented a serious menace against the errors and . . . the material interests of those editions that were more or less unfaithful to tradition."[33]

To catch a glimpse of this material threat, and the larger polemic to which it gave rise, we may return briefly to Jean Olive. His aforementioned editorial had, after all, criticized the typography of the Solesmes books only to recommend another, competing edition of chant from the diocese of Digne—an edition printed (by Mingardon, of course) in the larger squares that Dom Pothier called "modern notes." Olive preferred the Digne edition because he considered it not only "good value," but also a good deal more user-friendly. When the notes were larger, he argued, more than one singer could sing off a single book. To support this practical conclusion he had deferred to Théophile Beaudoire, the illustrious French printer whose opinion on such matters was known through a small but widely circulated pamphlet published the previous year and titled *Musique pour la liturgie notée.*[34] As we have seen, Beaudoire, the director of the general type-foundry in Paris, made his reputation in the 1850s by repackaging the past through his timely restoration of the Elzévir types.

His pamphlet is worth considering more closely, for he, too, opposed the Solesmes edition on the grounds of its unnecessarily complex typography.

Beaudoire's argument centered not only on the "historicism" of the Solesmes font (an aspect he considered excessive), but also on its difficulty. Indeed, Beaudoire seemed to think that Pothier's historically informed Gregorian types—perhaps like Morris's Chaucer font—made difficult work of the act of reading Gregorian music. He proposed avoiding all such beautiful difficulty in modern editions of chant by giving readers what they were most accustomed to: a modern plainchant notation, presumably one of the sort available at his own typefoundry.

Beaudoire had already expressed his musical preferences about four years earlier in his *Manuel de typographie musicale* (1891), a book in which he demonstrated both knowledge of typographic history and skill in producing older music types. An extensive table of neumes, not unlike those produced by Pothier, presented more than a dozen cursive forms impressively rendered in typographic "facsimile" (fig. 11). Yet the notes Beaudoire advocated for the actual printing of plainchant, essentially the same as that of Pustet or Mingardon, were far less complicated. His "modern" font, which we find on the same page, consisted of two basic shapes—a square and a lozenge—combined in various ways to yield the different species of neume. The typographic result, in his opinion, would be as cost effective as it was inviting to the consumer.

Not long after its release, Beaudoire's pamphlet, and its recommended notation, came under attack by a suspiciously named figure writing once more for Pothier's *Revue du chant grégorien*. The article in question, titled "La Typographie et le plain-chant," presented the opinions of an author very well informed about issues of music printing at Solesmes. So well informed, in fact, that I am tempted to conjecture that this gentleman, who signed himself simply "Schmidt," was actually using a pseudonym—based perhaps on the deceased Schmitt from the Solesmes press—to disguise his own (Benedictine) identity. The most likely candidate would seem to be Solesmes's head printer Etienne Babin, although Pothier, who himself contributed regularly to the *Revue*, runs a close second. In any case, "Schmidt" begins his polemic by rehearsing the well-known defense for the historical Gregorian font made by Pothier himself fifteen years earlier in *Les Mélodies grégoriennes*. Acknowledging the aesthetic "satisfactions" offered by the typographic neumes, he quickly turns to discuss their immeasurable advantages, and draws a startling conclusion:

> We must therefore attach great importance, for practice as well as for aesthetics, to these traditional forms, whose restoration is imposed as a consequence of the restoration of chant itself. . . . Not to displease, *Monsieur le directeur* of the General Foundry, but the abandoning of the traditional notation of plainchant had as its cause not economic factors, . . . which are here considered only accidental, but the actual abandoning of the true

Fac-simile des Neumes

Chaque figure a subi des transformations suivant les siècles.

Virga sons aigus	/ / 기 ٦ ٦	Climacus aigu-grave-grave	႙ 7**
Punctum sons graves	\ . - , ▪ ♦ ▪	Scandicus grave-grave-aigu	/ ⟩
Clivus aigu-grave	♪ ∧ ٦	Salicus grave-grave-aigu	/ - -
Porrectus aigu-grave-aigu	N ◥	Pes subpunctis grave-aigu-grave-grave	✓·.
Podatus grave-aigu	✓ ✓	Climacus resupinus aigu-grave-grave-aigu	/·./
Torculus grave-aigu-grave	∧ ∧	Strophicus sons prolongés	// /// 77 777

Toutes ces figures étranges correspondaient aux notes et groupes de notes ci-dessous :

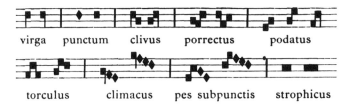

virga   punctum   clivus   porrectus   podatus

torculus   climacus   pes subpunctis   strophicus

Figure 11. Neumes designed by Théophile Beaudoire in his *Manuel de typographie musicale* (1891).

principles of execution. The practice of hammering the notes inevitably led to the graphic disjunction of the notes. The writing suffered the same fate as the execution. Like the latter, the former was left to the barbarians, destroyed and massacred.[35]

The passage's bellicose metaphor gives the topical notion of typographic vandalism a new twist. Here it becomes clear that the real vandals were not printers but barbaric singers, whose loathsome voices wrought havoc on the graphic tradition. The relentless attacks of such voices shattered the beautiful neumes into countless broken pieces, leaving behind shards of squares, a Gregorian humpty-dumpty for hapless moderns clumsily to piece together again.

The remedy for such comprehensive wreckage—as should by now be clear—was certainly not to be found in the patchwork squares of Pustet's or Mingarden's or Beaudoire's modern editions. Indeed, when Monsieur Schmidt pauses over the Gregorian music printed by Beaudoire, his judgment recalls the frightening landscape of modernity, whose electric lights and industrial sounds, as Huysmans and the fin-de-siècle followers of Baudelaire knew all too well, had irrevocably changed the sensory world into something intolerable. Beaudoire's modern notes revealed, in Schmidt's view, "just what the decadence of plainchant has led us to: the notes are of such a caliber as to make you blind, the sounds of a force to split your ears."[36]

It is an arresting image. However disgusting Dabin's "beetroot alcohol" might have seemed to a delicate French palate, this hyperbolic conclusion implied a physical condition infinitely more serious. Gazing at Beaudoire's Gregorian chant, Schmidt suggested, was actually hazardous to the health—so offensive to the senses that it had the power to destroy both sight and hearing.

Voices in Print

With this bizarre picture of a cantor made both deaf and blind by print, we negotiate a sudden turn into performance. It is admittedly an unexpected shift of focus for a discussion concerned primarily with the materiality of print. But Schmidt's strange rhetoric brings into view an important aspect of the typographic book that might otherwise have remained invisible—an aesthetic dimension apparent, one might say, not so much *on* the page as *in* it. His remarks suggest that there is indeed more to typography than meets the eye. The idea that ugly musical signs could produce equally disagreeable sounds assumes a basic connection between the physical properties of print and the activity it stimulates, between the sign and its performance. Typecast letters, he seems to say, always imply the voice that reads or sings. The material *nota* gives rise to an ephemeral *vox*.

The rapport between sight and sound, writing and reading, prompted by Schmidt's image of a painfully "loud" type should thus not be dismissed as the ranting of a polemicist. We recognize the same sort of rapport, in fact, in the very ideal of "legibility" that dominated turn-of-the-century discourse on typography. As we have seen, the notion of legibility referred to the way printed characters enabled the act of reading. It was said that a legible type "reduced fatigue"—that is, made for easier reading by offering printed characters paradoxically both more distinct and more consistent in form. For the conscientious typographer, this condition amounted to an unacknowledged contract between the printer and his potential customers. Stanley Morison expressed this obligation in the form of an anecdote: "If my friends think that the tail of my lower-case r or the lip of my lower-case e is rather jolly, you may know that the fount would have been better had neither been made."[37]

What this formula makes abundantly clear is that, in order to do its job properly, the ideal letter should never be noticed—not even by the printer's best friends. In an essay from some years later we find the matter put more directly. A "good" type, Morison explains, is "one that, while not drawing attention to itself, confers distinction, authority, elegance, and appropriateness upon the text in hand." He goes on to offer a conclusion that is nothing short of a commandment: "A high sense of discipline in letter-designing and book-designing are the paramount virtues unless, which God forbid, the printer is to come between the reader and his chosen author."[38] When a printer stayed obediently out of the way, the reader and his "chosen author" evidently had the opportunity to meet on some mutually agreeable ground. But this encounter could never be "face to face," since a reader was not even supposed to *see* the typographic face of the author. No, what the reader would discern on a well-designed page, with any luck, was that ephemeral element known as the author's voice.

This was the great, unspoken truth of legible type. Morison suggests that anyone skilled in the art of printing knew about this truth: the powerful relation between sight and sound, between the graphic representation and the voice of the text. We can certainly impute this sort of understanding to the more extreme experiments of William Morris, whose "difficult" Chaucer font achieved its desired effect by a similar logic. The archaic, black letters—dense, well formed, closely spaced—required a different kind of reading, demanding that the text be consumed in an entirely new way. It was this novel experience (which, of course, entirely escaped the reader's notice) that refreshed the Middle English text: as if, in the transformed time-space of reading, one would be able to imagine the historical Chaucer "coming through" the text in a new and compelling way, to perceive the strange accent of his archaic tongue. As Yeats would later put it, Morris's Kelmscott Chaucer evoked a "living voice," recalling a time when "the ear and the tongue were subtle, and delighted one another with the little tunes that were in words."[39] A beautiful page had the power, then, to transform what was known as "silent" reading into a blissful interval of listening.

Mallarmé's late-nineteenth-century poetic experiments with great blanks of white, though different in kind, might well be defended in similar terms. For as he set out to give the worn-out alexandrine of French classical poetry a new life, he also looked to typography to realize his goal. The path of a career that began with *L'Après-midi d'un faune* and ended with *Un Coup de dès* might profitably be traced in those white spaces that signaled the emergence of a new kind of poetic rhythm. Indeed, as the blanks began to consume more and more of the page, what became increasingly palpable, audible, was the sound of the text, a quality, or voice, that Mallarmé called simply "Music." Some years later the American poet Louis Zukovsky would articulate a principle that rehabilitated a sense of this Mallarméan experiment. The typography of a poem, he judged, "will help to tell us how the voice should sound."[40]

With these examples in mind, we may return to Dom Pothier. When he exclaimed to his fellow monk in 1876 that he would go to Belgium "to produce the purest Saint Gregory possible," we can imagine that he believed Desclée capable of producing not just the beautiful face of Saint Gregory's music, but the very voice in which he had uttered it. The Desclée font was going to be so "good," in Morison's sense of the term, that readers would finally be able to meet the good pope, to hear—indeed, to feel—his perfect song reaching through the page, a sweet caress on wholly unsuspecting ears.

Such a phenomenon was nowhere more clearly represented than on the opulent first page of the first book of chant produced by that Belgian press, which we have already examined (see fig. 10). The illustrations surrounding the opening chant of the liturgical year portray the effect the typography was to have on its fin-de-siècle readers. They reveal, in two drawings, two holy figures from the past being taken unawares, hearing voices that rend the fabric of their ordinary existence, that sing things never before imagined. On the left, the Virgin kneels on a prie-dieu before an open prayer book, a glimpse of her bedchamber in the background. She inclines her head away from the prayer book—listening—in the direction of the Angel, who holds a banner bearing the inscription "Ave gratia plena": "Hail, you who are full of grace." The Angel's right hand is raised, finger pointed upward, while a dove flies between the two figures, just below the banner, in the direction of the Virgin's left ear. It emerges from the banner, sailing on rays of light issuing from the words themselves. The voice of the Holy Spirit travels through these words of the Angel, his enunciatory "Ave" constituting what grammarians would call an ejaculation, and penetrates the unsuspecting listener as she hears them. The whole illustration depicts the scene of the Annunciation, the sacred instant in which the Messiah was mystically conceived through the ear of the Virgin Mary.

This scene on the left-hand side of the page is beautifully echoed in the triptych on the right, a tiny drawing that portrays another scene of immaculate listening. This time the holy one who hears is not a woman but a man; the penetrated ear is not the left but the right. It belongs, in fact, to Saint Gregory himself, who is caught in his own mystical act of listening, a divine moment in which, Christian hagiography tells us, he received the Church's song from the Deity, who came to him, again, in the form of a dove. Saint Gregory assumes a posture that combines those of the Angel and the Virgin depicted to his left. With one hand poised in midair, and another lifted, pointing, he is shown as both speaker and listener. Indeed, he is singing back the song he hears, a song that a dutiful scribe writes down. Framing the picture is a hymn that celebrates the scene in song, preserved in the same antique Gregorian notation that the scribe himself presumably writes. The text of the hymn proclaims:

> Sanctissimus namque Gregorius
> cum preces effunderet ad Dominum
> ut musicum donum ei desuper in carminibus dedisset
> tunc descendit Spiritus sanctus super eum
> in specie columbae et illustravit cor ejus
> et sic demum exorsus est canere
> ita dicendo: "Ad te levavi."

> When the most Holy Gregory
> poured out prayers to the Lord
> that He might surrender to him from above a musical gift in song
> then the Holy Spirit descended upon him
> in the form of a dove and enlightened his heart
> to such a degree that at last he began to sing
> saying thus: "Ad te levavi."

"To thee I have lifted up my soul." The opening notes of Gregory's original song appear at the very end of the hymn, as if to form an intertextual connection with the book inside of which the poem takes place—the *Liber Gradualis* that, as legend has it, Gregory himself had ordained. The song within the song functions to create a huge ellipsis, stopping the myth midstream, just as Gregory is about to sing the cycle of chants that will define the entire liturgical year, a cycle that began, of course, on the first Sunday of Advent, with the Introit "Ad te levavi." This chant then appears, as if in a *mise en abîme*, just below the triptych, on the very same page. In the drawing, the chant's opening notes are rendered in the cursive neumes that occupied the lower stages of Pothier's evolutionary chart, the first traces of music writing in the history of European music. Below, the chant reappears, almost larger than life, in the beautiful "fourteenth- and fifteenth-century neumes" that supposedly marked the culmination of such writing. The two halves of the page thus offer an image of history completed, from origin to end, *alpha* to *omega*.

Indeed, the tiny illustration at the top of the page seems to shed light on the original meaning of the neumes in much the same way that the Holy Spirit himself was said to have illuminated Gregory (the hymn in fact says "illustrated," from *illustrare*, to make bright). It reveals a direct connection between writing and singing, between the graphic representation of chant and its performance—indeed, the first musical performance of Christian history. The composition of that opening page, like that of so many medieval manuscripts, maintains a didactic rather than merely decorative function—leading us as if along an invisible path backward through history, from fifteenth-century neumes, to a ninth-century hand, right into the mouth of the singing Gregory. Readers of this historic Benedictine gradual could now imagine emanating from the page the very voice of the chant that the scene attempted to depict, a voice that "announced" the mysterious chant of the past to the unsuspecting listeners of the present. Through exquisitely legible signs they could not see, it sang to them the sweet, barely audible song of history.

3

Gregorian Hands

ot long after the publication of the much-awaited *Liber Antiphonarius*, Dom Pothier left Solesmes. In 1893, responding reluctantly to the call for a new prior, he moved to the Abbey of Ligugé—the monastery to which the converted Huysmans would repair in 1899. Pothier did not, however, remain long enough to make the aging writer's acquaintance. In the very next year he was again transferred, this time to a more promising post at the Abbaye Saint-Wandrille in Normandy, a spectacular house—complete with thirteenth-century ruin—that had recently been reclaimed by the Benedictines in the hopes of fostering a revival of monastic arts even more extensive than that at Solesmes.[1] (No less an artist than Maurice Maeterlinck spent twelve years living in this abbey, where he organized several twentieth-century revivals of *Pelléas*, and dreamed with Georgette LeBlanc of someday turning Saint-Wandrille into his own Bayreuth.)[2] On Christmas Day 1894 Pothier was named prior of the monastery; within four years he had become its abbot.[3]

Pothier's installation at Saint-Wandrille marked the beginning of a new era at Solesmes. For in 1896, just about a year after he had moved to Normandy, his former Abbaye Saint-Pierre witnessed two very different but equally important events that were to transform its public image. The first was the groundbreaking ceremony for the already discussed Gothic renovation of the monastery, whose sumptuous new façade literally put the abbey on the map, making Solesmes and its now famous singing monks a more enticing stop for sightseers—a unique fin-de-siècle tourist attraction. The second event also concerned a kind of renovation—one with consequences equally, if not more, significant for the abbey's public image. This was the publication at the Solesmes press of the first *Liber Usualis* (known in French as the *Paroissien romain*). The unique little book combined in a single volume the chants from both the gradual and the antiphoner, together with texts from the missal, for Sundays and the principal feast days of the year. With its manageably small format, the book represented a departure for the Solesmes press. Huysmans's Durtal had complained in *L'Oblat* about the unwieldy Solesmes prayerbooks "as big as post office dictionaries." The *Liber Usualis* now offered a practical alternative: a miniature volume that dispensed with a measure of typographic artistry in order to make the chant available to a larger body of the faithful.

This book was, in other words, a functional publication in whose purpose we begin to see another, very different image of the Gregorian reform at Solesmes. In the words of one turn-of-the-century Benedictine, it represented "a first attempt to popularize the chant—and the results surpassed all expectation."[4] With this portable book the Solesmes monks expected to enhance not so much the aesthetic value as the actual distribution of the music, and thus "en-chant" the public in a more literal sense: by getting the music into the hands of more and more worshippers. The distinctly pragmatic agenda signals a new phase in the Gregorian restoration—the emergence of, as some would call it, a "practical school" at Solesmes, a kind of Gregorian *école normale* aimed at increasing knowledge of the authentic chant through general education both within and outside the monastery.

Significantly, it is not to Pothier that we look for this pedagogical restoration. The impetus came entirely from one of his *confrères*, an industrious young monk called Dom André Mocquereau. Fourteen years Pothier's junior, Mocquereau did not enter the monastery until 1875, the year of Guéranger's death and the beginning of the most intensive period of preparation for the forthcoming *Liber Gradualis*. Having arrived at Solesmes with some prior musical experience (he played the cello), he soon became involved not only with the edition but also with matters of performance. Within a few years he had gained permission to train a small *schola* of advanced singers to improve the quality of chant in daily worship. By 1889, just a decade after his ordination, he had replaced Pothier as general director of the choir. It is thus hardly surprising that in the 1890s the direction of chant research should also have fallen into his hands and—especially after Pothier's departure to Saint-Wandrille—changed course. Under Mocquereau's influence, the Gregorian repertory at Solesmes was to acquire not just a new direction but a whole new look—a renovation as impressive, perhaps, as that of the abbey itself.

· · · · ·

The first, most significant sign of this renovation had become visible as early as 1888, in the inauguration of a monumental new project, entirely of Mocquereau's design, to be published by the Solesmes press. It was the announcement of a series of volumes in which the Benedictines would bring out, over the course of several years, all the principal manuscripts of Gregorian chant in photographic facsimile. Combe reports that Mocquereau first intended to call his grand scheme *Les Mélodies liturgiques*, but, as the name suggested an uncomfortable similarity to that of Pothier's 1880 treatise, he was encouraged to come up with another.[5] The series eventually bore the more esoteric title *Paléographie musicale*.

The whole endeavor showed more than a little ambition on Mocquereau's part. For one thing, the idea of producing a series of phototypes required a skill that the head printer Etienne Babin, however gifted at typography, did not necessarily possess. For another, such a monumental series—what amounted to a Gregorian *Denkmal*—would no doubt pose some financial risk to the monastery. But Mocquereau, after setting out to raise money himself through subscriptions, managed to convince both Dom Babin and the abbot Dom Couturier of the project's value. The first volume appeared in 1889. By 1896 the press had published four more, which, in addition to the impressive facsimiles, contained some of the more important extended essays on Gregorian theory to be produced at Solesmes.[6]

Despite the esotericism—and apparent extravagance—of the publication, the *Paléographie musicale* had originally been imagined as a pragmatic enterprise, and thus might be viewed as an early manifestation of the so-called practical school at Solesmes that eventually developed under Mocquereau.[7] He claimed to have conceived the series of facsimiles as a supplement to the recently published *Liber Gradualis*, a means of demonstrating the indisputable authenticity of the new Benedictine edition. Pothier himself had imagined, as we have noted, that the sheer beauty of his new edition would convince those with any taste at all, especially the reigning Pope Leo XIII, of its obvious superiority. But he was mistaken. Even with the timely release of their gradual the pope did not, as the Benedictines hoped, revoke the privilege previously bestowed on Pustet of Ratisbon, a privilege that in 1883 was in need of renewal. In two letters to Dom Pothier in 1884 the Holy Father made it clear that, although he recognized the value of Benedictine scholarship, his seal of approval would remain firmly attached to the Ratisbon edition.[8]

The papal brush-off was an obvious setback for the progress of the Benedictine restoration. Indeed, now that Leo XIII had spoken, the monks found themselves in an awkward position. In order not to appear disrespectful of the Holy See, they essentially had to avoid promoting their own publication. Mocquereau's series thus offered a kind of solution to the dilemma. Its pictures would save the Benedictines, in effect, thousands of words, silently proving—to anyone with eyes to see—the superiority of their new edition over that of Pustet. "The

principal goal of publishing these manuscripts," Mocquereau wrote in 1887, the
year he came up with the scheme, "is to prove to all, *through the sources themselves,*
the truth of Dom Pothier's doctrine, and of the chant offered in his Gradual."[9]
Through the evidence of the manuscripts, Mocquereau would confer onto
Pothier's modern gradual a new value, a truth it had been unable to claim for
itself.

From Print to Script

The series planned to lay out that truth in good order, beginning with the very
earliest sources. Mocquereau chose for the first volume an impeccable specimen
from Saint-Gall, the Codex No. 339, featuring the so-called primitive neumes
that had occupied the first rung of Pothier's evolutionary ladder (fig. 12). The
ancient handwriting in this source bore little resemblance to the perfect square
notes of Pothier's *Liber Gradualis*. The points and slashes that floated above the
Latin text were perhaps more like the notation found in the tiny, handwritten
hymn that formed the outer border of the triptych discussed at the end of the
previous chapter, on the *Liber*'s first page. But the neumes of Saint-Gall, floating
above the words without the aid of Guidonian staff lines, looked even more
primitive than those in the little illustrated hymn. If they resembled anything, it
was the odd bit of writing that appeared at the very center of the triptych: the
completely illegible marks covering the tablet of Gregory's scribe. It was here,
evidently, that Mocquereau focused his attention, as if to pick up where the neo-
Gothic illustration had left off. He would defend Pothier's edition by reproducing a much more precise picture of this ancient Gregorian hand and its first mysterious strokes.

However, these indecipherable neumes hardly offered a perfect defense for
Pothier's book. If it were proof Mocquereau wanted, it would certainly have
been more expedient to begin with one of the many fourteenth-century manuscripts that resembled Pothier's edition. What did the Saint-Gall notation provide that the more legible sources could not? In the explanatory preface to the
first volume of the *Paléographie musicale* we begin to find an answer. Mocquereau's final essay, "The Origin and Classification of Different Neumatic
Notations," presented a detailed rationale of the Gregorian handwriting his readers were about to see—an *écriture* he referred to as "oratorical" or "chironomic"
writing. The qualifiers alone suggested that he perceived much more on the page
than an arbitrary collection of points and slashes. What he found, in fact, were
the outlines of three basic accents (grave, acute, circumflex) that were themselves
the signs of another sort of movement, an expressive impulse he traced, with a
little help from Quintilian, back to classical oratory.

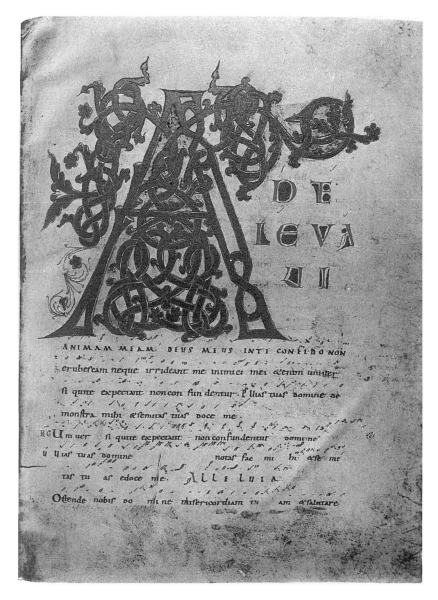

Figure 12. Opening folio of Saint-Gall Codex No. 339, from the first volume of Mocquereau's *Paléographie musicale* (1889).

His argument as a whole focused on the orator's performance. The heat of rhetorical passion produced, in Mocquereau's view, not just a flow of words but a spontaneous movement of hands, gestures that marked the natural cadences of the orator's speech: "In the act of speaking, the hand and the voice obey the same movements of the soul." From this image he spun a wonderful tale of the origins of music notation:

> The accents could have been born in one of two ways. Either the grammarian, when attempting to notate the intonation of syllables, took the gestures of the orator as a model: in this respect, the accents would represent nothing but a sort of pictography, analogous to what we find in the origins of language. Or (and this is the preferable explanation), the grammarian, in tracing these two signs / \, instinctively obeyed the same interior force that directed the hand of the orator. Could there in fact be anything more natural, more primitive, anything less invented or conventional, than the use of these two marks directed from low to high /, and from high to low \, to signify the rising and falling of the voice? . . . In the same natural movement that the orator lowers and raises his hand, the grammarian thus represented the intonation of syllables by means of accents.[10]

Through this story we begin to glimpse what Mocquereau himself saw in the old neumes, that natural writing he called "chironomic." The accent marks that interrupt the flow of his argument, displaying themselves in all their difference, seem to indicate that what he sensed was not "writing" at all, but something more basic, more physical—the natural undulations of hand and voice ("from low to high /, from high to low \"). It was a marvelous sort of synecdoche that turned the inky hand of primitive handwriting, the *manus* of the manuscript, into an entire, gesturing body. The very idea of chironomy, after all, referred to those hand movements through which a melody might be represented *without* notation, suggesting a displacement of the writing hand. The neumes' tight curves opened to become the majestic gestures of the orator who wrote his inspired performance, midair, for all to see. This was in fact Mocquereau's preferred explanation for the written accents: "it was the *hand of the orator himself* leaving on the parchment or wax tablets the trace of his ascending and descending movements."[11]

The proposition leaves us in no doubt about the authority Mocquereau associated with the primitive hand of the manuscripts. It also begins to suggest how the less-than-legible manuscripts he planned to publish in the *Paléographie musicale* might serve to uphold the Benedictines' perfectly legible *Liber Gradualis*. If Pothier's Gregorian typography could call forth the idealized image of Saint Gregory's lost voice, then Mocquereau's series of authentic Gregorian hands would accomplish a good deal more. The exemplars of ancient manuscripts would present not just an *ideal* voice but, in effect, the evidence of an entire monastic tradition of chanting—centuries of real, live singers who knew the repertory by heart. By reproducing these old hands Mocquereau intended to amass several volumes of medieval witnesses for Pothier's defense.

What lay hidden in these strange signs (as Mocquereau himself called them) was thus important not only for the whole Gregorian reform at Solesmes but presumably for Mocquereau himself—living proof, as it were, of his own monastic heritage. One of Mocquereau's first encounters with this inspiring heritage had taken place, we learn, some years earlier in July 1884, during his first trip to the Bibliothèque Nationale. After spending a day in the manuscript collection he wrote to Dom Couturier and confessed: "In the midst of all these old liturgical books, I feel at home. They remind me of the good old monks who wrote them for the divine office—the entire monastic past of the Holy Church is revealed."[12]

It was this feeling of communion with long-forgotten monks, the sense of being "at home" among the unfamiliar books of an urban library, that defined the peculiar and powerful effect of handwritten sources. The telling image of "good old monks" summoned from the lifeless pages of manuscripts marks a singular experience, an uncanny convergence of the strange and the familiar, that strikingly recalls the condition Michel Foucault has called the "fantasia of the library," referring to the experience of modern historians dreaming among their old tomes. In the nineteenth century, the "dusty volume that opens with a flight of forgotten words" represented, for Foucault, a site of scholarly work that was inescapably bound up with the imaginary. The modern scholar dreamed with eyes open, deriving a unique pleasure from "amassing minute facts," reducing monuments "to infinitesimal fragments."[13] Studying past monuments in all their glorious detail produced the fantastic vision known as scholarly knowledge.

Perhaps the most striking tale of such bibliographic reverie among music historians comes to us from Théodore Nisard, one of Mocquereau's more illustrious predecessors in the Gregorian reform. Nisard, whom we met briefly in chapter 1, was a cleric whose work on Gregorian chant at midcentury won him recognition from a number of historians, and not a little envy from his Belgian rival Fétis. In the course of a laborious study of primitive neumes an antiphoner from the Mazarine library in Paris fell into his hands; he made a remarkable discovery, the precise circumstances of which were published in an issue of the *Revue du monde catholique* from 1848:

I had been in Paris since 1841. A burning fever, resulting from the fatigue of my labors, kept me in bed when the Revolution of February 1848 broke out. From rue Princesse, where I was staying, I heard the alarm, a knell sounding from the towers of Saint-Sulpice, that announced together with gunfire the fall of a throne and the delirium of a people. I had the precious Antiphoner at the head of my bed, as always. All at once, a profound sleep seized me, despite the indescribable tumult outdoors, and I was transported to an old cathedral where the divine office was being celebrated. Wishing to join my voice with those of the cantors, I proudly opened the manuscript I had under my arm like an insep-arable companion. But at each of the written signs, I made sounds that aroused surprise and laughter from the choristers with whom I very timidly mingled. "Who is this new-comer?" they murmured. One of my imaginary companions took pity on my ignorance. He was a sweet, calm old man, with one of those beautiful faces admired by archaeolo-gists in the dazzling miniatures found in manuscripts from the fourteenth and fifteenth centuries. I assumed he was the head cantor. Taking me aside during the homily he kindly said to me, "My son, it appears you have not followed the lessons of our schola. Listen." And he made me understand, with a luminous swiftness, the symmetry of the neumatic notation.[14]

The outbreak of revolution in 1848, a people delirious with freedom: the details offer a bizarre narrative context for the comparatively cloistered work of the paleographer, for whom *liberté* meant something completely different. A scholar's freedom was born not of revolution but of reverie. Inspired by a delir-ium of another kind, Nisard reveals himself listening past the "indescribable tumult" to hear voices not from the present but from a long-forgotten history, voices that whispered the secrets of a silent script.

Making Facsimiles

These imaginary figures of Nisard's dream, the products of scholarly wish fulfill-ment, present us with a more extreme version of the "good old monks" Moc-quereau himself fantasized among the manuscripts of the Bibliothèque Nationale: both were visions stimulated by the illegible signs of ancient hands. Indeed, such imaginative responses could be traced back to a very particular aspect of the scholar's work habits. In order to study the neumes, a nineteenth-century historian had no choice but to copy them, to make his own facsimiles. Fantasy was linked, then, not just to reading but to writing the unreadable signs. The scholar's imagination was first unleashed with the tip of his pen, set free in the curves of a primitive notation.

E. T. A. Hoffmann beautifully thematized this effect of exotic script in his modern allegory of writing, "The Golden Pot," a tale of a young clerk, Ansel-mus, and his marvelous encounter with the archivist Lindhorst. Installed in Lind-horst's library, Anselmus is put to work copying Arabic manuscripts, with "pens, sharply pointed and of strange color, together with paper of quite uncommon whiteness and smoothness." The writing soon brings pleasure. Anselmus, we are told, begins "to feel more and more at home in the remote and lonely room." The beautiful *arabesques* he reproduces by hand—signs with no clear signified—

stimulate a fantastic vision of paradise. His methodical task becomes a dream, the stuffy library an enchanted Eden, and a wonderful new knowledge is offered through a voice—a phantasm of the illegible—that speaks to him from the parchment leaves. It is Serpentina, the murmuring truth of serpentine script, who transports the young scribe into a world where the unknown signs are utterly familiar.

These working hours had been and continued to be for him the happiest of his life; still surrounded by lovely music, ever and anon hearing Serpentina's encouraging voice, he was filled to overflowing with a pure delight which often rose to highest rapture. . . . In the new life which had risen before him, as in serene and sunny splendor, he seemed to apprehend all the wonders of a higher world, which hitherto had filled him with confusion and even with dread. His copying proceeded with rapidity and ease. For he felt more and more *as if he were writing characters long known to him.*[15]

The earliest studies of Gregorian chant, which required the same task of transcription, must have stimulated a similar kind of knowledge. To reproduce these cursive characters was, then, to invent stories of meaning, to dream, in the very act of writing, of a time when such writing was not contrived but completely "natural." Indeed, for Mocquereau the act of transcribing manuscripts involved a kind of channeling across time, an imaginary movement toward countless unknown scribes who were singers, conductors, orators. It was in this sense, perhaps, that Mocquereau imagined the manuscripts as a unique corridor to the past, living proof of monastic history. Retracing the neumes by hand, the modern scholar put himself directly and palpably in touch with that history, as if moving in concert with forgotten monks of old. The entry for "fac-similé" in Larousse's 1872 *Grand Dictionnaire universel* signals this condition with a quotation from the historian Casse de Saint-Prosper: "The facsimile," he says, "makes us live with that which no longer exists."[16]

In the 1860s Dom Pothier might have explained the purpose of the new Solesmes scriptorium in very similar terms. The very act of copying allowed the monks in this atelier not just to get their hands on a manuscript but also, as we observed with Pothier's handmade *Processional monastique*, to step right into its charmed world. Making reproductions was, after all, the quintessential monastic pastime, the means by which humanistic learning had been preserved during that bleak interval of Western history known as the Dark Ages. The Solesmes scriptorium, a latter-day monument to such monastic perseverance, provided its own copyists with the same indispensable knowledge, a marvelous new vision of Gregorian practices—a vision they acquired, so to speak, firsthand.

Such insight was virtually impossible to attain any other way. Like Hoffmann's Anselmus, Pothier and the other modern scribes of Solesmes possessed an intensely personal knowledge of Gregorian history, an experience that in many ways resisted description. What they knew could not be readily conveyed to someone who had neither seen nor touched a manuscript. It was a point Mocquereau himself raised in the first volume of the *Paléographie musicale*. His introductory essay described the whole "business of facsimiles," in fact, as a direct consequence of this problem of seeing. Scholars began reproducing the neumes, he argued, because "one could not speak to the public about these strange signs without first putting them before its eyes."[17] Seeing really was believing. His own series would provide a similar kind of service, a resource for all those who lacked direct, "hands-on" experience of the sources. Indeed, by publishing this evidence, making the Gregorian secrets accessible to all, Mocquereau significantly extended the scope of the paleographic work begun by Pothier and Jausions. He managed, in effect, to put the private world of the scriptorium, and its exotic writing, on public display.

· · · · ·

He was by no means the first scholar to make the attempt. Almost four decades earlier, in 1849, the Jesuit Louis Lambillotte had undertaken a similar venture—perhaps the first of its kind—when, in a significant departure from his career as a composer of sentimental sacred choral music,[18] he was inspired to produce a complete facsimile of the most precious manuscript housed at the Saint-Gall monastery, the Codex No. 359. He believed the source to be the "autograph," as he put it, of Saint Gregory's original antiphoner, hence the oldest surviving manuscript of Gregorian chant. His *fac-similé* presented, according to his title page, "an authentic copy" of this vast codex, whose 130 pages Lambillotte had reproduced with the aid of a professional calligrapher—after considerable resistance from the conservative Saint-Gall librarians. It was worth the trouble. The edition, first released by the Parisian publisher Poussielgue in 1851, continued to be so popular that by 1867 it required a second printing.[19]

The distribution of this antiphoner constituted an important event not only for Lambillotte and his publisher but for all midcentury *musicistes*. As Mocquereau observed, the obvious success of Lambillotte's facsimile "proved that lovers of religious music attached a high value to possessing, in its original form, the traditional chant of the church."[20] Yet despite this evidence, no one had followed Lambillotte's lead. After forty years, the *Antiphonaire de Saint Grégoire* remained the only complete facsimile of Gregorian chant—a shameful state of affairs, by Mocquereau's account, especially when compared with those "monumental publications currently available in all the other branches of science and art."[21] He hoped to fill the void, to supply the public with the musical sources they lacked. "It was by no means a question of rivalry with the different sciences," the monk demurred. Nor, he continued (protesting now a bit too much), "a sterile exercise in making a vast collection of original notations." No, the *Paléographie musicale* was simply "the most appropriate means of fulfilling the demands imposed by musical science today."[22]

What this musical science demanded, in a word, was rigor. Things had evidently changed in four decades. Those "*amateurs* of religious music" Mocquereau associated with Lambillotte's antiphoner had slowly evolved into a more sophisticated body of *connaisseurs*, professional scholars who required a different kind of evidence to satisfy their critical needs. Mocquereau signaled this new professionalism in the very first sentences of his inaugural volume: "There is not a single scholar today who has not adopted the law that the *Ecole des chartes* imposed on young paleographers the moment it unlocked its doors: 'The sources, always the sources—never be content with second-hand works.' "[23] What better justification for his own series? The imperative came, after all, from France's premier center of paleographic study, a school that just happened to be celebrating its fiftieth anniversary in 1889—the very year in which the *Paléographie musicale* was launched. Mocquereau revealed the extent of his commitment to the *Ecole* and its philosophy in the discussion about facsimiles that followed in his preface, an argument that drew liberally from the work of Léopold Delisle, one of the school's chief paleographers.[24] All copies, they argued, were not alike. Indeed, some of the most ambitious of the century's facsimiles suffered from a fatal flaw, a problem linked to their very mode of reproduction.

Lambillotte's famed *Antiphonaire* was a case in point. The copy had been produced by a common lithographic process known as *calcage*, in which an original manuscript was first copied by hand, then traced (*calqué*) with an oily ink that would easily transfer when rubbed onto a stone, yielding the inverted image necessary for the lithograph.[25] This labor-intensive operation—the only method of reproduction available until around 1870—thus required not one but two stages of painstaking calligraphy. It was the extent of this manual labor that caused the concern. However important *calcage* may have been for early paleographers, in Mocquereau's view, it "presented two serious drawbacks: on the one hand, the enormous expense of [its] execution; and, on the other, the difficulty— let us say the very impossibility—of realizing by means of lithography a copy perfect enough to take the place of the monuments themselves, faithful enough to remain above all suspicion."[26]

Even under the best conditions, then, the *calque* could be nothing more than an unfortunate "ouvrage de second main." The dubious nature of the copy was, of course, directly related to this unspecified "second hand," an extraneous member whose actions required looking after. Lambillotte himself seemed to have recognized the problem, a fact made clear by the following little story, which explained the circumstances of the volume's production: "I sent for a young calligrapher, with a firm and clever hand, and, under my supervision [*sous mes yeux*], he began a facsimile of the antiphoner."[27] The wording of the testimony suggested that the problem of the calligrapher—this "second hand" in the facsimile—involved more than just the accuracy of the writing. It also raised a larger question of vision. Did the copyist see what Lambillotte himself would have seen? The Jesuit in effect begged the question, reporting that the facsimile had been completed "under *his* eyes," as if to guarantee, by virtue of his own authority, the fidelity of the (nameless) hired hand.

Stronger assurances, however, came several pages later, in the form of an affidavit appended to the volume's preface:

We, the undersigned Director and Librarian of the Abbey of Saint-Gall, certify and attest that the copy in FACSIMILE of the Antiphoner of Saint Gregory, sub No. 359, which Monsieur Lambillotte had executed at Saint-Gall by the calligrapher Monsieur Naef, *according to what we have seen*, conforms perfectly to the manuscript, especially in that which concerns the notational signs.

Given at Saint-Gall,
this second of June 1849
Ch. Greith, Doyen, Director
L. G'Mür, Librarian.[28]

This report only made the problem more obvious. Indeed, the more these eye witnesses tried to minimize the calligrapher's hand in the facsimile, to render him invisible, the more clearly he seemed to come into view. By the time the highest authorities at Saint-Gall had spoken, the "firm and clever hand" of Lambillotte's *Antiphonaire* had acquired a name, and therefore a presence, that no amount of testimony could erase. This so-called autograph belonged, then, as much to the artistry of a certain Monsieur Naef as to that of the legendary Saint Gregory. In order to sort out the differences, to get the real picture, a true *connaisseur* of Gregorian chant had no choice but to return to the original manuscript.

Pothier himself had felt compelled to do just that. During one of his first trips to Saint-Gall, Dom Froger reports, "he noted down, on three small sheets, about *seventy* faulty passages" in the published facsimile, the corrections of which were then "transferred into the margins of his own copy, directly across from the imperfect version." Not until many years later, incidentally, did the Benedictines learn that the mistakes were not, after all, the fault of the calligrapher. When in

1907, as Froger goes on to explain, the monks had the good fortune to study "*the first copy* of the codex made under the direction of Reverend Father Lambillotte," they found the document "far superior to the lithographic reproduction: its fidelity [was] almost perfect on all points."[29] This new evidence ultimately proved that the flaws issued not from Naef's "original" copy, but from a copy of that copy—most likely perpetrated by another, unknown hand in Poussielgue's print shop, which turned the near-perfect calligraphy into a mere *calque*, and thereby left its trace.

Getting Real

The question of where to lay blame, however, perhaps misses the real point: the *calque*, by its very nature "suspect," was a source that required investigation. The problems associated with Lambillotte's antiphoner ultimately began with lithography itself. Pothier's later handwritten corrections only confirmed the well-known "infidelity" of the medium, smugly looking back from the margins as if to shout "J'accuse!" at the printed page and all its errors, a page that would necessarily be guilty until proven innocent. What serious paleographers obviously required was a new, more reliable Gregorian witness—one, to recall Mocquereau's words, "faithful enough to remain above all suspicion."

Which is exactly what the *Paléographie musicale* provided. Mocquereau's series followed the impressive example of the *Ecole des chartes*, whose most recent publications had employed a new technology, a type of photographic reproduction called *héliogravure* that yielded, according to Delisle, "facsimiles of a rigorous exactness . . . independent of the imagination or skill of a given artist." This "marvelous art," as he put it, had "opened entirely new paths to paleography," through the undeniable fidelity, as well as economy, of the printed images.[30] By the late 1870s, when gelatin printing had been developed and perfected, photographic reproduction was the preferred method for facsimiles, far more faithful—and less costly—than *calcage*. As Mocquereau saw it, the economic advantage would greatly benefit the work of *vulgarisation* he hoped to foster at his own school, whose mission, as we have observed, was to put the traditional chant directly into the hands of the people. Both amateurs and professionals would now be able to own original sources. Photography had inspired, in his words, a "veritable revolution."[31]

This technological revolution promoted a new democracy of knowledge. The cloistered spaces in which scholars had formerly worked were radically opened; the dark library, the monastic cell, were filled with a new light. No longer secret, the Gregorian tradition could acquire a different kind of value, a truth that appeared more potent precisely because it was more accessible. Indeed, this truth seemed to be guaranteed by the very medium through which tradition was now represented. A photograph, after all, could tell no lies. The unerring fidelity of the photographic image, dispelling illusions, replaced idle speculation about the ancient chant with a picture of the real thing—a page whose "strange signs" appeared, in truth, even stranger than fiction.

The strangeness can be seen by comparing one of the newer photographic facsimiles with the reproductions they eclipsed. Let us return to the Codex No. 359 from Saint-Gall and examine a single folio, as reproduced first by the hand of Monsieur Naef (et al.) around 1850 and then in the so-called phototypes of Mocquereau's *Paléographie musicale* (figs. 13 and 14).[32] Already in 1887, Mocquereau himself had imagined the possibility of such a comparison. Dom Froger explains that Mocquereau had dreamed of publishing this very codex as the "beautiful debut for [his] future collection," a debut that would certainly have called the validity of Lambillotte's source into question. He changed his mind, however, figuring the series would make a bigger splash with a source that was not "already in the hands of all interested parties."[33] Yet a trace of Mocquereau's original plan does appear in the very first volume from 1889. In an appendix, he provided a facsimile of just one page of that "precious cantatorium," containing the responsory "Sederunt principes" for the feast of Saint Stephen. None of the interested parties who already owned Lambillotte's edition could miss the striking differences between the phototype and the earlier *calque*—most notable in the distinctive personalities of each scribal hand.

The lithograph reveals something of the struggle of transcription, a struggle recalling a question (discussed in chapter 1) that Viollet-le-Duc himself raised about copying the figures on the façade of Notre-Dame Cathedral. "Where is the sculptor," he asked, "who could retrieve with the point of his chisel the naïveté of past centuries?"[34] The modern lithographer appears to have faced a similar difficulty. While the page does capture a sense of the original, it appears more like a caricature than an exact likeness, a cartoon of medieval writing. The writing itself is often insecure, as if the pen were simply unequipped to deal with this ancient hand, to recapture its simple, "naive" movements. The modern scribe, in fact, shows himself least comfortable just at the point where the historical scribe is most nimble: in the delicate strokes that appear and disappear, like so many tiny birds in flight, into the folds of the parchment.

No doubt it is this eerie presence of parchment that defines the most powerful effect of Mocquereau's facsimile. For what the tinted surface of the phototype exposes is not just a collection of handwritten signs but the medieval page itself, stained, wrinkled, framed by timeworn edges. The faded folio visible within the image thus returns the ancient hand to an ancient home, literally filling a blank left by the lithograph. This grainy site of writing, in its utter realness, recollects the dark and richly textured past from which it has emerged. Materializing around the handwritten signs, the manuscript appears like a death mask, or a kind of specter—a ghostly image of lost time captured in the camera's impassive eye.

The photograph allowed scholars, in a very precise sense, to see more than ever before: it offered a kind of panoramic view of its objects that in turn promised entirely new levels of surveillance. The obvious advantages of this novel medium met the needs of an increasingly professional body of scholars who, in Mocquereau's words, were "anxious to have before [them] the reproductions, facsimiles, notes, and variants that both support an editor's restored text and *control his assertions*."[35] But the sense of extended vision provided by the camera's eye also suggested other, more creative uses. We have already discussed how William Morris, for instance, experimented with this technology in the course of designing his new roman type. In having Jenson's letters photographed "to a large scale," as he put it, Morris claimed an entirely new view of his source, in the hopes of perceiving the Roman Letter, as it were, in its essence, a perspective formerly unavailable to the naked eye.

The same sort of advantage caught the attention of Viollet-le-Duc. In the eighth volume of his *Dictionnaire raisonné de l'architecture française*, one finds him extolling photography as a providential technology, which, he says, seems to have appeared "for the very purpose of aiding the grand work of restoration." Not only did a photograph "present the advantage of supplying indisputable reports," but its remarkable perspective produced an even more startling effect: "very frequently a photograph discovers what had not been perceived in the building itself."[36]

It is precisely this effect that carries the sense of truth so often ascribed to the photographic medium. Indeed, an image that "could tell no lies" was, by definition, a kind of *exposure*, with the potential to reveal unexpected secrets.[37] In the scholarly applications of photography, such exposure suggested two divergent results. The camera afforded an intense proximity to the sources that controlled interpretive license—the dreaming of a midcentury scholar like Nisard—and, at the same time, recovered that potential in a new, more modern form. It was as if the dream now appeared, with unsettling precision, on the slick surface of photographic film, creating an effect that strangely recalls the definition of the "uncanny" that Freud borrowed from Schelling: the photograph reproduced something that "ought to have remained hidden and secret, and yet *comes to light*."[38]

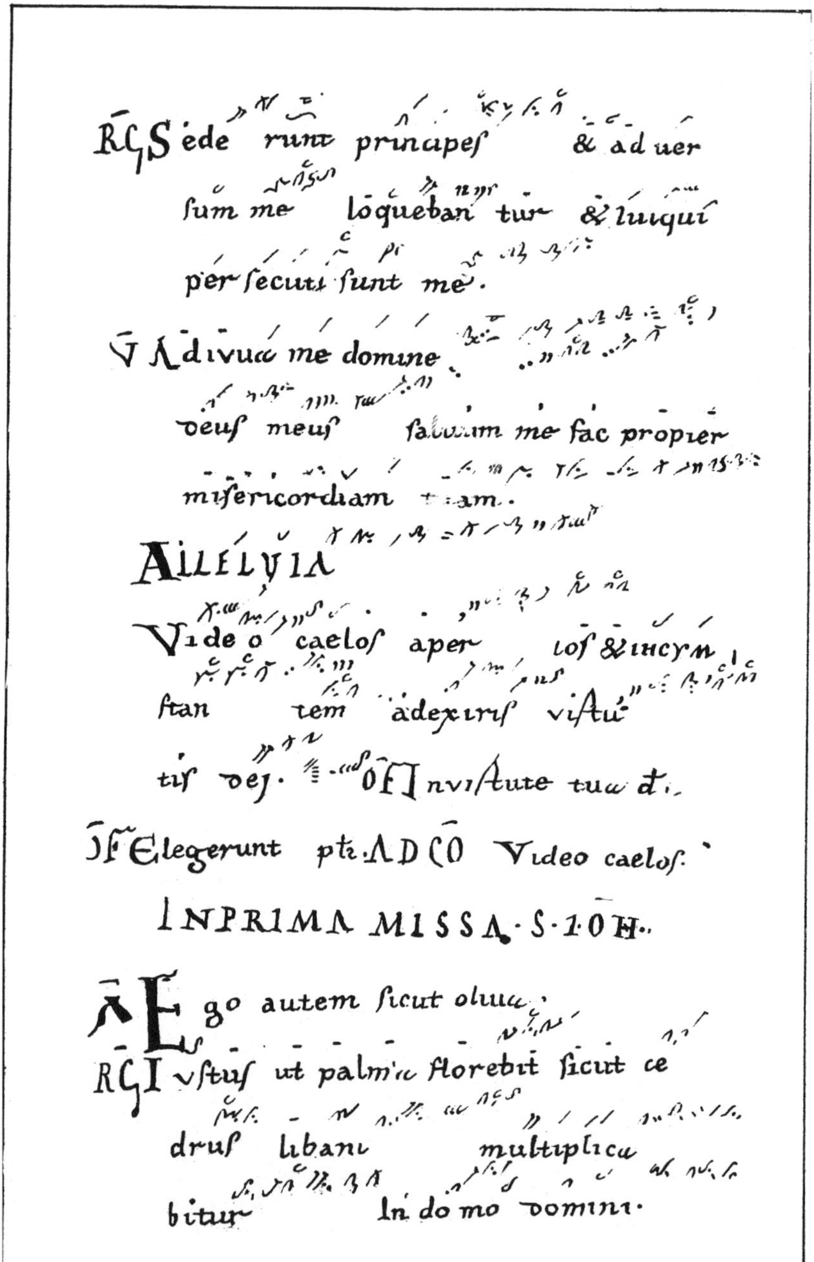

Figure 13. Page from Saint-Gall Codex No. 359, from Louis Lambillotte's *Antiphonaire de St. Grégoire*, a facsimile edition produced through *calcage* (2d ed., 1867).

Figure 14. Same page as in figure 13, here reproduced as a collotype in the appendix to the opening volume of Mocquereau's *Paléographie musicale* (1889).

It is worth digressing to consider one of the more astonishing examples of this uncanny photographic effect at the end of the nineteenth century. In May 1894, an Italian photographer named Secondo Pia took the first successful photograph of an underrecognized relic: the piece of ancient linen known today as the Shroud of Turin, which, as legend has it, covered the body of Jesus Christ after he was removed from the cross. The stained fabric was not much to look at; Pia himself admits to having seen nothing in his earlier encounters with it. But on this day something happened. As the art historian Georges Didi-Huberman relates, "There in the dark room, the moment the negative image took form . . . a face looked out at Pia from the bottom of the tray. A face he had never seen before on the shroud. A face that was, he said, *unexpected*. And seeing it he almost fainted."[39]

The image of Christ appeared to the photographer not in a dream but in a photographic negative, the play of light on film uncannily revealing "what one had never hoped to see on the shroud itself." Through the negative the stain thus became something positive, evidence of a miracle. Indeed, the sense of power associated with this evidence came in large part from its very status *as* a stain— a mark devoid of figuration. As Didi-Huberman points out, "The effacement of all figuration in this trace is itself the guarantee of a link, of *authenticity;* if there is no figuration it is because *contact* has taken place."[40] Not so much a figure as a deed, the stain left a trace of divine contact, the evidence of which was exposed—made eerily visible—through photography.

Now, Turin is about as far from Saint-Gall as a shroud is from a manuscript. But the story of the photographed relic may help us to understand the real value of the *Paléographie musicale* and the kind of evidence it offered scholars like Mocquereau. Through the photographs of the earliest sources, Mocquereau sought to expose Gregorian tradition, to uncover the truth hidden inside works like Pothier's *Liber Gradualis*. The most compelling truth revealed by photography was the very illegibility of this tradition, a fact that exposed something still more important. Consider once again Mocquereau's view of the ancient neume-accents. "Could there in fact be anything more natural, more primitive," he asks, "*anything less invented or conventional*, than the use of these two marks directed from low to high /, and from high to low \, to signify the rising and falling of the voice?" By this logic, the marks were "natural," "primitive"—that is to say, authentic—because they lacked the graphic techniques of conventional music notation, particularly those governing melodic concepts such as "high" and "low." In the absence of such figurative content, the neumes appeared more like stains than signs. They offered, like marks on a shroud, evidence of *contact* with the true Gregorian chant, a trace of its authentic performance. What Mocquereau saw, as we have already observed, was "the hand of the orator himself leaving on the parchment . . . *the trace of his ascending and descending movements.*"

This imaginative vision is not so much a fantasy as a phenomenon of photography, a medium whose very immediacy promoted the sense of encounter with the "real" hand beyond the signs. Mocquereau's vision emerges as a kind of second sight that expands the reproduced image, a condition that Roland Barthes has theorized as one of the supremely special effects of the photographic image. The utter realness of the photograph—which, in Barthes's view, stimulates a fantastic convergence between viewer and viewed—produces a moment of intimacy that is also a point of entry, a point he has called the *punctum.* "The *punctum* is what I add to the photograph and what is nonetheless already there."[41] Mocquereau's own description suggests that, for him, the *punctum* lay within the manuscript's acutely illegible marks. The tiny points produced by an ancient pen (the smallest of which were actually called *puncta*) ultimately pricked him, causing him to see something more in the notation: the irreducible reality of Gregorian tradition handed over by a human touch.

Tradition, Translation, Memory

Mocquereau attributed other qualities to these scribes behind the photograph, figures he designated (or personified) elsewhere in his essay as *neumistes.* Most important, his neumists possessed a memory, making the Gregorian music they knew part of what he called a living tradition. The idea of such memory was predicated on the very lack that defined the notation as "chironomic" or "oratorical." Indeed, in his account the neumists did not exactly read these partial signs; they simply reproduced, as he put it, "the melody already conserved within their memories." For these singers, then, reading music meant something else. It was not the sign on the page that evoked a specific melodic interval, but a remembered melody that "conjured up the meaning of the sign."[42] The incomplete neumes became an index of the memory of ancient *neumistes.*

Modern readers like Mocquereau, who lacked this traditional memory, obviously could not interpret the signs in the same way. Yet, as he points out, "we are not entirely without methods for reading the neumes." In the tenth and eleventh centuries, he explains, scribes began attempting to supply the traditional signs with the information they lacked, by "translating the melodies they possessed in their memories into open and clear notation."[43] This new, more musical notation clarified the sources by adding, so to speak, a second layer of data onto the existing neumes. In manuscripts such as the Montpellier tonary, alphabetic letters became a means of identifying specific *notae* within indeterminate cursive forms.

In the later, so-called Guidonian manuscripts, parallel lines provided a system of
loci with which to position neumes according to a relative scheme of high and
low. Taking all the sources together, modern scholars could reconstruct a sense
of the tradition by reading the later manuscripts first. Mocquereau referred to this
entire modern activity of backward reading as "translation":

> Fifty years ago, the neumes were for everyone an indecipherable scrawl. We worked
> for a long time to rediscover their forgotten meaning . . . .Many systems of interpretation
> were advanced, then recognized to be inaccurate or in contradiction either with the doc-
> uments themselves or with history. But since [quoting Max Müller] "every scientific sys-
> tem, however insufficient it may eventually become, is nevertheless a step forward," . . .
> we were finally able to see the light. Today, all professionals would agree that we have
> come to read the neumes . . . translating them with the aid of three families of manu-
> scripts that confirm and complete each other: the manuscripts without staff lines; the
> alphabetic manuscripts, and the Guidonian manuscripts.[44]

This benevolent view of translation—a totality of manuscripts "confirming
and completing one another"—distinctly recalls the redemptive program Walter
Benjamin himself described as "the task of the translator," a task whose ultimate
purpose fulfilled, as he put it, "the great motif of integrating many tongues into
one, true language."[45] Although Benjamin's essay originally assumed, in 1923, the
unlikely role of translator's preface to a German edition of Baudelaire, his unique
and often difficult view of translation illuminates, with unexpected clarity, certain assumptions that lay behind Mocquereau's paleographic project. It is helpful, then, to examine his claims, to contemplate the impossible task he attempted
to define. Indeed, pondering Benjamin's conclusions should eventually clarify a
larger implication of Mocquereau's *Paléographie musicale* that, in the end, would
appear to contradict its stated purpose.

· · · · ·

Among the more prominent images Benjamin employs to describe the condition of translation is that of the free passage of light. To carry words from one
language to another was ultimately to illuminate the condition of language itself.
A "real translation" was, in his words, "transparent": "It does not cover the original, does not block its light, but allows the pure language, as though reinforced
by its own medium, to shine upon the original all the more fully. This may be
achieved, above all, by a literal rendering of the syntax which proves words, rather
than sentences, to be the primary element of the translator."[46] Such a literal
approach was, in the case of Gregorian chant, completely necessary. Mocquereau
admitted that, in the absence of an oral tradition—of memory—modern scholars were forced to "proceed like those who, in the study of a language, start from

the word in order to arrive at the idea."[47] Neumes rather than melodies were the primary element of the paleographer. A complete translation of the Gregorian corpus required a neume-by-neume reading of the sources.

Mocquereau offered a glimpse of these sources in more than a dozen exemplars appended to the first volume of the *Paléographie musicale*—a kind of preview of what was to come. In the very next installment, however, he brought the monumental task of Gregorian translation fully into view with an impressive anthology including more than two hundred facsimiles of a single chant, "Justus ut palma florebit." It was a kind of comprehensive photo-essay that sought to present, through manuscripts of every era and provenance, the complete story of one chant, fully translated. The innovative project in fact seemed to clarify, in retrospect, an unusual claim made by Mocquereau in the opening essay of his first volume. Acknowledging the evident difficulties of the ancient neumes, he had promised to provide the necessary translation in modern notation. "This translation will [eventually] be published," he said, "but it will not come from us. It will be supplied by the very same documents we will subsequently release."[48] The promise suggested that the task of translating the traditional neumes was, in effect, already complete in future photographs. The facsimiles themselves would do the job, ultimately providing a translation so transparent—so "real," in Benjamin's terms—as to be completely invisible.

What would shine through this invisible translation was, he believed, the authentic Gregorian tradition. Mocquereau's understanding of tradition in many ways resembled the notoriously ineffable substance of translation that Benjamin called "pure language." As Benjamin described it, pure language was a kind of hermeneutic chimera, an intention "no single language could attain by itself, but which was realized only by the totality of [the] intentions [of all languages] supplementing each other."[49] Mocquereau thought he could recognize something of the same intention in the very proliferation of Gregorian *écritures* that appeared in sources across several centuries. Indeed, he speculated that if "a single man, in a single monastery," had curtailed such graphic experimentation by conceiving of a "unique notation that would be adopted by all churches," the force of tradition

> would have been singularly diminished; for that tradition would now rest on nothing but a single witness, one that could be mistaken, and therefore deceive us. The melodic uniformity of the manuscripts that followed this discovery could no longer serve as an argument for their authenticity, since all the versions of the Gregorian repertory would simply be copies of the work of this innovator.

In other words, the authenticity of tradition could be proven only through a diversity of representations, a diversity that, paradoxically, yielded a much more compelling sense of "unity." Mocquereau's conclusion, which echoed the well-known dictum of Dom Guéranger, presented tradition itself as this unifying force: when "monuments from all countries, in every form of writing, present an astonishing uniformity . . . we can conclude with certainty that the chironomic and diastematic manuscripts are identical. *Tradition alone could bring about such unity.*"[50]

The true Gregorian tradition seeped out, then, between the lines of different manuscripts, becoming part of what Benjamin would call the "eternal afterlife" of works of art. "All great texts," Benjamin claimed, "contain their virtual translations between the lines; this is true to the highest degree of sacred writings."[51] This virtual translation, as should now be clear, would emerge over time not in a single authoritative version but in the resonant space that was the afterlife of countless translations. Indeed, one of the few things a translation could hope to accomplish was to locate this lingering resonance or (to use Benjamin's most suggestive image) reproduce an "echo": "A translation does not find itself in the center of the language forest but on the outside facing the wooded ridge; it calls into it without entering, aiming at that single spot where the echo is able to give, in its own language, the reverberation of the work in the alien one."[52]

Benjamin no doubt caught these reverberations from Baudelaire himself. The image of an echo lurking deep within a dark "forest of symbols," which unmistakably recalls Baudelaire's poem "Correspondances," encourages us to view the task of translation itself as a mystical correspondence between languages. The pure language posited by Benjamin would thus be akin to the merging of sound, color, and scent that the poem famously likened to "long echoes mingling in a shadowy and deep unity" (de longs échos qui de loin se confondent / Dans une ténébreuse et profonde unité).

Mocquereau seems to have imagined the goal of his *Paléographie musicale* in strikingly similar terms, a goal he anticipated with the "Justus ut palma" project, published in 1891, one year after the thirteenth centenary of Gregory the Great's installation as pope. The reverberations of that volume, in fact, continued to be felt for some time, as can be seen from a memo Mocquereau addressed to His Holiness Pope Leo XIII ten years later: "Holy Father, after such an investigation, to which we were able to add more than three hundred manuscript witnesses, we had the right to consider this melody a multiple and faithful echo of the thousands of voices of Christianity, which, since Saint Gregory's time, sang the suave musical inspirations of the Roman Church."[53] The emphatic pleading gives us new insight into Mocquereau's paleographic project. Through the reproduction of hundreds of Gregorian manuscripts, faithful "witnesses" to tradition, Mocquereau imagined that he had done something far more powerful than collect mere pictures. Rather, he had reproduced evidence of the very memory by which the traditional melodies had been preserved for centuries. His photographic collection functioned, then, as a kind of modern *re*collection that mediated the space between past and present. It was the perfectly invisible substance of translation that recovered this memory, this stuff reclaimed by means of photography in which the melodies were liberated from their sources like an echo. But this echo was not the same decayed sound—the precious remainder of a natural Gregorian voice—that Gontier had imagined back in 1859. Mocquereau's echo was a more modern phenomenon, signaling the existence of a "pure language," a virtual substance that reverberated not so much within as *between* the ancient sources to call back the forgotten Gregorian tradition.

Science, Technology, Power

The lost memory was recovered by sifting through the layers of evidence buried in manuscripts, piecing together the "fragments," as Benjamin would have it, of the larger vessel that was the Gregorian language. The process that Mocquereau understood as "translation" bore, then, the trace of another discipline, the modern human science he and his contemporaries referred to more generally as "archaeology." Archaeology held out the promise of forgotten civilizations, the promise on which Mocquereau's scholarly hopes rested. Like an archaeologist, he believed that the Gregorian tradition could be recovered from fragments turned up in metaphorical digging, and that it would echo from the bottom of a metaphorical space hollowed out by science itself.

What was perhaps most striking about such archaeological work was the level of confidence scholars like Mocquereau could maintain with regard to its apparently ineffable goals. The confidence emerged in part from the technologies now available to him, technologies that by the end of the nineteenth century had transformed the very sciences on which their existence depended. First among these, as we have seen, was photography. No wonder we find Mocquereau, in the opening essay of the *Paléographie musicale*, marveling at this new technology, checking off a long list of exotic activities that "photography had made possible": "Without leaving his study . . . the artist can walk through the catacombs, consider the paintings, read the graffiti that cover their walls; the antiquarian can follow step by step, so to speak, in all parts of the world, the excavations of archaeologists in search of ancient civilizations."[54] Several years later, in 1896, the theorist Jules Combarieu would be far more dogmatic about such benefits. Recognizing the obvious importance of photography for Mocquereau's paleo graphic series (by then five volumes strong), Combarieu looked back on the efforts of Dom Pothier and offered stern judgment: It is "to be regretted," he

observed, "that [Pothier] has not surrounded his ideas with the arsenal of experimental proofs demanded by the modern spirit. One must say it over and over
again: without study and the direct reproduction of the original sources (to allow
the reader to be in control) no musical archaeology is possible."[55]

To be in control: this was the ultimate benefit afforded by modern scientific
technologies. The most significant activity enabled by photography was that of
surveillance; it allowed scholars to scrutinize a multitude of historical sites in a
single viewing and, in so doing, to enjoy a new kind of power, not of seeing, but
of *overseeing* history. It was this very advantage—the arsenal of proof provided
by photographic facsimiles—that Mocquereau's colleague Dom Cagin proudly
recounted in an essay from 1904. Describing the work of the Solesmes school,
he concluded an account of the monks' elaborate paleographic workshop with
this telling anecdote:

> Last year a German doctor of music came to consult Dom Mocquereau . . . about a
> work he was proposing to undertake. In the presence of the master and his pupils, gazing
> on the number of manuscripts at their disposal, their incomparable tool for studying
> them, and how they were making use of it, he went away, somewhat discouraged, saying
> that it was impossible to follow them in such a path, and that they had such a start, and
> such resources, that nothing could prevent them being always and everywhere ahead.[56]

More than a decade later, Mocquereau's own version of this paleographic vic-
tory sounded rather different. In 1921 he would tell a far less amicable tale about
not one but a whole group of scholars (guided, as it happens, by another unfortunate "German doctor of music") who supported that Gregorian anomaly
known as the Ratisbon edition. At the end of his story, the misguided scholars
return home not just discouraged but defeated by the powerful Solesmes archaeologists. Mocquereau described the strategy by which the monks prepared to
answer the spurious claims of these so-called Mediceans, who believed that the
chant of Saint Gregory was either lost or impossible to decipher:

> To these gratuitous assertions it was necessary to respond, but in such a way that no
> counterattack would be possible. Journal articles, reviews? These were tiresome. This type
> of flimsy weapon could no longer suffice. The battle had been going on for fifteen years
> (1868–1884), and it had to end. In fifteen more years, the famous thirty-year privilege
> would expire; and at that moment Rome would have to see the light, a light vibrant
> enough for truth to triumph.
>
> But what machine of war would be capable of knocking down all the obstacles and
> hurrying along victory? We had to find a kind of scientific "tank" [*une sorte de «tank» sci-
> entifique*], powerful, invulnerable, capable of driving out all enemy reasoning.[57]

The bellicose sentiments would have delighted Marinetti. Mocquereau's
unexpectedly futuristic tale of scholarly strategy put an entirely new spin on the

power of technology. An apparently innocent series of photographic facsimiles became, all at once, a piece of heavy artillery, a weapon with which to wage intellectual war. The aggressive image served to bring one of the most powerful effects of the photograph—and therefore of the entire *Paléographie musicale*—into sharper focus. For to photograph (or, perhaps more appropriately, to "shoot") the principal Gregorian manuscripts was not simply to capture the tradition on film, but to render its particularity, its overwhelming difference. The science of the photograph, in other words, literally changed the image of tradition. It blew the repertory apart, making it available for scholarly scrutiny as a series of discrete fragments. Through a continuously expanding photographic collection, Mocquereau exposed Gregorian tradition not as a single, idealized creation but as a staggering diversity of representations—a condition that reflects back on the nature of photography itself. As Susan Sontag has observed, "Photographic images are pieces of evidence in an ongoing biography or history. And one photograph, unlike one painting, implies that there will be others."[58] Mocquereau's radically expanded vision of the Gregorian repertory, which implied more and more photographs, was an inevitable consequence of the very technology through which he sought to restore it.

It is in this fact of multiple exposures that we begin to see how much Mocquereau's ultramodern endeavor departed from the work of his predecessor Dom Pothier. Indeed, it could be said that, by its willful proliferation of images, the *Paléographie musicale* functioned less as a defense of the *Liber Gradualis* than as a kind of silent critique. In the opening pages of his preface, for instance, Mocquereau used the words of Léopold Delisle to sound a warning against the pitfalls of all printed editions: "A typographic reproduction, however rigorous one imagines it, even when executed with special types, will never forestall all the qualms of the meticulous reader."[59] But even more serious was the speculation he offered at the end of the same preface. Who could not think of Pothier's typographic masterpiece at the moment Mocquereau spoke of a "single man, in a single monastery," inventing a "unique notation that would be adopted by all churches"? The moral of the story, we recall, was that such an innovator would, by the very uniformity of his invention, "diminish the force of the Gregorian tradition."

With this observation, we return briefly to Benjamin's task of translation and consider one final implication of Mocquereau's high-tech, archaeological project. In its very attempt to be a *translation*, we could say, his series presented the most powerful critique of the new Benedictine edition. For his view of a "totality of manuscripts confirming and completing one another" obviously opposed the idealized image of Saint Gregory that shone from the pages of Pothier's restored gradual. In the *Paléographie musicale*, tradition was represented by many *écritures;* in the *Liber Gradualis*, by just one. If, as Mocquereau believed, the pure language—the echo—of tradition lived within the manifold writings represented by his own series, then Pothier's edition had to be viewed not as a perfect representation of Saint Gregory's song but as a single effort that should, eventually, be superseded by others.

In a recent essay on Benjamin, the philosopher Alexander García Düttman has summarized this pluralistic dimension of translation in a conclusion that unexpectedly echoes the aggressive view expressed by Mocquereau in 1921: "If translation is a practice that reflects an art of combining and a technique of montage, if the translator must be in a position to implement the means at his disposal, . . . one may conclude that translation destroys the fetishism, canonization or glorification of language; *becoming, finally, a kind of war machine.*"[60] The conclusion is clear enough when we consider the montage effect of the "Justus ut palma" project. In the sheer multiplication of images, this volume, far from supporting the Benedictine edition, served in a very real way to undermine it by destroying, in Düttman's terms, the "canonicity" of its single, beautiful text. The utterly realistic photographs, at a basic aesthetic level, declared war not only on Pustet of Ratisbon, but on Pothier himself.

· · · · ·

We should thus not be surprised to learn that, from the moment he first heard of Mocquereau's paleographic plan in 1888, Pothier opposed it. His objection was so vehement, in fact, that Dom Couturier was nearly obliged to call the whole thing off. Pothier feared, Combe reports, "that the new collection would constitute a revision of his Gradual."[61] But his concern extended to the public dimension of the project, the discomforting fact that the sources, no longer the private property of monk-scholars, would now be put before a wide readership, placed into the hands of the people. Mocquereau related this resistance, quoting Pothier in a polemic from many years later:

> "Yes," [Pothier] said, "this project seems, at first glance, very seductive, filled with promises; but on closer inspection the results will be disastrous. It could bring about the ruin of the Gregorian restoration that we have attempted at Solesmes. . . .We will see the birth of the most extravagant theories on origins, on reading the neumes, on the modes and rhythm of Gregorian chant, etc. In sum, struggles, controversies, battles which, if not conducting the Gregorian restoration to its ruin, will certainly retard its progress for many years."[62]

The image of facsimiles bringing about the "ruin" of Pothier's efforts confirms the power associated with Mocquereau's new "scientific tank." From Pothier's perspective, the photographed manuscripts were indeed dangerous. By their very

ability to stimulate reflection—in Barthesian terms, to prick the viewer's imagination—the pictures had the power, he feared, to generate all sorts of fanciful
theories, far too many for a single scholar to answer. What is more, the multiple
(and potentially conflicting) *écritures* they exposed would necessarily raise questions about his editorial decisions. How many sources did he in fact consult? This
was, presumably, the most threatening dimension of Mocquereau's project.
Armed with photographs, readers who desired to "be in control" would be able
to go straight to the source, and in doing so they just might discover that Pothier had not always followed the evidence of the manuscripts.

Indeed they might. This possibility is nowhere more clearly evident than in a
copy of the 1883 *Liber Gradualis*, still housed at the Solesmes library, whose title
page bears the portentous inscription "ad usum A. Mocquereau." On appearance
alone, this copy could be described as a very real sign of the deglorification
accomplished by the work of translation, a destruction of Pothier's autonomous
work of Gregorian art. For the sense of Pothier's original edition is very much
obscured by the particular "use" Mocquereau makes of it. Bound in between its
pages we find countless frayed, blank leaves of four-line Gregorian staff paper, on
which alternative versions of chants have been copied in Mocquereau's hand, at
different times, in differently colored inks. On some pages we even see cursive
signs penciled directly over the printed types. The book resembles in many ways
the edition that, years later, would be known as the *Graduel neumé* (or *Graduale
Triplex*), an innovative text that purposely combined typographic and handwritten neumes on the same page in order to present the chant's graphic profile at a
glance. Mocquereau's book *ad usum* was a less systematic compilation, of course,
but its effect was no less powerful, the added leaves and notations turning Pothier's gradual into something more like a working notebook. Collected from the
evidence of manuscripts, his variant readings were transcribed into the existing
pages with the idea that they might eventually appear in a revised edition. The
alterations bore witness, that is, to an ongoing project of restoration, a project
whose very continuity anticipated Mocquereau's more modern view of Gregorian "tradition."

The handwritten revisions thus had the obvious, but still somewhat disturb-
ing, effect of demoting Pothier's beautiful edition to the compromised status of a
rough draft. The page containing the offertory "Perfice gressus" for Sexagesima
Sunday offers one of the more telling examples. Glued overleaf, on a bit of scratch
paper, a tiny comparative table in Mocquereau's hand reveals no less than eight
variant versions of the opening formula extracted from some of the most reliable
Gregorian witnesses: Saint-Gall, Laon, Chartres. All of the variants, as can be seen
in figures 15a and b, agreed with one another; it was only Pothier's version that

differed, showing a *pes* in the opening position where the sources showed simply a *punctum*. This addition revealed, in a single stroke, the authentic Gregorian hand decisively undermining Pothier's authority—indeed, presenting a visible, legible threat to his perfect Gregorian types. Destroying the very integrity of the Benedictine edition, the handwritten signs compromised its future glory.

Interestingly enough, no public sign of this threat was to be found in the second edition released by the Solesmes press in 1895. Nor did it come into view in the more popular *Liber Usualis* of 1896, discussed at the beginning of this

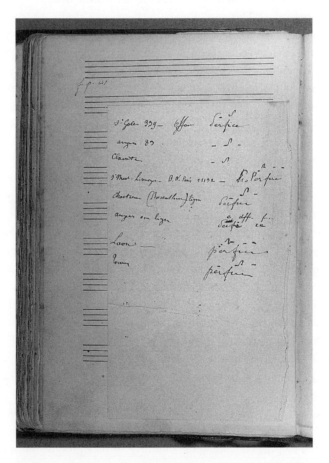

Figure 15a. Pages from Mocquereau's own copy of the Desclée *Liber Gradualis*, showing the Offertory "Perfice gressus" for Sexagesima Sunday with Mocquereau's handwritten corrections. Courtesy of Abbaye Saint-Pierre, Solesmes, France. Authorization No. 105.

Figure 15b.

chapter. The alterations did not show up, in fact, until 1903, when yet another book of chant was issued by the Solesmes monks under Mocquereau's supervision, a text that fully reflected the aims of his new critical school. All of the changes were assiduously collated in a newer, revised edition of the *Liber Usualis*—including, as it happens, one further innovation that would make the new volume, in the view of Mocquereau's followers, more practical, more democratic, and ultimately more modern. But our discussion of these events will have to wait. It is time to consider a very different kind of Gregorian enchantment, realized not in photographs or imprints but in the practices to which they eventually gave rise. We shall turn our attention from the inanimate to the animate, from the reproduction of books to their various readers. We shall reflect on the mysterious rhythms of chant.

4

Writing, Reading, Singing

ver the course of just two decades, from 1880 to 1900, the Gregorian restoration at Solesmes suffered a slow but radical transformation. From the exquisite books of the eighties to the sleek photographs of the nineties, a critical space began to open, a space that reflected the disparity between Pothier's edition and Mocquereau's manuscripts, between Gregorian art and Gregorian science. The different impressions left by the chant in each source, one imaginary, the other real, demanded a new kind of attention, inviting potential readers to reflect, compare, criticize. What Pothier had feared about the *Paléographie musicale* did indeed come to pass. The published manuscripts slowed the immediate progress of the Benedictine restoration by opening a new path to the future, a path soon crowded by eager lay musicians who could now study the chant for themselves. By 1901, when Mocquereau had completed the seventh volume of his series, he and his entire school had acquired a notable status beyond the walls of the monastery. Solesmes became a kind of model for a new and informed music scholarship—a practice that, flowing from the gap between the typographic edition and the photographed sources, was to be known as *musicologie*.

Musicologie was, at least, the term used by Pierre Aubry in a popular course taught at the Institut Catholique in Paris in 1898–99, a course that is said to have introduced the word to the French language.[1] Among the most prominent figures associated with Aubry's newly conceived science (he called it "sacred musicology") were, it turns out, the Benedictines of Solesmes, a fact made evident from Aubry's seventh lecture, titled simply *L'Oeuvre bénédictine*. He began by recalling the recent, sympathetic treatment of the monks by Camille Bellaigue in the *Revue des deux mondes* (discussed in chapter 1), then reminded his students of a crucial distinction: "The *Revue des deux mondes* is not any kind of scholarly journal," he cautioned, "and so Monsieur Bellaigue has reflected only the superficial, naturally attractive sides of the Benedictine life at Solesmes." Yet the monks, in his view, "deserved more than this," for these artistic souls were also "conscientious and prolific scholars."[2]

Aubry described exactly what these figures had achieved in the course of his next lecture, which concerned the application of philological method to music. "This new mode of musicological criticism has been introduced to us by the Benedictines of Solesmes," he announced, offering Mocquereau's "Justus ut palma" project, published in the second and third volumes of the *Paléographie musicale*, as "the best example."[3] It was not long, in fact, before Aubry himself would follow the Benedictine lead. In 1901 he brought out three critical editions of music from the Middle Ages, volumes that his publisher, H. Welter, proudly advertised as a "mélange of musicology," with a significant selling point: all the books, the advertisement promised, were printed "in the format of the *Paléographie musicale*."[4] The publisher was referring not so much to the size of the volumes as to their lavish images, involving the same *fac-similés en phototypie* that the Solesmes press had introduced to the public in 1889. Clearly, Mocquereau's innovative series represented a new standard for serious scholars like Aubry, who wanted to be doing *musicologie*.

I should like to linger over this new scholarly practice—to consider what it might mean to do musicology circa 1900—as a way of introducing a chapter whose subject is ostensibly Gregorian chant in performance. It is not stretching the term too far, I think, to consider the idea of musicology as a mode of performance, a particular way of executing music by a body of players—in this case, scholars who would call themselves musicologistes. While such execution does not immediately imply the production of musical sound, it does tend to imply a certain type of musical behavior. To do musicology requires, in effect, the same kind of agreement—a tacit cooperation among players—that underlies all musical performance, a cooperation that rests on established modes of interaction, standards by which players learn to measure their behavior and play in tune. The performance that unfolded in Aubry's *Cours de musicologie sacrée* represented, in short, the beginnings of that institutionalized practice we call a discipline.[5]

Significantly, the key players in this new performance were the monks of Solesmes. Indeed, it would seem—from Aubry's account, at least—that the emerging discipline of *musicologie* owed its entire existence to the Benedictines, in particular to the new principles of Gregorian restoration advanced by Dom Mocquereau's school, principles that had been borrowed from the field of comparative philology. Aubry was by no means the first to make the point. In 1896 Combarieu had already solidified Mocquereau's scholarly reputation by hailing him the "originator of a musical renaissance" and signaling the birth of a

marvelous new discipline at Solesmes, which he ventured to call, in conspicuously inverted commas, the "philology of music."[6] Combarieu was quoting, as it
happens, from Mocquereau himself, who in the long opening essay from the first
volume of the *Paléographie musicale* had coined the phrase in an attempt to clarify the special nature of his scholarly undertaking:

> Almost a century ago, a fertile thought extended and renewed the field of grammat-
> ical science. Instead of considering each language idiom in particular, scholars brought
> several of them together, "in order to observe" [in the words of Edmond Egger] "their
> progress over time, to grasp their original similarity and difference, to distinguish the point
> at which they were separated from a common root as well as the one in which they
> reconverge." . . . However daunting the study of such a large number of idioms might
> seem to us, it was nonetheless undertaken, pursued by linguists with an ardor, a wisdom,
> a method that should serve as our model. . . . [For] the science of linguistics . . . has
> already begun to trace for us, not only an isolated sketch of this or that language, but a
> magnificent scene of the whole, in which the evolutions of the principal idioms, dialects,
> and *patois* spoken in Asia and Europe were unfolded before our eyes, from the most
> remote times up to the present day.
>
> Why shouldn't musical experts, then, try to create in their turn—if you will permit
> me to use the word—a musical philology?[7]

The novelty of applying the methods of comparative philology to the study
of chant is made obvious by the tone of Mocquereau's rhetorical question. But
he had no reason to be defensive: by 1889 the importance of philology within
the so-called historical sciences had been established for nearly three decades. In
1863 Ernest Renan had pronounced the twin disciplines of "philology and
comparative mythology" as the most significant dimensions of contemporary
scientific thought, disciplines he ranked somewhere between history and geol-
ogy for their ability, as he saw it, to take the scholar "almost to the origins of
human consciousness."[8] In the same decade the Swiss linguist Adolphe Pictet
(first teacher of Ferdinand de Saussure) imagined a form of "linguistic paleontology" that could extrapolate a whole history of language from a single word.[9]
And Mocquereau himself was acquainted with Friedrich Max Müller's path-
breaking lectures published as *The Science of Language* (through its 1876 French
translation), which endorsed comparative philology with similar enthusiasm: as
a new sphere of knowledge that allowed scholars to perceive the underlying
unity within the apparent disorder of the natural world.[10] By entering this
sphere Mocquereau's *école* sought to gain an equally comprehensive view of the
Gregorian language, to arrive at a "magnificent scene of the whole" in which the
origin and development not only of individual chants but of the major dialects
would be made to unfold before the eyes of all.

This application of philological method to the realm of ancient music yielded a new discipline, then, as well as a neologism. Aubry's *musicologie* was little more than a fusion of these formerly disparate realms, a portmanteau that henceforth marked *philologie* as something specifically *musicale*. Inspired by the promises of this hybrid science, Combarieu himself soon founded a new scholarly journal, the *Revue d'histoire et de critiques musicales*, as a forum dedicated exclusively to its concerns. The opening editorial of the first issue, published in January 1901, was nothing short of a manifesto, calling for a complete reassessment of music within the human sciences. Combarieu and his fellow editors saw their new field of music history and criticism as a legitimate contender for professional recognition alongside the more traditional academic disciplines. "Music has the right," the editors claimed, "to occupy a place in the *official* programs of our universities."[11] Among the august scholars who appeared with him on the masthead were Romain Rolland, Louis Laloy, Maurice Emmanuel, and Aubry himself. Dom Mocquereau was listed as *collaborateur*.

Mocquereau's collaboration within this newly official field of musicology—his performance within an ensemble of secular scholars—had significant consequences for the Benedictine restoration, consequences that, as we shall see, impinged on the very concept of Gregorian performance. What began with Dom Guéranger as a liturgical problem had developed, with Mocquereau, into a true science, with impressive critical methods now being imitated by lay scholars pursuing different ends. Combarieu had elsewhere acknowledged that, at the Solesmes school, "the study of plainchant had become secularized," a development for which, he admitted, "we of the world cannot be too grateful."[12]

Yet this development had another, more serious outcome. The very secularization that Combarieu welcomed had the effect of transforming, one might say, the ontological status of sacred music. Under the guise of a more rigorous philology of music, the Gregorian song was changed from a strictly liturgical object into an object of scientific analysis—what philologists would call a "text." For evidence, we may look to Mocquereau himself, who in 1904 began an important lecture on the Solesmes school by saying, "Here is how we at Solesmes go about establishing *any musical text from the Gregorian repertory*" (Voici comment nous arrivons à Solesmes à l'etablissement *d'un texte musicale quelconque du répertoire grégorien*).

The terminology is important. From a philological perspective, a Gregorian text will always be a plural phenomenon, a collective suggested by etymology itself. *Textus* means "woven," yielding the idea of "a web of words," as Richard Crocker reminds us, or—to use the more elaborate formulation of Jerome McGann—"a laced network of linguistic and bibliographic codes."[13] However one chooses to define it, what the philologist calls a "text" has always referred to a form that is itself a complex of forms, written many times over. The philological practice known as textual criticism, which gained currency in the first half of the nineteenth century among scholars of ancient biblical and classical texts, accounted for these multiple writings in the same way that the linguist traced the filiation of multiple dialects: first by exposing all the known forms of a given passage, then by reconstructing their genealogy in the form of a *stemma*.[14] If in the 1840s Dom Guéranger was beginning to imagine the application of such a practice to Gregorian studies, it was not until Mocquereau began photographing chant manuscripts that the concept would be fully realized—for the first time in music's history.

The *Paléographie musicale*, as we have seen, enabled this new comparative approach to musical texts by exposing the written forms of the chant page by page, melody by melody, a process that allowed the enormous complexity of the tradition to come into view. It was no wonder that Combarieu and his university colleagues considered this kind of exposure "secularizing." By releasing chant from its sources, the photograph liberated the music from its immediate liturgical and performative contexts and, at the same time, made it available to a new kind of reception—a reception in which the chant's "performance" could now be understood as a form of pure analysis. In the abstract, collective space of comparative philology, a melody like "Justus ut palma" inevitably fell silent, becoming nothing more than a lattice, a matrix, a grid.

. . . . .

Such a colossal phenomenological shift deserves closer scrutiny. If we look back at the opening volume of Mocquereau's *Paléographie musicale*, for instance, we see a small but telling sign of this new textual condition in a single musical example intended to show forms of neumatic notation and their modern translation (fig. 16). Mocquereau reproduced, for the aid of his readers, a precise typographic transcription of the Introit for the first Sunday of Advent, "Ad te levavi," which was to appear some fifty pages later as the first folio of his photographic facsimile (see fig. 12). The transcription was, of course, infinitely more legible than the manuscript, owing to its two levels of notation: above, a row of exquisite cursive neumes (rendered in types that would have put Beaudoire to shame); and below, their analogous square forms shown on a four-line staff. But there was something else. Hovering over the signs was a row of numbers: 23, 3, 3, 2, 1, 3, 2, 1, 24. . . . They referred the reader to a "table of principal neumes" on the preceding page, which identified each of the signs by name. This top layer effectively dismembered the whole into parts, causing the complete "Ad te levavi" to

EXEMPLES DE NOTATION NEUMATIQUE AVEC TRADUCTION

INTROIT DU PREMIER DIMANCHE DE L'AVENT

Figure 16. Musical example of cursive neumes and their translation into Guidonian notation, reproduced in the first volume of Mocquereau's *Paléographie musicale* (1889).

appear, from another perspective, like a random series. The taxonomy bore the distinct marks of archaeological research, through which the ancient neumes arrived at a singular fate. Separated, catalogued, numbered, they were unearthed from the ancient manuscript only to be laid alongside the more legible square notes—like so many bones outlining the ghostly form of some ancient, unknown mammal. Gregorian paleography revealed itself, in this meticulous display, as a kind of musical paleontology.

This example was, however, merely an abbreviation of the more elaborate dismemberment that would define the philological work of the new Solesmes school. The process of separating and numbering a given melody into its constituent parts belonged to a larger critical apparatus that Mocquereau described in an extended essay from 1904. In order to keep track of the photographs, the monks required an *instrument de travail*, as he called it—a tool for analyzing the facts released from the sources: "From the confused mass of our manuscripts we had to extract methodically the component chants one by one and passage by passage, and then assemble each of the versions in clear order . . . capable of immediately supplying the quickest and best classified means of proof on a given point." The tool was nothing more than a synoptic table, an elaborate Gregorian matrix that had the capacity to "provide at will either the entire history of a passage . . . or the neumatic account of each of its component parts."[15] This was the incomparable philological instrument by which the monks, tabulating the evidence from the sources, turned Gregorian song into a modern historical text.

A table of the Christmas "Alleluia" will illustrate the point (fig. 17). Mocquereau summarized the process by which the monks set about preparing it:

One of us gets the [oldest layer of] manuscripts . . . and transcribes once for all from left to right, on as many horizontal lines as there are manuscripts to be perused, the whole reading of the Christmas "Alleluia," just as he finds it. He takes care in this transcription to leave spaces between the neumes, and to place corresponding neumes from other manuscripts below, along the same vertical axis. Thus he has a vivid presentation of them in order on separate rows, enabling him to follow, from top to bottom, the various possible vagaries of the neume whose history he is tracing. Generally, through a luxury of clarity, which is not without its advantages, each one of these analytical and synoptic columns of neumes has its number.[16]

Whereas Pothier had understood Gregorian "luxury" (*luxe*) in terms of the aesthetic of an impeccably printed page, Mocquereau connected it to an act of numbering. Reconstructing the Christmas "Alleluia" as a series of widely spaced, numbered events, his synoptic table presented the Gregorian melody as multiple, isolated pieces of data. Significantly, the tables were prepared on large sheets of graph paper, a feature that underscored the sense of discipline surrounding his philological workshop. For the parallel lines were more than just a convenience: they served literally to keep the Solesmes workers *in line*. And as each neume assumed its position in the precisely numbered sequence, individual parts took on a new kind of significance, the vertical columns generating whole vistas of new evidence that overwhelmed the unity of a single melody.

It was this textualizing of the Gregorian repertory that ultimately redefined the idea of its "restoration." Through a powerful new technology of knowledge, Mocquereau in effect broke down the same melodic corpus Pothier had so assiduously labored to rebuild, revising the status of the restored chant with a series of methodical strokes more calculated than any revolutionary vandalism. The Christmas "Alleluia" from Pothier's 1895 *Liber Gradualis* disintegrated into fourteen melodic positions, each with its own history, its own secrets.

In contemplating this disintegration—the stark difference between the lone Alleluia at the top of the table and all its distant relations below—we can perceive most clearly the gap separating Mocquereau's work of Gregorian restoration from that of the first *Liber Gradualis*. For Pothier what lay behind any

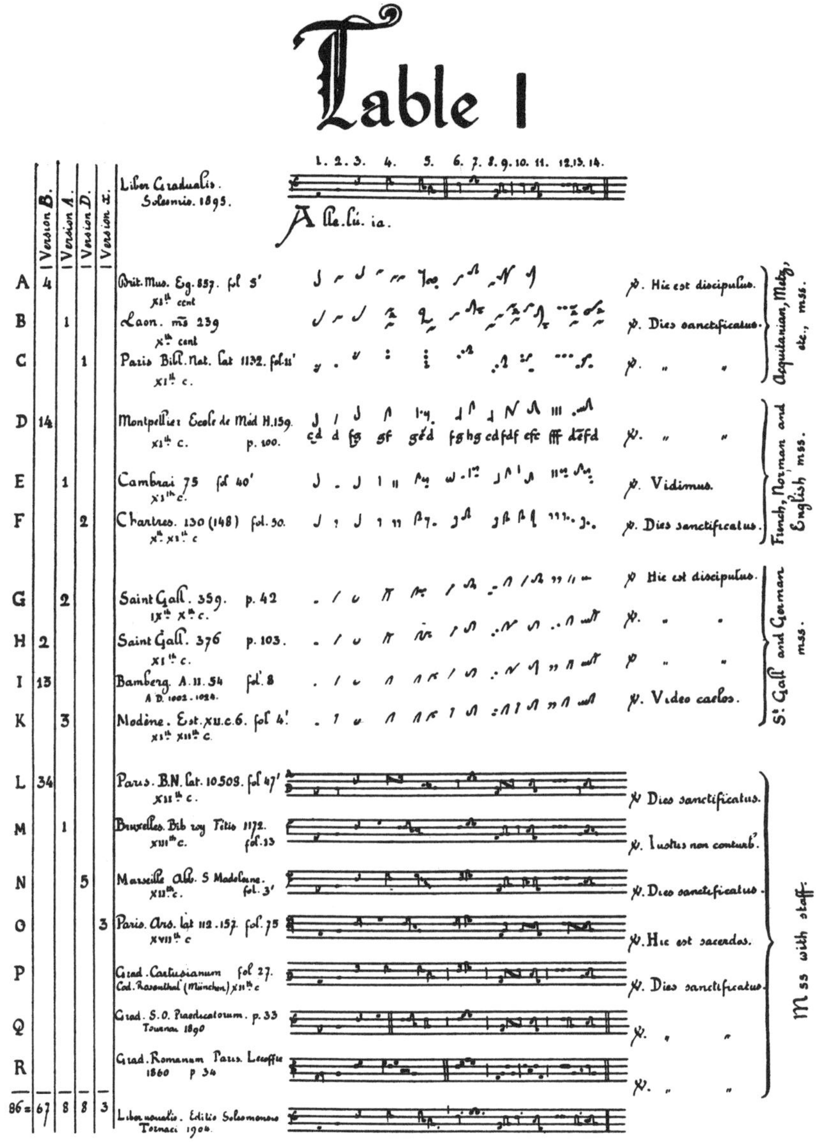

Figure 17. A synoptic table showing the Christmas "Alleluia" and its sources, published by Mocquereau in 1904. Courtesy of the Eda Kuhn Loeb Music Library, Harvard University.

concept of restoration was, as we have seen, an equally compelling notion of decadence: his purpose was to fix the Gregorian corpus he found broken within modern books and performances. Like Viollet-le-Duc, he intended to fix it for all time, gathering the shards of evidence along a single, aesthetic horizon and producing a composite form whose very aesthetic excess, he believed, would recover the aura of the lost Gregorian past.

Mocquereau's response to this historical illusion was essentially to dismantle it—by reproducing, with the aid of more modern tools, the precise forms in which chant *did* exist in different times and places. Through the camera's lens the chant was refracted; through philology, its composite form undone. Mocquereau's discipline thus revised the aura of the already restored melodies, systematically exposing the layers of tradition, the secrets frozen within Pothier's beautiful types. Yet far from dispelling the sense of decay preserved within these artistic reconstructions, Mocquereau simply reproduced it in a new form, his systematic breakdown of the Gregorian melodies offering another example of what Nietzsche called "the sign of every literary decadence": the moment when life, as he put it, "no longer dwells in the whole."

> The word becomes sovereign and leaps out of the sentence, the sentence reaches out and obscures the meaning of the page, the page gains life at the expense of the whole . . . Indeed, the whole no longer lives at all: it is composite, calculated, artificial, artifact.[17]

If Pothier's beautiful books were one form of the "decadent enchantment" that defined the Gregorian restoration at Solesmes, Mocquereau's Gregorian tables presented another, more modern version of the same phenomenon. Under the heat of scientific scrutiny, the chant now appeared to evaporate into countless Gregorian molecules, an image that recalls the unsettling condition Marx identified with modernity itself: all that was solid melted into air.[18]

La Méthode Bénédictine

These reversible perspectives on the restoration of Gregorian writing—like two sides of the same historical coin—reflected similarly opposed ideas about the practice of Gregorian reading, a subject that leads more or less directly to musical performance, that is, to singing. In many ways it was the singing of Gregorian chant that represented the site of the most obvious disagreement between Pothier and Mocquereau, a site where their differing views on Gregorian restoration come more fully into view. A sense of this disagreement emerges, in fact, in two brief passages that discuss neither reading nor writing but the slippery space between: the liminal stage of spelling. Mocquereau regarded spelling, simply enough, as a convenient metaphor for the analytical work implied by Gregorian philology. The process of naming the individual notes in a chant was more or less analogous to the careful identification of neumes within his synoptic tables. Thus in the first volume of the *Paléographie musicale* we find Mocquereau defending one of his neume-for-neume translations in the following terms: "Before appreciating a text, it is necessary to know how to spell it."[19]

He must have known that his *confrère* did not share this opinion. The effects of spelling represented, for Pothier, another of the evils to be expunged in the course of chant's restoration. It was a position he broached early in *Les Mélodies grégoriennes* when, meditating on the "excellence of liturgical chant," he stopped to consider the causes of its modern decadence:

> It must be said: in our era, especially since the sixteenth century, the liturgical melodies are no longer what they used to be. They are neither understood nor enjoyed in the way our forefathers understood and enjoyed them; nor are they interpreted in practice as our forefathers interpreted them. We have come to a heavy and monotonous style of execution, one that removes from the chant all rhythm and color, that destroys the charm— how shall I say it?—the very essence of the melody. For sounds that follow one another uniformly, like the syllables of a child spelling his lesson, are no more a chant than the child's syllables are a reading.[20]

In order to reverse this heavy and monotonous style of execution, to get from childlike spelling to the charmed readings "enjoyed by our forefathers," Pothier advocated, as noted in chapter 2, the restoration of traditional Gregorian neumes. In contrast to Mocquereau, however, Pothier saw this restoration as a means to an end. For him, the purpose of the neumes had less to do with bona fide paleography than with performance, bypassing spelling to reach what was the more important goal of a restored Gregorian reading. Pothier conceived the old notation, in other words, not as *notae*—silent Gregorian letters—but as the long-forgotten *vox* of the chant, its ancient, animating breath.

The difference of opinion is key. This subtle revaluation of spelling in the work of our two monks recalls, for instance, the larger cultural shift in what Friedrich Kittler has called the *Aufschreibesysteme*, the notation systems or "discourse networks" of 1800 and 1900. (David Wellerby has conveniently translated these categories, in the foreword to the English version of Kittler's book, into the more familiar ideologies of "Romanticism" and "Modernism.") Pothier's concern for restoring the ancient voice of the text in fact echoes the aims of a whole generation of European educators circa 1800, who sought to reform the pedagogy of reading. Kittler surveys the introduction of new reading methods based on phonetics, citing the foreword to an 1807 primer by the Bavarian school official Heinrich Stephani that warned teachers of the pitfalls of the older "spelling method." The passage could have been written by Pothier himself:

> To grasp the uselessness of this method, take for example the word *ship* and mentally spell it out for a child: *es ach i pe*. Can you imagine that a child would know how the *sounds* of the first two letters are spoken together after having repeated the *names* of the letters? We do not connect names when we pronounce a word . . . but rather sounds. . . . If you teach your child to pronounce the *sounds* of these two letters, first individually and then together, the child will have completely learned how to read the word.[21]

In Stephani's method the voice took primacy over the letter. Spelling, no longer advocated as a precondition for reading, was simply left out. The teacher helped the child to translate the written signs into sound, putting phonemes right into his mouth. Without the intermediate step of naming letters, reading turned directly into expression, becoming a "natural," rather than mechanical, act.

Yet it was this very natural act that, a century later, would be submitted to a new kind of technological scrutiny. By 1900 the study of reading had less to do with enabling than with *measuring* the process by which a reader turned letters into sounds. Kittler describes the early experiments in psychophysics that attempted to determine such measurements, the complex set of mental operations that led to the comprehension of a written word:

> Following the procedure of Helmholtz, who built device after device to measure reaction-time thresholds, the psychophysics of the nineties went to work measuring reading with kymographs, tachistoscopes, horopterscopes, and chronographs. There was intense competition among these machines to determine the smallest fraction of time in which reading could be measured. . . . Experimental subjects . . . sat, chained so as to hinder or even prohibit movement, facing black viewing boxes out of which for the duration of a flash . . . single letters shone out.[22]

To quantify reading through scientific research was to break down the Romantic pedagogy of the natural voice. Turned into experimental subjects, readers in fact lost their voices, watching, immobile, while whole words disintegrated before their eyes. This scientific transformation had the unexpected effect of renewing the status of written letters and thus, as Kittler notes, "of spelling, which had generally come to be viewed with contempt." A researcher from 1900 concluded that "even the educated fall back on the 'most primitive spelling' as the minimum *and* standard of all reading."[23]

In such attempts to get behind the act of reading, to analyze its parts, we recognize the effect that motivated Mocquereau's study of Gregorian texts, an effect that strongly colored his perception of Gregorian performance. Whereas Pothier would advocate, like Stephani, a phonetic approach to the chant in order to fix the broken melodies, the ancient sounds that lay fractured in the mouths of modern singers, Mocquereau would eventually seek to enumerate the contents of this restored performance. He intended to spell out, as it were, the complex set of behaviors that constituted proper Gregorian chanting. Dom Jean Claire reports, in an article of 1980 commemorating the fiftieth anniversary of Mocquereau's death, how the young monk, upon entering the order, found himself completely mystified by the method of singing practiced at Solesmes, a style Pothier and his fellow monks took to be completely natural.[24] In the seventh volume of the *Paléographie musicale* Mocquereau made his first serious effort to solve the mystery, to quantify the effects of the natural performance that, by 1901, had come to be known as *la méthode bénédictine*.

The mystery centered on the single most *un*quantifiable dimension of the chant: its rhythm. Gontier had claimed as early as 1859 that the secret to the singing at Solesmes lay in a rhythm that was not at all measured but "free." The further discussion of this Gregorian performance practice by both Pothier and Mocquereau reveals just how elusive such freedom could be. The divergence in their theories lay not so much in the idea of free rhythm as in its representation—the set of terms with which each one attempted to capture it, to preserve its sense of mystery. Although it is possible to ascribe the difference in such representations, as Dom Jean Claire has suggested, to the fourteen years that separated the master from his pupil—a sort of generation gap—such a conclusion fails to account for the dynamic nature of the separation. To posit a generation gap is to invoke the almost static condition of a personality conflict. Yet the distance between Pothier and Mocquereau was not merely a matter of individual temperament.

In their differences, the two figures would seem to manifest the very temper of the epoch they inhabited—that queer, historical interval we call the "fin de siècle." This was an era whose definition proved as difficult for commentators in the previous century as it is for historians today. Eugen Weber opens his monograph on the period by musing over this difficulty, citing, among other sources, a weekly newspaper published toward the end of the 1890s—called, naturally enough, *Le Fin de siècle*—whose editorial agenda was expressed in the following terms: "All is mixed, confused, blurred, and reshuffled in a kaleidoscopic vision."[25] The Benedictine restoration represented a similar fin de siècle muddle, a reform movement that, at the century's turning, was in a notable state of flux. Nostalgia for a lost Gregorian past came face to face with futuristic science; art crossed paths with technology. Pothier and Mocquereau might be read, then, as figures—Romantic and Modern—for such confusion, the difference between them realized not as a fixed space but as a kind of undefined movement, a shuffling between competing ideologies.

Indeed, it was a form of this very movement, with its surface of freely changing possibilities, that seemed to reappear as the secret, inscrutable essence of
Benedictine chant. The mysterious rhythmic freedom of Gregorian song could
thus be viewed as a potent sign of the times. Free rhythm becomes a figure for
the whole mixed-up historical era, whose undefined pulse not only accentuated
but ultimately shaped the differences between Pothier and Mocquereau. To
consider the narratives of free rhythm in their work is to encounter the central, defining mystery in the Gregorian restoration at Solesmes, a mystery
whose multiple faces may serve, finally, to illuminate the complex meaning of
fin-de-siècle enchantment.

Dom Pothier's Ear

Pothier introduced the freedom of *chant liturgique* in the opening chapter of *Les
Mélodies grégoriennes* by invoking the notion of a music that was not exactly
music. His argument turned on the ambiguity of the very term he was attempting to define. The French word *chant* does not translate directly into the genre
of music we call "chant" but refers more generally to the whole phenomenon of
song, the natural music produced by birds and humans whenever voices are
raised. Such natural music constitutes a singular mode of expression, a musical
act falling into the blissfully undefined space between speaking and singing. For
Pothier this kind of expression was simply a "cry": "There is in the Catholic
liturgy of the Church a music that . . . is at once a word and a song [*une parole et
un chant*], a rich and powerful music that is also simple and natural, a music that
does not seek to be music, does not listen to itself, but is released as the spontaneous cry of religious thought and feeling."[26] The explanation recalled something of the ethos of lyric poetry as it had been defined, almost a century before,
by the Romantics. In a letter to his friend Zelter from 1809 we find Goethe, for
instance, musing over the connection between word and tone in song in similarly evocative terms, representing music as a force whose ecstatic union with
words created "something unique," a fusion of poetic and sensory experience.
"We think and feel," Goethe claimed, "and are carried away by it."[27]

In its most elementary form, this unique fusion of thought and feeling was,
for Pothier, nothing more than what the ancients called an "accent." The concept embodied the same kind of ambiguity that invaded the idea of song, a phenomenon that belonged equally to *parole* and *musique*. The notion of accent designated the natural rising and falling of the voice, and thus, in Pothier's view,
referred to "a species of modulation for which properly musical modulation was
but a development." He argued the point by means of etymology: *accentus*

derived from *ad cantus*. Not only did the idea of song (*cantus*) emerge at the very heart of the concept *accentus*, but, as Pothier goes on to say, "several authors have observed [that] accents are called tones (*toni, tenores*), which is also the name given to the musical modes."[28]

This etymology of the accent, which appeared in Pothier's chapter on neumatic notation, only enhanced his view of Gregorian writing. Like other nineteenth-century scholars, he conceived the neumes as an ancient script used by both grammarians and musicians to represent vocal inflection, the rising or falling strokes marking the rise and fall of the voice that defined proper elocution. The notion of the equivalence between musical and prosodic accents—between the early neumes and accent "marks"—was first observed by Edmond de Coussemaker in his *Histoire de l'harmonie au moyen âge* (1852) and, as Leo Treitler has shown, became the reigning paradigm for explaining the origins of musical notation not just in the nineteenth but well into the twentieth century.[29] Treitler has strongly objected to this origin myth as a "red herring" that "is misleading not only about the nature and origins of the neumes directly, but indirectly about other aspects of the relationship between language- and music-writing, and about the relationship between music-writing and the chant tradition itself."[30]

It is precisely this last relationship between music writing and the chant tradition that I should like to examine by reading Pothier's account of *accentus*. My goal is not so much to demonstrate how the account may have been "misleading" as to understand its rationale: what the concept of accent actually signified for nineteenth-century scholars like Pothier. For Treitler the "accent theory of origin" is wrong because it supports a view that the essentially oral tradition of chant was, from its beginnings, a *written* phenomenon. But the objection fails to acknowledge how the Romantics themselves actually understood this writing. Indeed, through Pothier's account we begin to see that perhaps the most compelling aspect of the concept of *accentus*—at least as he understood it—lay in the way it transcended the written to embrace a notion of writing that was, however paradoxically, an *oral* phenomenon.[31] For scholars like Pothier the upward and downward strokes of *acutus* and *gravis* represented something far more natural than mere writing because they were, above all else, signs of pure vibration, evidence of that ineffable substance we call the voice.

To prove the point, Pothier needed nothing more than a single Latin word. In the fourth chapter of *Les Mélodies grégoriennes* he demonstrated how long and short syllables of the word *Roma* yielded, in their difference, three temporal units, a quantity he attempted to represent with a revised spelling: *Rooma*. The alteration was telling, for the doubled vowel of the first syllable, which obviously showed

Figure 18. Example showing the phenomenon of word accent at work, from the fourth chapter of Pothier's *Mélodies grégoriennes*.

the effect of its doubled quantity, also evoked the actual sound of the spoken word. Respelling *Roma*, in other words, disturbed the integrity of the graphic sign, a disturbance that in turn foregrounded its aural or vocal dimension. Pothier's demonstration would further emphasize this sounding element by introducing diacritics to represent the syllable's precise inflection, a movement whose most natural form, as he pointed out, was to "fall again after having risen." The three time units of *Rooma* thus embodied a threefold accent, moving high to low, *aigu* to *grave*. The word became *Róòmà*, the compound vowel revealing the incipient form of the circumflex (*Rômà*). The combined accent outlined a single rise and fall of the voice. Pothier completed the proof by offering a picture of this singular speech act in easy-to-read Guidonian notation (fig. 18).

The example makes Pothier's notion of the chant's origins completely clear. We witness the word *Roma* undergo a graphic distortion until it is made to deliver something beyond the mere letter. Wrung from its fluid form are three precious drops of sound—three *puncta*, like vowel points, that showed the natural vocalization of *o* and *a*. The vowel is, etymologically speaking, a sign of the voice (in Latin, *littera vocalis*), an audible *vox* breathing life into the inert *notae* of writing. Formed by the relatively unobstructed passage of air, vowels are letters that represent pure sound, occupying that dimension of speech closest to a cry, or to music. Pothier's example derives Gregorian music by pronouncing the name of the Catholic Church's symbolic home, emancipating the ancient *vox* from the written sign and thus returning the word *Rome* to an originary state of pure vibration.

The demonstration recalls one of the important precepts of early Romantic philology, a science that, as described by Foucault, conceived of language as a phenomenon of sound, of speech rather than writing. In the work of scholars like Grimm and Bopp "language is treated for the first time," Foucault explains, "as a totality of phonetic elements":

> This explains the new interest, shown by Raynouard and the brothers Grimm, in nonwritten literature, in folk tales and spoken dialects. . . . By means of the ephemeral and

profound sound it produces, the spoken word accedes to sovereignty. And its secret powers, drawing new life from the breath of the prophets, rise up in fundamental oppositions (even though they do tolerate some overlapping) to the esoteric nature of writing . . . .[Language] has acquired a vibratory nature which has separated it from the visible sign and made it more nearly proximate to the note in music.[32]

For Romantic music scholars like Pothier the secret power of chant originated in such ineffable vibrations: "An art like Gregorian chant," he said, "borrows its best effects from the science of language . . . [and] nothing is as delicate as the phenomenon of speech."[33] Ecclesiastical Latin preserved traces of a music that was something like the original dialect of the Church, an idiom that harked back, as we have seen, to Saint Gregory himself. This music was to be understood, then, not as an adornment—a musical layer added *to* the words of the liturgy—but as a sound that issued naturally *from* them. Chant was, finally, nothing more than highly expressive speaking. As an elocutionary act raised to a higher power, so to speak, it captured in its syllables a music that was the accent of religious devotion.

Pothier's concept of Gregorian rhythm grew out of this accent. "Rhythm always flows from the accent of speech," he once said, "as from its primary and natural source." The essence of Gregorian speech encompassed, in other words, not only a bending of tone but a shaping of time—a temporal inflection that issued, once again, from the pronunciation of Latin, with its alternating patterns of weak and strong syllables. In a chapter on the "diverse values of notes" from *Les Mélodies grégoriennes*, Pothier revealed the character of this movement in a simple formula: the accented syllable was always "strong without elongation," the unaccented "long, but weak."[34] The accent so concentrated the energy of the word that it functioned, in his words, as an *élément condensateur*, a "condenser element," forcing the tone of the strong syllable upward without increasing its time value. Only through the release of such tension did time pull back, the relaxation of both pitch and rhythm producing, in the unaccented syllable, a slight elongation. The same speech accent that caused a natural rise and fall in the voice created an equally natural push and pull of rhythm.

Pothier would later develop this insight into a more rigorous theory of movement, a fully fledged notion of rhythmic tension and release, expressed by the Greek terms *arsis* and *thesis*. In a series of articles from the 1890s, Pothier attempted to demonstrate the practical application of this theory by transcribing several familiar Gregorian melodies into modern notation.[35] The transcription, for instance, of the hymn "Ave Maris Stella" (whose trochaic rhythm he barred, in triple meter, $\frac{3}{4}$ Á-|ve____ Má-|ris____ Stél-|la____) revealed his basic understanding of the terms. All accented syllables were placed, then, on the third beat of the measure, which would correspond to the arsis, or rising part of the meter; the final, weak syllables came to rest on the downbeats, corresponding to the thesis, or cadential part. It was this striking reversal of the conventional paradigm that presumably accounted for the mysterious—and therefore ancient—allure associated with the Benedictine method of chanting.

Far more difficult to explain were the individual rhythmic values contained within these rising or falling movements, which necessarily varied, as Pothier asserted in his *Mélodies grégoriennes,* "according to circumstances." Longs and shorts became longer or shorter depending on whether a given syllable fell at the beginning, middle, or end of the word or of the whole phrase. In syllabic recitation, a simple *punctum* could thus represent as many as four or five slightly different values in a single line of text. The situation became only more complicated with neumatic or melismatic chants. The inflections represented in the compound neumes such as *pes, clivis,* and *torculus,* or in the combination of these neumes, inevitably caused the already elastic syllable to swell or contract further. Pothier attempted to illustrate this elasticity in another musical example whose melismatic inflections yielded no less than fourteen ways of executing the strong and weak syllables of the text.

This was the sense in which the rhythm of Gregorian chant could be called "free." The nature of traditional notation made it impossible to specify precise durations, since the same neumes could represent longer or shorter values depending on their position within the chanted phrase. The note forms themselves had no fixed value. Thus, although Pothier could articulate the general principle that governed Gregorian rhythm, he was unable—and unwilling—to calculate its individual *rhythms,* those infinite nuances that flowed from the ancient Gregorian dialect. He considered such an activity, in fact, not only pointless but unnatural. "Even though, as one can see, there are long and short notes in Gregorian chant, as in all speech, it is not on this object that we should focus our attention. Who dreams of scanning his words while speaking? It is sufficient that one take care to pronounce them well and distribute them well according to the natural divisions of the phrase."[36]

The real value of the neumes resulted "spontaneously," as Pothier put it, from good pronunciation, creating rhythms so natural they never had to be written down. Such spontaneity recalled Pothier's original description of the Gregorian song, in whose accents he had heard a similarly instinctive expression—the "spontaneous cry of religious thought and feeling." Before concluding his practical discussion of note values, he returned somewhat abruptly to this primal state of devotion in order to reconsider the meaning of chant's rhythm. "If rhythm is the soul of the chant, devotion is the soul of rhythm," he reasoned, adding the following caveat: "It is better to feel devotion than to define it." With this logic, Pothier decisively removed his account from the theoretical to the visceral, from thinking to feeling. It was not by calculation but by inspiration that one came to know the real values of this sacred music. The most important fact was thus not so much to quantify rhythm as "to feel it and express it," which required the performer simply "to be inspired by the divisions of the text and the phrases of the chant."[37]

. . . . .

It was this inspiration that Pothier attempted to explore in his next chapter. He began his account of "the characteristic rhythm of Gregorian chant" by tracing the rhythmic instinct to its source, locating it within the one sense organ designed to collect nature's sounds: the ear. The natural rhythms of all speech, and therefore of chant itself, originated not in abstract principles but in the basic requirements of this sensory apparatus. In order to ensure intelligibility, he argued, the ear demanded certain reasonable divisions within a sequence of spoken sounds: "Too continuous, they would offer the ear nothing but a confused progression; too disjunct they would become absolutely unintelligible." Pothier developed the point with some help from Cicero's *De Oratore*:

> In speech, syllables are grouped in such a manner as to form words, clauses, and sentences. These divisions, brought about by the natural distinction of ideas, and required by the necessity of respiration, are at the same time *a need for the ear*. So much so, says Cicero, that we would not be able to stand an orator whose lungs allowed him to say everything in one breath without stopping: *si cui sit infinitus spiritus datus, tamen eum perpetuare verba nolimus*.[38]

The ear's authority only became more prominent as Pothier went on to consider the nature of these oratorical divisions, an inquiry that led him immediately to the subject of proportion. The discernible sections within a discourse, he argued, could never be "haphazard or arbitrary" because "the ear had received from nature the feeling and need for proportion." It was this natural sense of proportion that served as the basis of Pothier's understanding of rhythm. Whereas, in the measured rhythms of poetry, the proportions among individual phrases unfolded according to a single metric principle, in speech no such regularity reigned. This so-called free rhythm of discourse—which Pothier referred to as "number"—involved no fixed measurements, only "the natural instinct of the ear": "The number [of discourse] rests on a measurement determined not by fixed rules but by the intimate feeling whose organ is the ear. This organ contains naturally within itself the measurement of sounds, and thus judges what is too long or too short."[39]

This striking image of the ear as the original arbiter of speech, which Pothier gleaned from the fifty-third chapter of Cicero's treatise,[40] made its way into other nineteenth-century origin myths. An 1879 treatise on French versification by an exact contemporary of Pothier, the critic Louis Becq de Fouquières, described the development of measured speech in remarkably similar terms. It was not until natural man began to organize his instinctive cries into language that he conceived the idea of measuring his discourse, an impulse that Becq de Fouquières ascribed to the power of the ear: "The ear required authoritatively that the voice regulate its emission—that is to say, it was not to send an arbitrary or indeterminate sum of sounds for which it could not calculate the number or duration. It became necessary to assure the regular play of the voice and to subjugate it to a unit of measure." The number that best satisfied this regular play, and to which the ear was most sensitive, turned out to be twelve—the precise length of one alexandrine—which, by his reasoning, allowed "the elements to be grouped in the greatest number of combinations."[41] Thus Becq de Fouquières, rediscovering the essence of number in sound, derived the natural origin of classical French poetry.

Pothier affected to do very much the same thing for chant. Yet his theory of Gregorian number also drew support from another, more compelling tradition, a medieval Christian narrative that traced the ear's putatively natural feeling for chant to a divine origin. We return to the primal scene of Gregorian history, the site of Gregory's original inspiration. This occasion has been depicted, through an iconography extending at least to the tenth century, as an unmistakable moment of divine intervention *per aurem*. A version of this traditional illustration, as we have already noted, adorns the opening page of Pothier's first *Liber Gradualis*, showing the saint in the act of dictating his song to a faithful scribe (see fig. 10). What the picture presents most clearly are the discrete stages of this transmission, which reads, as if along a sacred flow chart, from left to right, inside to outside. The chant that begins in Gregory's ear flows outward from his mouth to reach the hand of the scribe, who records the event in writing. It is the Holy Spirit, in the form of a dove, that sets the whole process in motion, infusing Gregory with the intimate feeling that first prompted him devoutly to raise his voice. The ear appears as the organ through which the saint was moved to measure his words, creating the perfect accents that, like his lifted hands, enacted the very meaning of that original cry: "Ad te levavi."

This picture of the first Gregorian speech act offers a useful angle from which to scrutinize Pothier's theory of rhythm. Indeed, the image preserves what was, for him, one of the most important truths of chant's origins—its secrecy. The feeling that moves Gregory to sing is clearly a private inspiration, here depicted in its most literal sense, as a dove whispering into (literally "breathing on," from *in + spiro*) the saint's ear. The ear becomes a crucial figure in this story of origins: a tiny cavity connected to an unseen interior, it represents the corridor to inspiration, a dark path leading to all that is intimate, personal, hidden. In an article from his 1874 *Grand Dictionnaire universel du XIXe siècle*, Larousse concludes his etymology of the word *oreille* by observing that the linguist Frederic Eichhoff had "related the Latin *auris* and its analogues to the Sanskrit *usa*, 'vase' or 'cavity,' from the root *us*, meaning to penetrate or pierce."[42] It is no wonder Pothier chose to place the image of Gregory receiving the chant next to that of the Annunciation, the most spectacular story of divine penetration in Christian mythology. The intertextual link between these two subjects served only to heighten the sense of mystery that surrounded what Gregory himself spontaneously conceived. The image of his penetrated ear signaled that the chant he sang was, from the beginning, a private, interior phenomenon—an inspiration whose indescribable rhythm, Pothier claimed, the ear knew intimately, as if "by a secret instinct."

Throughout his *Mélodies grégoriennes*, Pothier gave priority to this interior sensibility. Placing himself in the position of the speaking subject, of Gregory himself, he theorized chant's movement as a subjective phenomenon, constructing what was essentially a Romantic theory of rhythm. From this insider's perspective, it was always an unseen impulse, like the breath in Gregory's ear, that moved the subject to speak well—to mete out his thoughts. By remaining hidden, rhythm thus joined the world of vibrating phenomena that constituted the essence of language for the Romantic philologists, a world of invisible sensation whose proper organ was not the eye but the ear. Here is Pothier's last word:

> We should say of chant what Quintilian says of discourse: in a well-composed discourse there is number, and a kind of meter, but this number and measure is not so clear as to be marked by the rising and falling of the hand. On the contrary, this measure is the free measure of which Horace speaks: *numerisque fertur lege solutis*. It is the number that exists in discourse *without appearing to be there*. We feel it, the ears are deliciously affected by it, but we cannot say what it is.[43]

· · · · ·

Mocquereau would not be so sure. It was precisely this invisible phenomenon that he would attempt to articulate in his own theory of Gregorian rhythm, which he began formulating as early as 1901. Reversing the terms on which Pothier founded his idea of musical number, Mocquereau gazed on the primal scene of Gregorian history as if from the opposite direction, and from this perspective he drew entirely new conclusions about the nature of Gregorian performance. Viewed from right to left, the scene of Gregory's first song reads very differently indeed. The emphasis shifts from ear to eye, from inside to outside, bringing into relief one element of the traditional iconography that seems to have constituted, for Pothier, a significant blind spot: the figure of the scribe. From the vantage point of the scribe, the Gregorian song is, after all, not just audible but visible. Not only does he notate, in clear signs, the accents of this song for all to see, but the marks on his tablet appear to be related to something he himself witnesses: the movements dictated by Gregory's uplifted hands.

The status of these hands designates one of the clearest points of divergence in the theories of Pothier and Mocquereau. Whereas Pothier, in the remark above, concludes that the performer, like the orator, simply remains still in the act of intoning the chant (the rhythm too subtle "to be marked by the rising and falling of the hand"), Mocquereau imagines manual movement as a necessity of good performance. As discussed in the previous chapter, the hand gestures of writing itself represented a basic rhythmic concept, corresponding to a chironomy, as he called it, that was eventually to become the basis of a more complex rhythmic theory. What Mocquereau himself would highlight in the picture of Gregory's transmission of the chant was not, then, the private sensations of the ear but the more public activity of the hand. Indeed, the concept of "accent" for Mocquereau required an understanding of *two* different hands: both that of the singing Gregory and that of the scribe who writes his performance.

Dom Mocquereau's Hands

It was through the figure of the scribe that Mocquereau in fact acquired a kind of optical distance on the subject of Gregorian performance, a position that prompted him to take on the task Pothier himself had refused to broach: the analysis of rhythm. In the opening pages of his ambitious treatise on Gregorian musical number, the first volume of which appeared in 1908, Mocquereau announced his intention to expose the mechanism that drove the mysterious free rhythm that Pothier's theory had relegated, in the end, to inspiration. Indeed, Mocquereau argued that in the free rhythm of speech, music, and dance one could discern, as he put it, "the tiniest rhythmic subdivisions," whose recurrence suggested an even more profound mystery, a phenomenon he articulated as a fundamental law: "at the foundation of every rhythmic composition there exists a series of primary beats [*temps premiers*], grouped in units of two or three."[44]

A long footnote referred the reader to a recent study that confirmed the point, a piece published, of all places, in the first volume of *Harvard Psychological Studies*. The American psychologist Robert MacDougall, reporting on the structure of simple rhythmic forms, had concluded, from "the positive evidence of experiments," that the numerical limit of such forms comprised just "two rhythmical units . . . of two or three beats respectively."[45] In experimental work conducted at the Harvard Psychological Laboratory in 1902, MacDougall had measured the responses of his experimental subjects using an impressive mechanical apparatus, a photograph of which was included in the published report. MacDougall's study of rhythm thus fell squarely within the world of tachistoscopes and horopterscopes—the machines of psychology—that defined Kittler's "discourse network" of 1900. By citing this study Mocquereau revealed not only his breadth of reading but also, and more important, the ultramodern positivistic bias of his scholarly undertaking. His theory of Gregorian rhythm would not rely on the same vague notions of "feeling" that had sufficed for Pothier. He intended systematically to break feeling down into its smallest components, to recover its essence. Aesthetic phenomena like rhythm were—in the words of psychologist Hugo Münsterberg, who wrote the preface to the Harvard volume—"of all the feeling processes those which can be produced in the laboratory most purely."[46]

The purity of such a study required that rhythm be separated from the contexts it formerly inhabited. It was, again, the vantage point of the scribe that encouraged this analytical disintegration, which distinguished the part from the whole, the rhythmic dimension of chant from the act of singing itself. In the introduction to his treatise, Mocquereau announced his plan to study rhythm in isolation "from everything that could veil it, complicate it, denature it." His hope was to see rhythm for what it was, "to penetrate it in all its truth, all its nakedness."[47] This was perhaps the clearest expression of the theoretical reversal of his whole approach. It was no longer a matter of rhythm penetrating the ear of the subject, as in the Romantic theory advanced by Pothier, but of the subject—the theorist—working to penetrate the essence of rhythm:

> The study of pure, naked rhythm, divested of all melodic and oratorical ornament, is ever more necessary in our era, where so many musicians . . . mistake for absolute laws of rhythm facts that are nothing but special applications of one language or one type of music. To untangle rhythm from all these matters that entwine it, to make its true nature known—this is the work that should occupy the student.[48]

The biggest such snarl involved the sacred words themselves. Mocquereau's treatise, organized in three parts, left this topic for last, commencing with the origins of rhythm proper and the rhythmic dimension of melody before turning, in the final part, to "les textes liturgiques." Readers, however, would have to wait some time before learning Mocquereau's thoughts on this last subject. The third part of his treatise did not appear in print until 1927, four years after Pothier's death. For Mocquereau, the most basic element of speech—the *paroles* that in

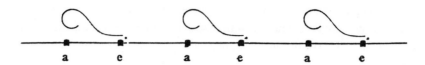

Figure 19. Example showing the principle of *élan* and *repos*, from the first volume of Mocquereau's *Nombre musical grégorien* (1908).

Pothier's theory served to define the chant's free, or oratorical, rhythm—presented something of a problem, one that he would not resolve for another twenty years. His new theory of oratorical rhythm depended on simply getting oratory out of the way.

Clearly, the act of speaking no longer represented for Mocquereau the "natural" activity it had been for Pothier. Speech had become complicated. Far from calling on expressive instincts, Mocquereau advised the modern student of Gregorian rhythm to avoid "all preconceived notions, derived either from our occidental languages or from modern music." On this point, once again, he sought confirmation from an American expert. This time he cited the classicist Charles E. Bennett from an article on Latin prosody published in the 1899 *American Journal of Philology.* The passage included the following stark reflection: "At all events, it is certainly of the first importance, in approaching so delicate a problem as the pronunciation of a language whose data we can no longer fully control, first to rid ourselves as completely as possible of all preconceived notions derived from our own language which might mislead us."[49] The talk of data and control seems a far cry from the Romantic vibrations that echoed in Pothier's description of Gregorian accent—and a good deal closer, perhaps, to the ethos of Mocquereau's synoptic tables, the power tools of comparative philology. From Bennett's perspective, responsible scholarship required one to begin by acknowledging the fruits of such comparative study, taking into account, as he put it, "the great divergence of human speech along with the often radically different character of spoken languages." The comparison of languages, in fact, revealed so many patterns that one's own speech habits could only complicate, rather than illuminate, the study of an ancient dialect like Gregorian.

Mocquereau therefore did not begin his treatise by attempting to squeeze Gregorian music out of the name of the Church's ancestral home. He started, in fact, without a word, without pronouncing so much as a syllable. His first examples did not even employ a musical staff—just two pure vowels, *a* and *e*, marked by two *puncta*, unfolding along a single, horizontal axis (fig. 19). Two, he explained, was the smallest number of events that could constitute a rhythm. The note pairs were distinguished by a small dot following the second *punctum*, a mark meant to show their difference, short and long. Mocquereau went on to explain the intimate relationship between these two elements: "The short appears as a beginning, a point of departure, a momentum [*élan*]. It seems animated, living. It is in motion. The long, on the contrary, appears as an ending, an arrival, a cadence or fall. It is a stop, a rest [*repos*]. . . . No need of a text, of an ancient manuscript to prove to us this truth: it is inside us. Even the savage without culture must be aware of it."[50]

This primordial iamb, which Mocquereau considered the "very essence of rhythm," recalled the principle of tension and release, the arsis and thesis adumbrated by Pothier in 1891.[51] But there was a difference. Mocquereau wrested the arsis and thesis from the prosaic trappings that had weighed down Pothier's understanding—not only the modern transcriptions, whose strong, vertical bar lines were, in his view, easily misinterpreted, but also the Latin text that fell heavy on the tongue. Indeed, in his imagination Gregorian rhythm embodied such a lightness of being that it should simply float. By breaking apart the Latin word and dismantling melody, Mocquereau released this pure motion, the soul of the chant, which now appeared ghostlike on the page, hovering over the two vowels in the form of a gentle curve, a sign that was also a sigh, suggesting the endless lift and droop of rhythm, its weightless *bercement*.

Stripped of every encumbrance, the rhythm of chant thus became ephemeral, evoking a world of the spirit that renounced the heavy materiality of language to embrace the mysterious, immaterial properties of music. In a chapter on rhythmical movement from the first part of his *Nombre musical grégorien*, Mocquereau described the delicacy required to sustain such weightless material in performance, citing an aphorism of Nietzsche: "The Beautiful is light. All that is divine walks on delicate feet."[52] The reference formed a poetic pun, implying that the *percussio* marking the metrical iamb and trochee, the "foot" of Latin prosody, had nothing to do with the divine properties of Gregorian rhythm. For Mocquereau, the mysterious freedom of this rhythm was not, then, a matter of the free combination of prosodic elements—the freedom from regular meter, as suggested by Pothier—but a freedom from the very idea of meter, whose inevitable force would weigh the rhythm down. "Take heed," Mocquereau warned. "Force, in rhythmics, brings us always closer to the material element, the striking of a hammer on the anvil, or the release of the piston of a locomotive. The use of this force in Gregorian rhythm—so ethereal, so virginal—should be constantly tempered by the immaterial power that gave it birth."[53]

Mocquereau guarded against the danger of such hammered performances by keeping the chant's rhythm at arm's length. The *percussio* of which the ancients spoke was not, as he explained, "a force of the *voice*, but a noise of the foot or hand beating, scanning the rhythm."[54] Such scansion was the proper jurisdiction of the choirmaster. At the time of the Greeks, Mocquereau explained, it was the *choryphee* who indicated rhythmic undulations "with hand or foot." In Hucbald's time, this figure was known as the *prior scholae*, who likewise ruled the singers by his own hand, according to a specific *chironomia* (from *chiro*, hand, and *nomos*, rule), or, as Mocquereau would translate it, *chironomie*.[55] He considered such manual gestures an absolute necessity for rhythm's proper performance, the local movement serving to represent, as he put it, "a vocal movement that was otherwise untranslatable except by analogy."[56]

A footnote to his original discussion of *élan* and *repos* made this necessity especially clear, entreating the modern choirmaster to trace the same curve whose outline he had left on the page, by "raising his hand quickly on the short note and lowering it on the long."[57] It was precisely this show of hands that constituted the difference between the rhythmic theories advanced by our fellow monks. Mocquereau sought to understand—quite literally, to grasp—the immaterial, spiritual element of Gregorian movement by exposing it, taking rhythm from the hidden interior of Pothier's ear and transferring it to the body's surface, a public site where it would be seen as well as heard. His pedagogy forced the choirmaster, like a doubting Thomas, to learn the secrets of rhythm by touching it with his own hands.

The shift might best be understood as a question of *tact*—a notion whose two opposed meanings very nearly match the distinctions between the theories of Pothier and Mocquereau. In one sense, tact refers to a sensitivity, an internalized feeling for what is proper, realized, as it was for Pothier, in *speaking correctly*, having an ear for the chant. Yet tact also refers, more basically, to the sense of touch (from the Latin *tactus*), suggesting the direct, manual involvement of a body with an object. It is this sense of tact that we find in the work of Mocquereau. To have Gregorian tact would mean to get in touch, in a literal way, with divine singing, a condition that recalls both Gregory and his scribe capturing the soul of the chant—in the air and on the page—in the rise and fall of an exquisite cursive.

Nowhere is this condition more strikingly displayed than in Mocquereau's analysis of the Gregorian antiphon "Cantate Domino canticum novum," which concludes his chapter on Gregorian chironomy in the first volume of *Le Nombre musical grégorien* (fig. 20).[58] The remarkable reading he offers seems to fulfill the command of Latin text ("Sing to the Lord a new song"), presenting a picture that transforms the ancient chant into something more fresh and original than any modern *mélodie*. Most arresting is the graphic representation of the rhythm, in living color, which transcends the rigid parallel lines of conventional

Figure 20. Full-color illustration of "Gregorian chironomy," first published in volume 7 of *Paléographie musicale* (1901), and later reproduced in Mocquereau's *Nombre musical grégorien* (1908). Although Mocquereau does not explicitly credit the artists, the illustration appears to be the work of the nuns of Sainte-Cécile.

notation. A graceful curve atop the melody, it loops among the red notes, leaving in its wake a froth of sea-foam green that engulfs the musical staff. The Gregorian chironomy turns the hymn into a gently cresting form that floats right off the page. Here is the divine movement of which Nietzsche spoke, rendered in all its mystery, a movement borne by feet so delicate they walk on water.

"Mystery," the French ethnologist Michel Leiris once wrote, "can be represented as a border, a fringe encircling the object, isolating it at the same time as it emphasizes its presence, masking it at the same time as it qualifies."[59] In Mocquereau's diagram, the pale green wash encircling the melody attempts to make such mystery visible on the page by representing the same, graceful movements that the choirmaster would reproduce with a wave of his hand, pulling Gregorian rhythm out of thin air like a conjuror. For him, the source of this mysterious movement was found not in the Latin words—which fall like lead weights to the bottom of the staff—but in the wash of melody itself. What he called the "quasi-spirituality of Gregorian rhythm" belonged to the immaterial realm of musical sound, to singing rather than speaking.

Mocquereau's pedagogy encouraged singers to experience this mystery themselves, by tracing the gestures written by the choirmaster. To Pothier's rhetorical question "Who would dream of scanning his words while speaking?" Mocquereau in effect answered, "I would." The most efficient means to rid performers of preconceived notions was to fill them with new notions, by training them in the unfamiliar ways of the ancient Gregorian music. To this end, Mocquereau included a series of musical exercises in the second part of his treatise. For him, it was not inspiration but, so to speak, the act of drilling that would cause the chant's elusive rhythm finally to penetrate the ear of the student.

The exercises were to be executed in three distinct stages, beginning with what Mocquereau called a "rhythmical reading." As he explained, the student would begin the exercise by "reading the notes without singing them," while at the same time "executing with his hand the rhythmic movements" represented by the chironomic line. To this silent reading he added, as a second stage, a rhythmical pronunciation of solfège syllables, after which the student finally graduated to singing itself, in the form of vocalise. "To make the transition from solfège to vocalise, you will repeat the same melodic exercises, this time suppressing the consonants of the solfège syllables. In other words, instead of singing *do, re, mi*, you will sing *o, e, i*." The vowel sounds, he cautioned, "should conform to the official Roman pronunciation, which will be taught in the third part of this treatise."[60]

There were about fifty such exercises in all, starting with melodic patterns generated by simple neumes, and moving slowly to more complex neumes and their various combinations. Figure 21 shows the beginning of the twenty-eighth drill, which presented melodic patterns formed by "simple juxtaposition." The exercise, like all the others, was accompanied by a heavily edited transcription in modern notation, complete with the chironomic line the student should have in hand. This encircling figure, along with the additional expression marks, complicated the transcription to the point of near illegibility, as if to show just how different Gregorian singing was from modern practice. By comparison, the neumes that preceded the transcription, separated in neat bunches, appeared pristine.

The Gregorian neumes in these exercises were pristine in another sense, for they in fact represented no particular chant at all. The pattern was nothing more than an isolated melodic fragment—*pes, clivis, porrectus*—rearranged in a sequence, like a small particle extracted from some unknown Gregorian melody for closer examination. Mocquereau's drills served, in effect, to break down the sacred *cantus*, reducing it, piece by piece, into a more elemental form whose purest manifestation was vocalise. This was archaeological method in performance, Pothier's cry taken to the laboratory. Stripped of all melodic interest, all liturgical meaning, the Gregorian song was restored to a state of unadulterated

1. Mode.

a   a   a   a

Même exercice, transcription musicale.

Figure 21. Example from Exercise No. 28 from Mocquereau's *Nombre musical grégorien* (1908), a chironomic vocalise developed to drill neume groups "joined by simple juxta-position."

sound, rendered by the purest open syllable, *a*. The exercises thus fulfilled Mocquereau's most pressing scientific objective, articulated at the beginning of his treatise: to isolate Gregorian rhythm in all its imagined purity.

Indeed, Mocquereau ensured that such a goal would be reached even before the singers opened their mouths. His opening instruction signaled the first, radical stage of purification, effectively uncoupling the written from the oral, separating the chant from the voice. Students would begin their drill, Mocquereau advised, by "reading the notes without singing them," contemplating the Gregorian rhythms in reverent silence, drilling them into their bodies without any noise at all. By moving their hands, they created of themselves the perfect container, a vessel to be filled with sound. The chironomic line became the script by which students learned to change their musical behavior. In this primary act of reading, the chant momentarily transcended song's realm, the interior of the body where sound is born, and became, for a few silent minutes, pure dance.

· · · · ·

In this respect Mocquereau's pedagogy would seem to resemble the efforts of another early-twentieth-century theorist, who sought to reform music education through the art of dance. As early as 1898, the Swiss pedagogue Emile Jaques-Dalcroze had begun publishing essays concerning the problems of young pianists, offering solutions that eventually developed into a systematic pedagogy that called for the engagement of the student's entire body. As he explained, "I set my pupils exercises in stepping and halting, and trained them to react physically to the perception of musical rhythms. That was the origin of my Eurythmics."[61] A 1907 article, "The Initiation into Rhythm," opens with a principle that resonates strongly with Mocquereau's own ideas: "To be completely musical, a child should possess an *ensemble* of physical and spiritual resources and capacities, comprising, on the one hand, *ear, voice* and *consciousness of sound*, and, on the other, the whole body . . . and the *consciousness of bodily rhythm*. . . . By means of movements of the whole body, we may equip ourselves to realise and perceive *rhythms*."[62]

To foster this rhythmic consciousness, Dalcroze, like Mocquereau, advocated starting with rhythm first, uncoupling movement from sound: "If at the commencement of a lesson, sound is eliminated," he argued, "rhythm attracts the whole attention of the pupil." In developing soundless exercises to help students become aware of this so-called plastic rhythm, to perfect their movements in time and space, he drew heavily—again, like Mocquereau—on the authority of antiquity, especially on the idea of the Greek *orchesis*, which, as he explained it, was a complex art that consisted in "expressing every emotion by means of a gesture."[63] Photographs of students from Dalcroze's Eurythmics Institute, taken in Geneva around the time of the First World War, reveal scores of ladies, barefoot and bedecked, à la Isadora Duncan, in sheer Greek pepla, enacting elaborate classical tableaux—leaping, running, holding hands—as if bringing to life the inert figures painted on a Grecian urn.

Mocquereau's pedagogy did not go so far, settling for a more decorous movement of hands where Dalcroze would have advocated the full body. But the suggestion of choreography was never far from his mind. As he explained, the principle of the arsis and thesis, the primordial rhythm governing all movement, belonged, from the time of the Greeks, to the world of dance:

> In dance, [the Greeks] called *elevatio* (arsis), ascending movement, the rising up of the body, and *positio*, or *depositio* (thesis), the lowering, or falling of the body toward the terminal point of its movement. In consequence, in music . . . and in poetry, what they called *arsis*—elevation, rise—referred to the sounds and syllables that corresponded with the rising of the body, and *thesis*—lowering, rest—referred to the sounds or syllables that were sung at the moment the dancers *touched the ground*, whether it be a simple touchdown in order to rise again, or a definitive rest that completed the movement. It is from the movement of dancers that the terms *arsis* and *thesis* come to us.[64]

It would be left to Mocquereau's American protégée Justine Ward to develop this insight, to translate Mocquereau's chirography into a fully fledged choreography.

In 1923, after months of study with the Solesmes monks, she published a text on Gregorian chant for the use of children in Catholic schools. Her teaching, as Mocquereau himself noted fondly in the preface to the volume, involved a twist on the master's own pedagogy that suggested a notable influence of Dalcroze. In order to feel the rhythm properly, she argued, children must be given training in movement. Ward's greatest concern was to develop, through exercises, a feeling for the lightness of being that informed Mocquereau's understanding of Gregorian rhythm, a feeling she hoped to instill by means of an unexpected pedagogical innovation:

> Each child should be provided with a light veil of tulle or similar filmy material with which to carry out in action the rhythmic exercises of the early chapters. These veils are no mere ornament but a fundamental element in acquiring that vocal lightness, smoothness and legato, that soaring quality, that ethereal flight wherein lies the charm and beauty of the Gregorian phrase. The eye helps the ear and the muscle sense reinforces both.[65]

It is a suggestive image. The picture of small Catholic children dancing, like sprites, amid yards of tulle gives Mocquereau's idea of the "quasi-spirituality" of Gregorian rhythm a strangely literal touch. But Mrs. Ward's methods served only to bring out more clearly what Mocquereau had implied all along. The veil functioned in three dimensions as the pale green wash over the "Cantate Domino" had functioned in two, the hazy film materializing what was, finally, an immaterial phenomenon: the movements of the singing voice that carried rhythm's mysterious freedom.

Hieroglyphs

The act of singing—as Ward called it, the "ethereal flight of the Gregorian phrase"—became, of course, all the more ethereal when no one was singing. Perhaps this is why, in Mocquereau's theory, Gregorian consciousness was supposed to develop in the absence of sound, where the musical rhythm could be completely uninhibited. Falling silent, students drew patterns with their hands, leaving no sound, no mark, just the trace of movement. The activity represented, finally, the complete inversion of the rhythmic concept advanced by Pothier. Whereas he had theorized Gregorian rhythm as the exclusive domain of the ear, belonging to the invisible but audible realm of vibrating language, Mocquereau's pedagogy put the movement before the eyes, making it visible and, in the process, temporarily *in*audible. Translated into gestures, Gregorian rhythm became an exquisitely soundless dance of writing.

What Mocquereau created through these chironomic movements might be described, then, as a unique kind of phonographic notation. Certainly, the curling lines that adorned the musical transcriptions of his treatise bore an odd but striking resemblance to the sound-writing—those endless spirals carved in wax—that covered the surface of the gramophone cylinder. The "ligne chironomique" represented, like this waxy *écriture*, but a trace of the sonorous movement preserved in the Gregorian melody itself. In 1905, Emile Gautier would describe such writing as one of the most compelling features of the modern technology of sound recording. Records were, in his words, "cabalistic photographs [in which] sound can outlive itself, and leave a posthumous trace, but in the form of hieroglyphs that not everyone can decipher."[66] Unlike conventional music notation, the curves of chironomy were not signs *for* musical sounds, but gestures that appeared to contain sound within their very shapes, yielding, like the gramophone record, a direct and pure form of music writing. It was in this sense that Mocquereau's wave could be called hieroglyphic: its form both exposed and concealed the movements of Gregorian melody, preserving their mystery.

This novel sound-writing enacted, then, a textualization of performance analogous to the marvelous textualization of Gregorian melody that formed the basis for Mocquereau's musical philology. In his synoptic table, multiple layers of neumes served to expose that elusive truth of the Gregorian melody, the same substance—appearing, as it were, between the lines—that Benjamin would call "pure language" and Mocquereau himself understood as the echo of tradition. It was through a similarly layered music writing that Mocquereau's chronomic notations sought to reveal the essential element of performance known as pure rhythm, a divine ether whose written form aptly reproduced the condition of the spirit world from which this non-material issued. The silent inscriptions reified, like an unmoving gramophone record, the profound silence of the dead. Through the chironomic drill the singer was allowed to take this stuff of spirits directly in hand, and thus—like the "recording angel" who formed the Gramophone Company's first trademark—to get inside the sacred groove.

·   ·   ·   ·   ·

Such rhythmic scribbling underwent, however, a complete transformation in the Solesmes editions. The difference appeared to be, once again, a question of Gregory versus his scribe. In order to fit on the page, the mystically waving hand of the master had to become manageable, translated into a more practical system of encoded dots and slashes, like the marks transcribed onto the first wax tablet. Mocquereau worked, then, to distill the larger gestures of this imaginary waving hand into a kind of shorthand, inventing, like the scribe, a practical rhythmic notation that could be written in the chant books themselves. Indeed, he justified his invention in terms of a significant scribal tradition. In the manuscripts associated with the monastery of Saint-Gall—such as the famed Codex No. 359 originally copied by Lambillotte—he found evidence of just the sort of rhythmic notation he himself wished to develop. The special markings in these sources transmitted a form of mnemonic writing attributed to the famous singing school at Saint-Gall established by Charlemagne's envoy Romanus, and hence were sometimes called the Romanian additions. The notation consisted largely of letters and abbreviations that, according to the ninth-century accounts of Notker Balbulus, stood for Latin modifiers (for example, *c* for *celeriter*, or faster, and *moll* for *molliter*, sweetly). There was also one additional diacritic, the so-called *episema*, which attached to the cursive neumes in different ways to enhance their rhythmic meaning.

"In the beginning," Mocquereau explained,

> this rhythmic tradition was expressed in the ancient neumatic notations perhaps even better than the melodies themselves. The schools of Saint-Gall, of Metz, of Como . . . attest to this fact. But this tradition was not long maintained: Guidonian notation only precipitated its decline. It suppressed completely the letters and signs that, in the primitive notations, indicated the rhythmic *allure* and, in this respect, far from being a development, was a step backward.[67]

The loss of this older tradition of writing, he claimed, was responsible for the regrettable disappearance of the ancient rhythmic principles he was now attempting to restore. Indeed, Mocquereau suggested that the chant's much discussed decadence and ruin resulted not from the destruction of the liturgy, as Guéranger had thought, but from *"the lack of precision in the teaching and the notation of rhythm."*[68] The final, glorious stage of the modern Gregorian restoration, as Mocquereau envisioned it, held out the promise of a restored singing body, a universal choir all of whose members were trained to perform the chant in the same way.

In a remarkable essay written shortly after the First World War, incidentally, Dalcroze imagined a similar, utopian future of performers united through rhythm. Musing over the benefits of his own pedagogical methods, he predicted that "a new demand for collective unity [would] drive numerous persons, formerly estranged from art, into association for the expression of their common spirit." He then offered this chilling vision of a crowd, rehabilitated through rhythmic training: "The call for a psycho-physical training based on the cult of natural rhythms . . . will fill an increasingly important part in civilized life. . . . We shall feel the need for a new technique in the grouping of crowds. . . . Only an intimate understanding of the synergies and conflicting forces of our bodies can provide the clue to this future art of expressing emotion through a crowd."[69] In 1908 Mocquereau's own goals were no doubt more modest. Yet he, too, envisioned a more rigorous discipline of collective singing as the natural outcome of the Gregorian restoration, a discipline he would foster in part through a rehabilitated rhythmic notation. If his pedagogy of Gregorian musical number trained performers to forget their preconceived notions and move *à la bénédictine*, his new, improved Guidonian notation would serve to keep the marks of this training in view at all times.

By 1899 Mocquereau had introduced the first of these notational improvements. A new *Kyriale* (produced in the same small format as the 1896 *Liber Usualis*) included in its preface a brief explanation of two new signs appearing in print for the first time: a tiny dot, which Mocquereau called the *punctum morae*, to indicate the *mora vocis*, or lengthening of the voice; and a miniature bar line to indicate a brief rest. Just one year later, another sign appeared in several new chant books, a *petit trait* or short horizontal line that Mocquereau derived from the *episema* found in the Saint-Gall manuscripts. It signaled a slight ritardando, enlarging the note without affecting its rhythm. In a longer preface, he offered a more complete defense of these additional signs. Introducing the fundamental law of binary and ternary subdivisions later developed in his *Nombre musical grégorien*, he argued that "a truly practical notation" would strive to make such divisions clear: "Many people have expressed the desire to see this development realized. We hope, at least in part, to satisfy them with our new edition."[70]

In 1901 yet another *Kyriale* offered the opportunity to produce one more sign—from the perspective of Mocquereau's rhythmic theory, the most important of all. It bore the somewhat unwieldy name of *punctum losangé avec ictus de subdivision*, a diamond with a short vertical line attached to its leftmost point. It was the vertical stroke that counted most, indicating the ever-so-subtle subdivision of the melody, the slight *touchement* within a moving phrase that the hand would render by a tiny loop. Mocquereau called such a touchdown the *ictus*. This sign represented the last, and certainly the most novel, of the putatively ancient notations to visit the Solesmes editions. In the end, then, no more than a half dozen modifications—a dot, a dash, a comma, a vertical slash—took their place alongside the Guidonian neumes. Over the course of two years, these tiny signs transformed the existing chant books, one stroke at a time, putting the Solesmes method into print so that performers everywhere might learn to reproduce it.

· · · · ·

After 1901 things changed. It would be many years before another edition issued from the Solesmes press, and for a compelling reason: the press, together with the monastery itself, was forced to shut down. In January 1901 a debate began in the

French Chamber over a new law that self-consciously attempted to repeat the moment in revolutionary history—the point at which our story began—when, in 1790, the Constituent Assembly deemed the religious orders "incompatible with the social order" and recommended their extermination. It will be necessary to shift our focus momentarily and consider this turn of events, whose repercussions were to have a profound effect on the rhythm of all future Gregorian productions.

The call for action came this time from the radical senator Emile Combes:

> Once again, the Catholic Church in France has organized itself into a despotic hierarchy, leading the people to an ideal totally opposed to modern society, plotting the destruction of the political and social edifice erected by the glorious French Revolution. In the last ten years, the religious congregations have multiplied tenfold. Citizens, we have to undo in a very short time the clerical reaction of a century.[71]

Combes's proposed solution to the problems created by this burgeoning clergy and their increasing wealth was the legislation known as the Associations Law. Passing in both chambers by July 1901, it denied religious communities the right to form legal associations, and therefore to own property. Not long after its passage, thousands of stunned religious left the country.

Most of the Benedictines, including Dom Pothier's community from Saint-Wandrille, relocated to Belgium. Solesmes was the sole exception. Led by their abbot, Dom Delatte, they abandoned their monastery in September 1901 (fig. 22) and crossed the English Channel to settle at Appuldercombe House, a modest château on the Isle of Wight. The monks attempted to protect their rights to the evacuated buildings by entrusting the property to the marquis de Juigné, a local sympathizer.[72] The attempt was only partially successful. The full extent of the abbey's abandonment can be verified several years later in a bizarre postcard image of the entrance, photographed around 1905. On the right-hand door a crudely posted bill proclaims the buildings as a *dépendance*, a property under the official jurisdiction of the state (fig. 23). Parked to the left of the doors, as if adding insult to injury, we see a wagon bearing the insignia of Roger, the name of a popular turn-of-the-century flea circus.

Perhaps even more important than the buildings was the state of the printing press that had operated within. In an attempt to prevent the government's repossession of this lucrative business, the monks had quickly transferred all rights of ownership to Desclée of Tournai, the house that had brought out their first publications almost twenty years earlier.[73] From September 1901, Belgium became the official home of the Solesmes editions, a transaction that carried significant implications for the future of Dom Mocquereau's school. Desclée wasted no

Figure 22. Photograph showing the monks leaving their abbey for the Isle of Wight (1901). Photo: Claude Lambert Archives, Sablé, France.

time getting to work, issuing a *Manuel de la messe et des offices* in 1902 and, the next year, a new, improved edition of the *Paroissien romain*.

The preface of both books began with an autobiographical account of the painful circumstances that followed the monks' departure from France. Despite the sale of their press, the official government liquidators had confiscated most of the editions, both finished and unfinished, thus requiring the monks essentially to start all over again. "The losses," Mocquereau admitted, "were considerable." But there were gains. The 1903 *Paroissien* represented, more than any prior edition, the remarkable advances made by the Solesmes school in both science and performance. Not only did it include innumerable changes to the melodies themselves based on the comparative study of the manuscripts, but it also featured a full complement of rhythmic signs together with a long, unapologetic discussion of their practical value. In Mocquereau's words, this supplemental notation would make "the melodic line and its rhythmic divisions easier to grasp" and thus "easier to interpret with art and piety."

It is not insignificant that the new, improved *Paroissien*, with its small format, was also the most popular of the Solesmes editions. A few months after its release

4 SOLESMES. — *Entrée de l'Abbaye* — I.L

Figure 23. Postcard of the entrance to the Solesmes Abbey, ca. 1905, showing a wagon from a popular *cirque de puce* parked outside. Note the official bill posted on the gate.

Figure 24. Page from the Solesmes *Liber Usualis* published by Desclée in 1903, showing the Offertory "Perfice gressus" now corrected according to Mocquereau's specifications, with supplementary rhythmic notation. Courtesy of Abbaye Saint-Pierre, Solesmes, France. Authorization No. 105.

came two translations, the *Liber Usualis* in Latin and now—for obvious reasons—in English, translations that more or less guaranteed that the new publications would be used by choirs in every country. These reissued *Libri* thus had the profile (if not the look) of true *éditions belges*, in a literal as well as colloquial sense. They were reeditions that also represented a kind of betrayal, *contrafacta* that turned decisively against the older Solesmes books. An example of such musical betrayal can be seen clearly on the page of the 1903 *Liber Usualis* that contained the now revised Offertory "Perfice gressus" (fig. 24), the chant for Sexagesima Sunday discussed at the end of the previous chapter. Not only do we find the melodic text corrected along the lines of Mocquereau's handwritten changes (see fig. 15), but the notation itself is enhanced by the presence of numerous additional rhythmic signs, as well as a more nuanced barring. For Mocquereau, such additions were the only responsible option, as he explained in the introduction to his *Nombre musical grégorien*:

If we wish not to be disillusioned, to close our eyes to the most obvious facts, we must admit, loyally, after twenty-five years' experience, that the notation of the first books from

Solesmes, despite eminent qualities, responds neither to the requirements of the Gregorian rhythmic principles, which are today better understood, nor to the practical needs of
singers in every category. . . . In all these respects it is, in part, defective and incomplete.[74]

In attempting to reverse such defects, the edition from 1903 documented, in
all its materiality, the significant gap that separated Pothier's notion of restoration
from that of Mocquereau. It was a gap that resulted, as we have already noted,
from Mocquereau's discipline, in its dual aspect—both as *musicologie* and as performance. The rhythmic signs, Mocquereau asserted again and again, were a
practical measure, a means for getting singers to perform the ethereal Gregorian
rhythm, so to speak, in lockstep. But the notation also seemed to signal Mocquereau's erudition, his musicological discipline. The tiny marks on the page left
an undeniable impression of the scholarly apparatus behind the book, the evidence culled from real sources. In exposing rhythm, the notation thus marked
not only the *percussiones* but also the considerable *repercussiones* of the new
Solesmes school, measuring the impact with every dot and stroke.

. . . . .

The new *Liber Usualis*, in addition to everything else, was a timely publication.
For 1903 marked another decisive moment for Solesmes, one that brings us to a
final tale in our history of the Gregorian restoration: on July 20, after a reign of
twenty-five years, Leo XIII died. It was not so much this event as its consequences that proved significant for the Benedictines. Within two weeks a new
pontiff had been chosen, the former patriarch of Venice Giuseppe Sarto, who
took the name Pius X. Sarto's election surprised not only the college, but also
the humble cardinal himself, for he lacked the one diplomatic qualification that
had determined nearly every papal election since the fourteenth century: Cardinal Sarto did not speak French. His acceptance of this holy office would
change, in significant ways, the diplomatic relationship between France and the
Vatican that had existed for nearly four centuries.

It is all the more striking, then, that among the first decrees issued by the new
pope was one that would have direct bearing on the lives of the now exiled
French Benedictines. In November 1903, just three months after his election,
Pius X completed the legislation, *Inter plurimas pastoralis officii*, that formed, as he
called it, a "juridical code of sacred music." The statement legally bound
Catholic churches to institute Gregorian chant as their principal music for worship. The text, delivered *motu proprio*, or by the pope's own action, also expressed
opinions on the proper performance of sacred music, including the use of instruments in church, acceptable musical styles, and the preferred gender of singers.
Polyphonic music in the guise of Palestrina (what the text called "classical

polyphony") was permitted. Women were not. The pope also enjoined bishops to set up commissions in their dioceses to oversee the execution of sacred music, advising them especially to establish *scholae* for the proper training of singers.

The legislation said nothing about the books that should be used in performance, even though, by the time Pius X took office, there had been no officially recognized edition for two years. The papal privilege issued to Pustet of Ratisbon had expired in 1901, and Leo XIII, deciding this time not to renew it, put no new edition in its place. The new pontiff was keen to avoid the kinds of conflicts that had already arisen around this privilege and so maintained a laissez-faire policy. He did, however, favor the work of the Benedictines, introduced to him by his longtime advisor on musical matters, the Jesuit Angelo de Santi. Since de Santi was one of Mocquereau's strongest supporters in Rome, the exiled monks had reason to be confident about the possibilities for future success.

Indeed, the pope's benevolent view toward the Solesmes community soon became clear, when de Santi began planning an international congress to celebrate the thirteenth centenary of the death of Saint Gregory the Great. The congress would memorialize, in effect, two popes: Pius himself and his sixth-century forebear. For de Santi and many others, the new ruler appeared in the modern day to assume the role tradition had assigned to Gregory, dictating, by his own inspired motion, the sacred music of the Church. Scheduled to take place in Rome over several days during April 1904, the congress would feature both scholarly sessions and rituals honoring the popes at all the major Roman churches, culminating in a huge papal mass at Saint Peter's. On such occasions, the celebrant traditionally employed a missal made exclusively for the ceremony. Pius X requested that this time the task be completed by the nuns of Sainte-Cécile, also exiled on the Isle of Wight. Over the course of several months they carried out his wishes, fashioning, completely by hand, an illuminated missal with chants based on the most recent books produced by their brother monks. It was Dom Mocquereau who eventually presented their creation to the Holy Father, on April 9, just two days before the papal mass.

The meticulous artistry of the nuns, which we have encountered before, could only have made the Holy See more favorably disposed to the French Benedictines. From all reports, they outdid themselves. This was especially the impression given in the French Catholic newspaper *L'Univers*, which featured a lavish description of the book by an unnamed author whose style seemed to emulate that of the devout Huysmans:

> All the sweetness of Gregorian inspiration unfolds before my eyes. This Missal is a veritable poem. The Benedictine sisters have made a masterpiece of liturgy and of illumination, with delicacies suggesting a completely celestial mysticism. To say nothing of the

bindings, whose vermilion clasps are embellished with precious stones. In the illuminations we see a liturgical knowledge worthy of the faithful disciplines of Dom Guéranger. . . . At the moment of the benediction with incense, we see a deliciously virginal
angel recalling all the creations of Fra Angelico. . . . Little by little, as the solemn moment
approaches, the [book's] lyricism increases. The words of the consecration appear in letters of resplendent gold. . . . Then, a touchingly delicate thought: the *Memento mori* has
for a frontispiece the image of Saint Margaret—Margaret being the name of the mother
of Pius X.[75]

The missal itself culminated in music, which meant an equally poetic rendering of chants drawn, appropriately enough, from the Feast of Saint Gregory the
Great (fig. 25). No more virginal angels, only the business at hand. The borders
now narrated in pictures the history of sacred music that the congress was celebrating, beginning with an image that resonated most closely with the pope who
presided. As described by our unnamed author, it was a scene of "Gregory the
Great, lying on the bed where he was kept by illness, teaching music, rod in hand,
to the children of the *Schola cantorum*." Below the exquisite scene appeared the
Introit "Sacerdotes Dei," written in perfect twelfth-century neumes—that is, a
notation even more archaic than the one restored by Dom Pothier. Two lines
alone, black and red, formed a staff from which the languid melody suggestively
drooped. Saints Isadore and Ambrose looked on approvingly.

This marvelous ornament of liturgy, seen by only one pair of eyes in a ritual
reportedly attended by fifty thousand faithful, reminds us of the inspiration that
had first motivated Pothier, more than thirty years earlier, to fashion his own *Processional monastique*. The nuns' fanciful imitations, depicting a flawless Middle
Ages, revealed the kind of intense, utopian nostalgia that defined, as we have
seen, just one of the enchanting faces of Gregorian reform. But another face was
also to be seen at the congress, in the form of an equally enchanting technology,
which contrasted significantly with the nuns' Romantic handiwork. Indeed, the
very music reproduced *à la médiévale* by the Sainte-Cécile artists underwent a
second reproduction—this time not on parchment but on wax—employing the
most advanced twentieth-century science: Gramophone engineers came to
Rome to put the congress on record. Like Gregory's faithful companion, they
dutifully preserved the musical performances at Saint Peter's, as if to ensure, with
their modern machinery, the future of Gregorian history.

Phonography

It was not the first time they had come. Exactly two years before, in April 1902,
Fred and Will Gaisberg had traveled to the Vatican on a hunch, hoping to capture a few inspiring words of the ninety-two-year-old Leo XIII. When this novel

Figure 25. A page from a missal illuminated by the nuns of Sainte-Cécile in 1904 for the Papal Mass celebrating the thirteenth anniversary of the death of Gregory the Great.

plan fell through, they were forced to settle for the next best thing, recording instead the voice of Alessandro Moreschi, the "angel of Rome" as he was sometimes called—one of the last living castrati. The two engineers made about nineteen records on this occasion, which preserved not only Moreschi's strangely compelling soprano (we hear him take a spine-chilling top B in an arrangement of Gounod's "Ave Maria") but also the perhaps less-than-memorable sound of the Sistine Chapel choir, which he himself directed.[76]

At the 1904 congress, however, the Gaisbergs' purpose appeared to be more documentary than musical. It is hard to imagine that the Gramophone Company expected to sell the fifty or so discs they produced—the very first sound recordings of plainchant ever made—on the basis of musical interest alone. An advertisement for the recordings, released by London publishers Burns and Oates in 1905, suggested as much. Printed inside the back cover of a book about the exiled Solesmes monks, the ad's text began with the following sober description:

> By a happy thought the Gramophone Company has determined that the triumphs of voice-reproduction achieved for the Concert Room and the Council Chamber should be accomplished for the Church. Faithful "Records" of the Music performed during the International Gregorian Congress held in Rome on the occasion of the Thirteenth Centenary of St. Gregory the Great, 1904, have been taken with the full approval and assistance of the Holy Father and of the highest musical authorities. Such "Records" must provide intellectual and musical treats in Catholic homes and institutions.[77]

This dignified sales pitch warrants closer consideration. From the sound of it, the Gregorian Congress lay in a kind of uncomfortable space between council chamber and concert room, the intellectual value of the event clearly gaining the edge over music. The ad copy gives the impression that Burns and Oates themselves were hard put to persuade guilty English Catholics of the legitimate value of a Gramophone "instrument," a fact borne out by the next few paragraphs (fig. 26). Securing a nod from an official at the Archbishop's House, they reminded potential customers—somewhat pathetically—that the gramophone might generate "revenue for the School or Mission." In the meantime, they also managed to suggest that, safely installed inside the home, there was no reason the machine could not perform other, more palatable entertainments: "By a turn of the wrist, and at the slight cost of extra 'Records,' the same Gramophone which reproduces the Music of the Mass sung in St Peter's by Pius X, during the Gregorian Congress, will . . . revive Dan Leno or set Melba and Santley singing."[78] The observation made the status of the sacred music abundantly clear. Next to Dan Leno, plainchant could only sound, well, plainer.

No, the chant recordings were not so much musical as educational, recalling one of the important functions Edison himself had noted when first introducing

Gramophone and Plainchant

♪

BY a happy thought the Gramophone Company has determined that the triumphs of voice-reproduction achieved for the Concert Room and the Council Chamber should be accomplished for the Church. Faithful "Records" of the Music performed during the International Gregorian Congress held in Rome on the occasion of the Thirteenth Centenary of St Gregory the Great, 1904, have been taken with the full approval and assistance of the Holy Father and of the highest musical authorities. Such "Records" must provide intellectual and musical treats in Catholic homes and institutions. They will even be the allies of choirmasters, teaching choirs to interpret with exactitude the melodies which the *Motu Proprio* prescribes. By the aid of science, the literal Voice of the Church may be heard in the land.

* * *

With special interest, therefore, Messrs BURNS AND OATES announce the entirely successful completion of this great project. They are able to offer to their clients, on most favourable terms, the most perfect Instruments and "Records," all carefully tested for them by MR LAWRENCE PETRE, who, at Archbishop's House, Westminster, gave an approved performance before His Grace and a body of chief experts in Church Music. Explanatory Instructions are supplied to each purchaser; and five minutes will suffice to give an "operator," who has never seen an Instrument before, the complete mastery of its simple mechanism.

* * *

At 28 Orchard Street, London, W., an Instrument may be daily seen and heard; and no trouble will be spared, by correspondence or personal visits, to put every purchaser on perfect terms with the Instrument. Its capabilities are of the widest range, and its true and mellow tones have now exorcised the familiar twanginess of inferior Instruments. By a turn of the wrist, and at the slight cost of extra "Records," the same Gramophone which reproduces the Music of the Mass sung in St Peter's by Pius X, during the Gregorian Congress, will, for the further purposes of Public Entertainments or School Treats, revive Dan Leno or set Melba and Santley singing.

* * *

At Bazaars, the Gramophone easily earns its purchase-Money, and becomes a source of revenue to the School or the Mission.

[SEE OVER

Figure 26a. Advertisement for Gregorian plainchant "Records" sold through the London publisher Burns and Oates in 1904. Courtesy of the Eda Kuhn Loeb Music Library, Harvard University.

"THE VOICE OF THE CHURCH"

CARDINAL MERRY DEL VAL writes to the Italian Manager of the Gramophone Company:

"I am happy to inform you that His Holiness the Pope has received with many thanks the Gramophone which he has had the privilege of hearing. The immense success obtained by the apparatus is proved by the exact reproduction of the Gregorian Chants, and it will, without doubt, increase the fame of the Instrument, which marvellously unites to the originality of the invention absolute exactitude of Reproduction."

The GRAMOPHONES recommended by Messrs BURNS and OATES are the "Monarch Junior" £5 10s.

Tapered Arm; 10-inch Turntable; Side Wind, can be wound while playing; Handsome Cabinet; "Exhibition" Sound Box; 18-inch Brass Horn; Needles. The effects produced by this machine are lifelike.

Or where a smaller volume of sound will suffice:

THE No. 3a STYLE GRAMOPHONE

an entirely new style.   Price 50s.

This Machine has a handsome pyramid Cabinet, side wind, Concert Sound Box, 14-inch Nickel Horn, and includes box of Needles.

With these Instruments everyone in a Community-room will hear Plain Song as distinctly as he might have heard it in St Peter's at the Pope's Mass during the Gregorian Congress.

Larger Instruments are supplied at prices ranging upwards to £25.

THE PLAINCHANT "RECORDS"

These Records (amongst the many) are suggested as a beginning:

(54786) *"OFFERTORIO E COMUNIONE,"* della Messa di S. Gregorio. 10 inch, 5s.

(54784) *"INTROITO,"* della Messa Dell 'Assunzione. Sung by the Augustinian Fathers, conducted by BARON KAUZLER. 10 inch, 5s.

(54789) *"HAEC DIES,"* sung by pupils of the French Seminary, conducted by FATHER MOCQUEREAU. 10 inch, 5s.

(054752) *"GLORIA IN EXCELSIS DEO,"* sung by Sistine Choir, conducted by MONS. RELLA. 12 inch, 7s. 6d.

(54787) *"ALLILUJA,"* della Messa Dell 'Assunzione, sung by the Benedictines of St. Anselmo, conducted by FATHER POTHIER. 10 inch, 5s.

These records, together with the machine selected, will be sent to any part of the United Kingdom, at a fixed additional charge of 2s. for packing and carriage.

BURNS & OATES, LTD, 28 ORCHARD STREET, W.

Figure 26b.

his invention in 1878. He predicted, among other things, that the phonograph would benefit "the preservation of languages," by providing an "exact reproduction of the manner of pronouncing."[79] Messrs. Burns and Oates themselves suggested this advantage, noting the unique value of the gramophone for choirmasters, who were now enjoined by the *Motu proprio* to teach Gregorian chant in their churches. Indeed, with this novel machine the oral traditions of teaching could be transformed: the oral had, for the first time in history, become completely *literal*, fixed in a revolutionary form of writing. *Nota* and *vox* now claimed the same, narrow space. As Kittler points out, "Edison's invention was not called a phonograph for nothing: it registers real sounds rather than translating them into phonemic equivalences as an alphabet does. Emile Berliner's more modern device, which replaced rolls with records, was not called a gramophone for nothing: true to its name, it retains 'the sounds of letters' and has a writing angel as its trademark."[80]

The inverted commas enclosing the word *Records* in the Burns and Oates advertisement implied more or less the same thing. They reminded the reader of the dual personality of the gramophone disc: more than a written register, it preserved sound itself as a form of writing. The traditional symbol of the voice in writing, the quotation mark, served to mark this difference literally, keeping the record's voice in view. Such envoiced documents, the "allies of choirmasters," afforded new possibilities for the dissemination of knowledge, and thus enhanced teaching in an unexpected way. By employing the gramophone, the choirmaster actually yielded his voice, permitting the literal "Record" to take the place of his own oral teaching—to speak for him. And why not? Pius X officially "pontificated" the discs in November 1904, bestowing further authority on their already authentic sound. What is more, the infinite reproducibility of such "Records" meant that every choirmaster could now possess the *same* voice, a thought that evidently inspired Burns and Oates: "By the aid of science," they concluded, "the *literal Voice of the Church* may now be heard in the land."

The opinion had been expressed even more emphatically at the Gregorian Congress itself, when Baron Rudolph Kanzler delivered a talk on the value of the gramophone for music education—a subject on which he was fairly well informed, as *professore di canto gregoriano* at the Liceo di Santa Cecilia in Rome.[81] His speech, which also happened to make it on record, began by recalling the traditional nature of the Gregorian melodies, for which an oral tradition was, he stressed, "absolutely necessary":

> This is so true that Charlemagne, as everyone knows, requested Adrian I to send him two cantors from Rome, Romanus and Peter, who became the founders of the two famous schools of Saint-Gall and Metz. It would certainly have been very different if

Charlemagne had had the gramophone at his disposal! Not just two, but innumerable schools would have been founded all over the world, which would have faithfully followed the most minute details of every melodic phrase as performed by the school of origin.

Kanzler lamented the loss of Charlemagne's two cantors, but he pointed out that, because of both Dom Pothier and the newer Solesmes school, the Carolingian traditions bequeathed by these medieval pedagogues were now restored. Peter and Romanus lived again in the figures of our two monks. In order to protect this revived performance practice—to ensure the continuity of tradition— Kanzler proposed that the gramophone recordings from the congress be housed in "true scientific libraries, so as to make them available to scholars." If the baron's vision certified the documentary value of the discs, his conclusion further clar- ified the nature of what they would document. He went on to predict that lis- teners would hear "very little difference between the choirs" because "we all share the same views."[82]

While our story of the latter-day Romanus and Peter has perhaps suggested otherwise, it turns out that Kanzler was right. However unexpectedly, the his- torical recordings betray no significant differences between Mocquereau and Pothier as choirmasters—the former directing students of the French Seminary in Rome, the latter, a small choir of Benedictines from the monastery of San Anselmo. One gets the impression that the choirs—in these recordings, at least— were not performing at their best, the thin sound suggesting just a few singers huddled around the machine's horn. But the style of the singing preserved on the records is largely the same, with both choirs declaiming their chant in the relaxed, unmeasured cadences that characterized the Benedictine method. This smooth, one-note-at-a-time declamation was just as apparent in the perfor- mances of the other *scholae* featured at the congress, one of them directed by Father Antonio Rella, a professor of Gregorian studies at the pontifical *scuola*, the other by Kanzler himself. The similarity will perhaps seem less remarkable when we consider that de Santi had been strongly promoting the Benedictine editions in Rome, together with the French method of singing, for more than a decade. By 1904, the Benedictine aesthetic of "free rhythm" was clearly in no danger of competition.

Far more striking about these early records, however, is how familiar the per- formances still sound today. True to Kanzler's predictions, the modern tradition of chanting *has* been enabled by the gramophone, by a whole history of sound recordings—documents whose most notable contribution to performance prac- tice will always lie in their power to promote uniformity, to reduce stylistic differences.[83] Listening to these choirs of 1904 produces none of the eerie strangeness—the keen sense of loss—I feel when hearing Moreschi's voice, an effect recalling another one of the phonographic functions described by Edison. He had predicted in 1878 that his machine could be used to collect, like a kind of aural photograph album, the voices of the dead. Moreschi's recorded voice enacts exactly this sort of memorial: I am made brutally aware that not only he but an entire tradition has passed away. Yet, while the singers who chanted in 1904 are just as dead as this bygone angel of Rome, their recorded voices produce no such rupture—because the style has lived on. Through the power of mechanical reproduction, the practice that began exclusively as *la méthode bénédictine* has become what most of us regard as the *only* performance practice, a truly international style of singing that has largely defined the sound we associate with Gregorian chant.

Even the experimental performances of recent decades (made in the name of "early music") have done little to cancel this impression. Indeed, all too often such performances have tended only to confirm the importance of the Benedictine method, maintaining it as a kind of zero degree of performance, a default method against which the novelty of the experiments can always be measured.[84] To listen to these first Gregorian recordings is thus to recognize the power of the phonographic medium. The "literal Voice of the Church" first captured in 1904 has remained so fixed in modern practice that Baron Kanzler's prediction rings eerily true: the performances of chant heard on contemporary recordings reveal how much, even today, "we all share the same views."

There is one place in the 1904 recordings, however, where a sense of difference can be heard—a place where the inexorable pastness of the Gregorian past is glimpsed in all its chilling truth. It is in an instance not of singing but of speaking that we can perceive the gap separating the world of Pothier and Mocquereau from our own—and indeed, the two monks from each other, in their work of Gregorian reform. Both monks had been invited to address the scholarly sessions of the congress; both were also enjoined to record a portion for posterity. For Dom Jean Prou, the current abbot of Solesmes, these speeches remain the most precious items preserved on the historic recordings, for they return to us—unlike the musical performances we still recognize—something that really *has* been lost. As he writes, movingly: "Voices that have been silent for a half century are restored to us today. [They are the] voices of the great masters . . . of Gregorian chant in the nineteenth and twentieth centuries, each one having *its own character, vibration, timbre, accent*."[85]

What returns in the recorded speeches of Pothier and Mocquereau is, in a word, a *rhythm*. Not merely the content of their speeches but also their very *mode* of speaking reveals the character Dom Prou hears, a rhythmic phenomenon that recalls what Plato himself understood as *ethos*. As Philippe Lacoue-Labarthe has written, speaking of *The Republic*:

> Rhythm (measure and meter, prosody) is . . . judged fundamentally in relation to *diction* inasmuch as this imitates or represents a *character*. Rhythm manifests and reveals, gives form and figure to, makes perceptible, the *ethos*. . . . To this extent, then, it should perhaps be recognized that rhythm is not only a musical category. Nor is it simply figure. Rather, it would be something between beat and figure that never fails to designate mysteriously the "ethical"; for the word . . . already implies . . . the type and the stamp or impression.[86]

I myself listen for this impression, for the sound or mark that would designate something of the ethos of these two masters, something that would place them, quite literally, in their own time: in that difficult interval between the nineteenth and the twentieth centuries. I am struck first of all by what they say, by the character of the ideas they choose to store for all time on record. Pothier returns to the very inspiration with which he opened his first book on chant, the divine inspiration that transforms speaking into singing. He begins:

> Song is natural to man. So it is already in simple speech. Man, in speaking, naturally modulates his voice, and thus produces a kind of music, which is the accent of discourse. *Accentus, ad cantus*—by this [formula] we mean the vocal inflections that, without being a song in the strict sense, more or less approach it. "The accent is the soul of language," *accentus anima vocis*: When in speech, thought takes flight and feeling catches fire, the accent, in the same beat, rises up to be identical with what the soul feels. It then takes a richer and more powerful form. It turns into song.[87]

It is a touching exordium. The opening period rehearses the very theory of accent—the myth of the soul's flight into song—that informed Pothier's understanding not only of chant's origins but also of its performance. But the impression of these poetic remarks is distinctly enhanced by the sound of Pothier's almost seventy-year-old voice, delivering these words in a mode whose ethos can only be described as naturalistic. It is not so much the slightly guttural accent that conveys this impression (the frequent glottal stops betraying something of Pothier's class background) as the intonation of the phrases themselves, which imbue his story of origins with a singsong modulation, a rise and fall that has all the natural simplicity of Romantic verse (fig. 27).

The actual *notae* in figure 27 are approximate. My "transcription" shows nothing more than the relative modulation of Pothier's voice, tracing the outline of his short opening sentences—one *octosyllabe* and two *alexandrins*—punctuated by full stops. The repeated shape becomes a kind of reciting tone, hanging each time around the same tenor and closed by the same cadence, whose internal fluctuations, tiny modulations of the voice, tellingly reveal the (accented) final

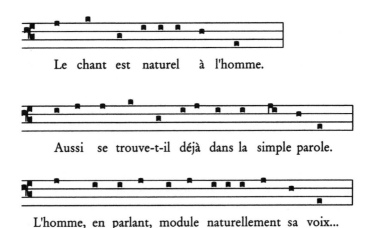

Figure 27. Musical transcription of the opening phrases of Pothier's address to the Gregorian Congress, recorded in Rome, April 1904.

syllables of every word, as if repeating the very demonstration by which, raising his voice, Pothier squeezed sound from the city of Rome.

Mocquereau's speech leaves an entirely different impression, discoursing not on song but on science, as he explains to the congress the nature of the editorial changes introduced into the most recent books published by Desclée:

> Here is how we at Solesmes go about establishing any musical text from the Gregorian repertory. I say "we," and this manner of speaking not only makes me more comfortable, for [the pronoun] is not at all magisterial, but it also expresses a reality that is good to know about. There is, in fact, an entire school, a whole workshop on trial, and the one who speaks to you at this moment, in the name of the ten or fifteen members of this school and workshop, is but one in their midst, subject himself to their mutual control, as they themselves are subject to each other and to his.[88]

His was evidently a very serious "we." Mocquereau spoke neither for himself nor for a vague idea of mankind, but for the body of workers who together formed the school of Solesmes. Within the confines of this workshop, with its built-in surveillance, the Gregorian chant was transformed into a "text," rewritten not as the spontaneous *vox* of inspiration but as the precise *notae* of mutual control. The image offers the starkest of reality checks to Pothier's Romantic vision of sacred song. But once again the mode of speaking enhances the impression of this difference. The first sentence alone (fig. 28) parses into three phrases to form a single period, unfolding in one, long breath that conveys an almost heroic ethos, in keeping with the proportions of the institution that Mocquereau invokes.

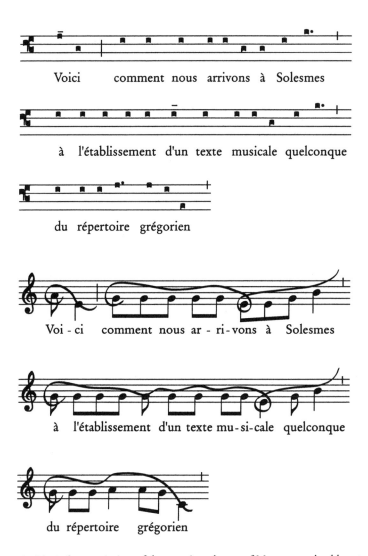

Figure 28. Musical transcription of the opening phrases of Mocquereau's address to the Gregorian Congress, recorded in Rome, April 1904.

My transcription of course employs the notation Mocquereau himself advocated for the representation of rhythm, the second layer conveniently exposing the *je ne sais quoi* of the younger monk's more elevated mode of speech. His long opening sentence remains magnificently suspended, never touching down, as if eschewing all the directness of Pothier's country accent. Indeed, in this context the implications of Mocquereau's supplemental chirography become clearer.

The curved line hovering over the notation gives the distinct impression of a force beyond the "natural," suggesting the elocutionary training by which an educated speaker learns to *conduct himself* in order to produce his more elevated diction. The additional mark conveys this something extra, the ethos of superior breeding, of civilized deportment. Indeed, the almost pedantic content of Mocquereau's address to the congress, with its dry exposition of men and manuscripts, takes on a notably different air through his particular vocal conduct, offering a sense of the magisterial task undertaken by the Solesmes atelier itself. Far from celebrating Gregorian nature, the workshop embraced a lofty new culture of Gregorian science.

What leaks through the recorded voice is, then, the exalted character of a restoration informed by scientific discipline, by *musicologie*. This was the immaterial force that hovered over Mocquereau's "we," controlling its collective movement in a rhythm that ultimately reshaped the Gregorian corpus, revising Pothier's naturalistic cry into a far more profound mystery—a mystery of silent signs that wove the marvelous text of modern history.

Postlude

Legitimate Imprints

arly in March 1904, it turns out, Pius X changed his mind on the subject of the chant books. His first thoughts on the matter, as mentioned in the previous chapter, had been simply to continue the precedent set by Leo XIII toward the end of his papacy; that is, Pope Pius hoped to remain aloof from the question of printed editions altogether, by granting special privileges to no one and thus leaving individual dioceses free to choose among available publications. However, this policy would be short-lived, for soon after the release of the 1903 *Motu proprio* on sacred music, interested parties from all sides—including Pothier and Pustet—began pressing the Vatican for a more specific ruling.

The Sacred Congregation of Rites attempted to resolve the matter as late as February 1904, when they deemed the most recent editions published by Desclée suitable for general liturgical use.[1] But this decision was apparently considered no more satisfactory than the first. Combe reports that, within a week of the announcement, not only Pothier, but the *abbé-primat* Hildebrand were in Rome lobbying for a completely new Vatican edition, to be based on Benedictine research. The Belgian arch-abbot, as head of the Benedictine order, naturally saw the matter (and its financial rewards) as his jurisdiction, especially since the best books had once again returned to Belgium—indeed, to a press founded by the very figures who had built his own Abbey of Maredsous. Pothier, on the other hand, having produced the order's first *Liber Gradualis*, seemed to want the job for himself. But the person actually responsible for the recently approved editions had not even been consulted. Only after an urgent entreaty from Father de Santi did Mocquereau, armed with *tableaux synoptiques*, leave the Isle of Wight for Rome, not only to join the negotiations but also to remind those gathered— or so it was hoped—of who had the control after all.

The pope would soon put an end to these discussions when, just a month before the Gregorian Congress, he privately announced a decision to undertake the publication of all the books necessary to fulfill the aims of his first decree, a task that would be realized in Rome at his own Tipographia Vaticana. In order to prevent any special privilege or monopoly, the Holy See itself would now control the copyright, granting any publisher who followed regulations the right to reproduce the edition. Because the books most suitable for immediate publication already existed at Solesmes, a spokesman for the pope wrote to Dom Delatte, "inviting" the monastery to turn over their rights, both to the melodies and to the notation. Needless to say, the abbot obeyed. The house of Desclée followed close behind. By the time the Vatican publicly announced the plan, during the Gregorian centenary celebrations, the pope, together with de Santi, had already begun drafting the legislation that would enact it. This appeared a little more than two weeks later in the form of a second *Motu proprio*, bearing the date 25 April 1904.[2] Known as *Nostro Motu proprio* ("By our [first] *Motu proprio*"), the document represented an addendum to the previous decree, making not just the sacred music, but its precise material form, a matter of canon law.

This legalization of chant forms the subject of my final discussion, bringing the story of Gregorian restoration, of fin-de-siècle enchantment, to a decisive— even abrupt—conclusion. Indeed, the Vatican's calculated appropriation of the Solesmes edition could be described as a form of *dis*enchantment, at least from the Benedictine perspective. Although the new ruling obviously elevated the Solesmes research, raising their edition to the status of an authoritative text, it also, quite literally, took the chant out of the monks' hands, thus removing a significant measure of their authority. For the good of the whole Church, the authorship of the Gregorian repertory would now belong to the Vatican alone. This shift would have serious consequences for the idea of history that guided the restoration of chant at Solesmes, producing a disenchantment of another kind. For if the captivating power of Gregorian history issued from the ever renewable mysteries of restoration itself, from historical secrets revealed one source at a time, the papal legislation all but dispelled this charm. With the second *Motu proprio*, the Gregorian restoration entered a new historical phase, one whose perfect temporality matched the tense of all canonical speech acts: the authoritative past of "Roma locuta est."

Past Perfected

This was, in fact, the tense in which the new decree began. The papal performative offered little in the way of mystery, yielding instead the exaggerated and ungainly cadences of legalese: "By Our *Motu proprio* of 22 November 1903 and the subsequent decree published on Our order by the Sacred Congregation of Rites 8 January 1904, *We have restored to the Roman Church her ancient Gregorian chant,* this chant which she inherited from the Church Fathers, jealously preserved in her liturgical books, and which the most recent studies have so fortunately returned to its primitive purity."[3] The next sentence set down the decision concerning the production of liturgical books, the project that would make the already completed restoration even more complete. "In order to furnish Our Roman Church and all the churches of this Rite with the common text of the Gregorian liturgical melodies, We have decided to undertake, with the types of Our Vatican press, the publication of liturgical books containing the chant of the Roman Church, reestablished by Us." The wording of this second passage, with its very literal reference to the printing process, offered a sense of the transformation the liturgical melodies were to undergo. Rendered in a Gregorian font that belonged no longer to Solesmes nor to Desclée but to the Vatican itself, the sacred melodies would leave a very different sort of impression, displaying the distinct character—indeed, the very *ethos*—of legitimacy. In the common text of the Roman Church, even the smallest *punctum* would be stamped with papal authority.

A series of additional regulations, now in the future tense, further specified the ethical dimension of this universal text—or, as it was to be known, the Typical Edition—by indicating the proper modes of conduct that were to govern its execution. The first article concerned the nature of the melodies themselves. These would be, the text stipulated, "reestablished in all their integrity and purity according to the readings of the oldest manuscripts, taking particular account of the legitimate tradition contained over the course of centuries in the manuscripts." The description sounded suspiciously like the work of a certain community of exiled French Benedictines, who, as it turned out, were identified in the very next clause. The Holy See made quite clear, lest the arch-abbot Hildebrand (or anyone else) have other ideas, who would take charge of preparing the Vatican edition. In the course of a single sentence, the name of the chosen ones appeared, in fact, not once but twice:

> Guided by Our special predilection for the Order of Saint Benedict, and recognizing the work accomplished by the Benedictines in the restoration of the true melodies of the Roman Church, particularly by those of the Congregation of France and the monastery of Solesmes, We will that, for this edition, the editing of the parts containing the chant be specially entrusted to the monks of the Congregation of France at the monastery of Solesmes.

With this benevolent gesture, the Vatican seemed to give back what it had just taken from Solesmes when the monastery handed over its copyright. But the monks' editorial rights were not fully returned. An additional clause laid out an

elaborate plan for keeping the newly reappointed editors in line, subjecting them
to an even stricter surveillance than that already enforced at their own workshop.
The edition they prepared, the decree stated, would be "submitted to the examination and review of the special Roman Commission recently instituted by Us
for this purpose."Ten names were appended to the document, directly below the
papal signature. Pothier appeared first on the list, as president of the commission,
accompanied by two other Benedictines, Dom Laurent Janssens, from the
monastery of San Anselmo in Rome, and, of course, Mocquereau. The other
Roman members included figures instrumental in the recent Gregorian Congress, not only Father de Santi but also Baron Kanzler and his colleague Father
Rella. Rounding off the collection were two more Italian clerics and two foreign musicologists, among them Peter Wagner, best known for his important
Einführung in die gregorianischen Melodien, a work that by 1904 had already
appeared in a revised, second edition.

The purpose of the commission was obvious enough. With a diverse body of
Gregorian specialists to supervise its production, the edition would remain above
criticism. In order to avoid the kind of polemic that had tainted Pustet's books,
the new *Vaticana* promised the approval of a collective—here established as a
symbolic committee of ten. The commission was admonished not to publish any
text "unless a proper and sufficient cause [could] be given." Even more tellingly,
the members were also "sworn to secrecy in all matters concerning the compilation of texts and the printing in progress." The rule essentially made public
disagreement among the commissioners illegal. No edition bearing the Vatican's
name would emerge blemished with tales of internal strife. On the contrary, the
chant would reflect unanimity precisely because of this enforced anonymity. All
those involved in the restoration would speak, like the Holy See itself, with just
one voice—which was the only voice imaginable in the silence of secret pro-
ceedings. Like the Gregorian performers whom Baron Kanzler had arranged to
preserve on record, the figures behind the Typical Edition were to present a
united front, a collectivity in which—through the future perfect imposed by
papal syntax—everyone will have agreed.

■ ■ ■ ■ ■

That, at least, was the idea. Things proceeded smoothly enough at first, when the
commission's duties involved relatively simple tasks of organization. At the initial meetings, just a few days after the signing of the *Motu proprio*, the committee
reached consensus on several issues, not least of which was the question of the
Solesmes rhythmic notation. The issue turned out to be less difficult than
expected, the monks having acquiesced once they learned, through their con-

duit de Santi, of the pope's preference for a more neutral face on the new *Vaticana*. Mocquereau, at any rate, had little cause for worry. His Jesuit friend had managed to safeguard the future of the notation by pushing through an additional, convoluted clause in the new legislation. Without mentioning the signs by name, it made allowances for certain, small changes in the published reproductions of the Typical Edition.[4] Mocquereau himself was nevertheless successful in persuading the committee to accept one "invisible" rhythmic marking. It was decided that, instead of a dot, a blank space would follow the Vatican neumes to indicate the longer value of the *mora vocis*.

Similar issues filled the agenda for the committee's next meeting, hosted by the exiled editors at Appuldercombe the following September. But the real work would not begin for several more months, when the proof sheets of the new *Kyriale*—the first installment of the Typical Edition—finally arrived. By Combe's account, these appeared shortly after Christmas 1905, more than eight months after the signing of the second *Motu proprio*. The long interval suggested that the Solesmes monks, far from repeating earlier research, were taking their charge seriously, making sure to collect enough new evidence, with the trusty *tableaux*, to defend their editorial decisions, keeping themselves above criticism. Yet Mocquereau had misjudged the potential effect of their scholarship. When Pothier received the first set of proof sheets, the tables, so to speak, turned. It was now the committee, in its collective wisdom, that had suggestions for the editors. Rather than accepting the lofty Solesmes method, Pothier saw room for numerous "improvements" to the melodies under review. It was no wonder. The proposed *Kyriale*, like the 1903 *Liber Usualis*, represented a significant revision of the first editions prepared at Solesmes—with changes based, Mocquereau reported, on the study of more than 120 manuscript sources. Pothier, apparently unable to recognize the melodies now put before his eyes, reacted with a certain resistance. In fact, he balked.

He was not alone. When in early spring the commission gathered in Rome to evaluate the proofs, so many corrections were proposed that Pothier had to adopt a working method to account for them all. A letter from the president, written in April, explained to the editors the ostensibly democratic procedure used to reach consensus:

> Everyone in attendance has a copy of the proofs to examine. The President has notated on his own copy the variants proposed by the absentees, in order to determine, in the event of discussion, the number of those in favor or opposed to one or another reading. The President begins by singing from the proof. When coming upon a passage on which one of the members has an observation to make . . . the President stops, and the case is discussed. . . . If the feeling of the assembly is evident, the discussion is closed. In the

opposite case, the President asks each of those present, one by one, his opinion, and the decision is made according to the majority. . . . As you can see, the method is fairly meticulous, but regular and sure.[5]

The image of Dom Pothier singing to the assembly from the trial pages of the *Kyriale* gives the idea of "proof" a very different spin. It was not the work of the printer but the melodies themselves (and thus, by extension, the Solesmes monks) that went on trial, cross-examined by one of the oldest living Gregorian experts, who tested the chants, one by one, by putting them into his mouth.

In other words, Pothier's method placed the burden of proof on singing. Rather than silently checking the printed pages against an original text, he turned the signs into sounds, privileging *vox* over *nota*, the performance of the chant over its spelling. The putatively meticulous—but ultimately very personal—process of correction advocated by Pothier offers further, compelling evidence of his ideological separation from Mocquereau, a distance we attempted to measure in the previous chapter. Pothier's musical sensibility, like that of the original Gregory, flowed from his own ear, the site of all good judgment. It was an internalized feeling that finally determined, for him, the truth of the melodies, a feeling that, by 1905, amounted to over two decades of Gregorian experience. Pothier had no need to check the edition against a material exemplar because he could rely on his own memory, bringing back the very first edition he had prepared in the 1880s. Since that chant book had also drawn its authority from acceptable Gregorian sources, an important question arose about which melodies were truer. The commissioners returned to a passage from the *Motu proprio* that linked the Gregorian restoration to a "legitimate tradition contained over the course of centuries in the manuscripts." What, they wondered, was legitimate? Pothier answered with the chant he knew by ear, and called it a "living tradition."

Mocquereau himself could not respond, having remained at Appuldercombe to continue his work, on the assumption that the proofs would speak for themselves. Understandably, he was alarmed at the committee's recent decisions, which he had learned through de Santi, and expressed his concern in a series of memoranda quickly dispatched to Rome. It was not just the bogus democratic method (with its specter of music made by committee) but the very implications of the method that caused him distress. Mocquereau had little patience for the idea of a "living tradition" if such a tradition rested solely on personal taste. The rigorously scientific criteria of his own historical discipline recommended, in fact, that one jettison all preconceived notions, reject acquired tastes, in order more completely to comprehend the artifacts of the past. History, after all, seemed much more remote—and therefore more truthful—when it was completely unfamiliar. The methods of comparative philology guaranteed this kind of alienation, blocking the historian's ears in order to create room for the strange new facts spelled out, in silence, before his eyes. For Mocquereau, a "legitimate tradition" could mean only one thing: the tradition exposed through the legitimating practices of modern historiography itself, which required the agreement not of committees, but of manuscripts. In his system, only notes could vote. And the older they were, the more they counted.

But to reconceive the democratic process in this way, shifting the burden of evidence onto the oldest sources, was to create other difficulties. Not least was the problem of amassing enough manuscripts to secure a good reading. Even though the Solesmes monks had managed to collect hundreds of photographed sources for their atelier, Mocquereau was still prepared to judge the evidence, especially in the case of certain repertories, as insufficient. When, for example, the sources for a particular melody yielded too many variants, judgments about what constituted the "legitimate tradition" obviously became more difficult. This was precisely the problem surrounding many of the chants from the *Kyriale*. Mocquereau had mused over this difficulty in an essay from 1904, published in the same month as the *Motu proprio*:

> What then to do? In such a case we begin by procuring a huge amount of information. This shows, by the way, how much, even with our *tableaux*, the work remains in some aspects provisional—how much it could be perfected by an inquiry that would exhaust all the usable documents, and thus how much it would be imprudent and premature of us to present our editions as definitive. In fifty years, perhaps, we could dream of it. Not today.[6]

His equivocal conclusion reveals another, more serious respect in which Mocquereau's aims conflicted with those of the Pontifical Commission— indeed, with the very papal legislation under which all parties now labored. The heroic critical methodology of his school demanded a deferral of judgment—a denial of closure—that, on the face of it, was completely at odds with the authoritative closure of the *Motu proprio*. From the perspective of the Solesmes atelier, both the present and the future tenses, in direct contradiction to the pope's speech act, were by definition *im*perfect, awaiting future discoveries. It was apparently less significant for Mocquereau's school that Rome had spoken than to know that certain manuscripts had not yet spoken.

Indeed, an anonymous English translator in 1905 found the assertive "not today" of Mocquereau's essay so potentially inflammatory, especially in view of the Vatican edition in press, that he hastened to add this conciliatory footnote:

> In this paragraph Dom Mocquereau is speaking of the "definitely final" musical text, which would satisfy the ideals of critical and exact scholarship. He would admit that the "passages" affected with uncertainty are not so extensive as to vitiate the general correct-

ness of the musical text as a whole. From the same point of view, if the Church had decided to wait til she could satisfy the ideal of exact scholarship, she might not yet have authorized the text of the Vulgate.[7]

The translator's explanation appeared, however, only to make matters worse, by spelling out, in the clearest possible terms, the difference between the Church's evidently makeshift decisions—which resulted in a flawed and incomplete Vulgate—and the more exalted "ideal of exact scholarship" that motivated the Solesmes workshop. For these scholars, the true texts of the past could be fully revealed only by digging up more and more sources. Legitimacy rested, in the end, on archaeology.

It was this problem of legitimacy that ultimately brought the work of the commission to a standstill, the proponents of "living tradition" facing off uncomfortably with the Solesmes archaeologists throughout the months of February and March. To resolve the conflict, Pothier finally resorted to a higher authority. By the beginning of April 1905 he had heard from the pope's secretary of state, Cardinal Merry del Val, who wrote: "His Holiness has charged me with declaring to your Most Reverend Paternity that, when He decided to return to the ancient Gregorian chant, He did not intend to make a work so exclusively favoring the archaeology of this chant that we could not admit today certain Gregorian melodies that have come down over the course of centuries." The letter went on to assert that "it would not be contrary to the intentions of His Holiness that the Pontifical Commission for the Vatican Edition of the liturgical books give preference to certain less ancient compositions, provided that they truly have the character of Gregorian music."[8]

The traditionalists had suddenly gained considerable ground. Still, the judgment was not forceful enough to convince the Solesmes editors themselves, who continued sending polemical missives to Rome in defense of their own work. According to Combe, by the end of June they had drawn up, with the support of de Santi and others, something of a manifesto to place before Pius X, in the hopes of reversing the actions of the Pontifical Commission. The document's central paragraph asserted, once again, the unimpeachability of the Solesmes scholarship, whose scientific methods exceeded even the limits of canonical authority. The authors cheekily pointed out that the pope himself could not have imagined such results:

> Because the School of Solesmes offers us such an ensemble of guarantees, and because the difficulties raised by their opponents have no solid foundation, lacking all basis in science, we, the undersigned, declare ourselves ready to support the authors of a work undertaken for the honor of the Church, a work that until now has not only justified *but surpassed the Holy Father's highest hopes.*[9]

The manifesto did no good. Within days, a second letter addressed to Pothier from Merry del Val brought the dispute to a decisive end.[10] It announced a change of plan—a "simplification," the text stated euphemistically, "in the work of the editors." The new Vatican edition would be based on the Benedictine gradual published at Solesmes in 1895, a book that represented, as everyone knew, the work of Pothier, containing the so-called living tradition that he knew by heart, and that Mocquereau had labored to correct by hand. But the cardinal's letter announced that, from this point on, it would be Pothier alone who took charge of any corrections to the melodies, using, as he saw fit, the "paleographic studies pursued under the wise direction of the most Reverend Abbot of Solesmes." An additional clause put these exalted studies in their proper place, stating that "the Holy Father [would] take under His supreme authority and protection the special edition of the liturgical books that He called Typical, otherwise leaving the field free for the studies of learned Gregorianists." The Vatican did not prohibit scientific research with this ruling. It simply relegated such research to an undesignated "free field," as if condemning the monks to the very site on which Mocquereau, and later his entire school, had first staked their scholarly claims—the world of the staffless Saint-Gall neumes, whose signs floated freely, as they say, *in campo aperto.*

· · · · ·

It was not exactly Siberia, but it was a punishment nonetheless. The Solesmes monks were, with this decision, indirectly censured for their extremist position regarding the Church's musical traditions. In this respect, the conflict surrounding the Vatican edition—and the pope's reaction to it—would seem to anticipate another, more serious conflict that visited Pius X during the same decade, the crisis involving what, in Catholic circles, was tellingly known as modernism. The term referred to the teachings of certain Catholic intellectuals around the turn of the century, scholars who sought to update traditional theology through historical discipline. Alfred Loisy's *Histoire critique du texte et des versions de la Bible* (1892), to cite just one example, had transformed the field of hermeneutics by applying the methods of modern textual criticism to the interpretation of biblical texts. Later, in *L'Evangile et l'église* (1903), he argued on similar grounds that dogma itself could be subject to revisionist readings. Deeply suspicious of this intellectual trend, the Holy See reacted defensively, condemning the modernists in its 1907 decree *Lamentabili*, not only listing their sins but calling on the whole Church to cooperate in their censure.[11] "The problem as it stood," explains the theologian Yves Congar, "was concerned with the relationship between historical documentation and tradition as the Church lives it, and as theology, the science of faith, can and should conceive of it. Was tradition reducible to the demands and limitations of history, or does it go beyond them, and if so, how, and under what conditions?"[12]

This, in a sense, was the same, unanswerable question that divided the members of the Pontifical Commission. Although no one actually called them "modernists," the Solesmes editors so insisted on their own historical methodology that they appeared—to some members of the commission, at least—as subversive as the theologians Pius X would soon denounce. An unforgiving account of the monks by Peter Wagner, published the same year as *Lamentabili*, related the polemic that ensued after the Vatican's change of plan, describing the ex-editors in terms that were at least as condemning as those in the pope's encyclical:

> How the crisis was brought about is well known. Far from finally bringing their procedures into harmony, the archaeological party offered to the Catholic world the disedifying example first of an anonymous, then open "war" against the Vatican chant-books. Having projected their own notions, in spite of innumerable requests from the most varied sources, they have refused to collaborate even to the present hour. Unlike obedient children of the Church, who would deem it as an honor to join in the realization of a noble Papal initiative, they somehow consider it as honorable to stab this initiative in the back; they arouse and maintain an opposition to *an adequate and standard praxis of the whole Church*, one which, moreover, comes into the world with the seal of the Holy Father.[13]

Nearly a century later Wagner's reactionary account, with its dark insinuations of deviance and violence, sounds more than a little paranoid. But the tone of his essay gives us a clear idea of the threat posed by modern disciplines on a traditional institution like the Church. Far from unearthing the Church's lost traditions, the newfangled Gregorian archaeology was viewed as a means of destroying them, a method that turned its back on "standard practice." Wagner astutely critiqued the Solesmes *tableaux* from this very perspective:

> The Solesmes "critical" method investigates each single note or group in accord with its manuscript tradition; the melodic text of each individual portion is established on the basis of the whole material. This method certainly testifies to much labor, to diligence, and high endeavor. But is it free from bias? This question I cannot answer in the affirmative. For the possibility is that we end up with a mode of singing which has never and nowhere existed. The newly employed statistical investigation of the materials of the readings for individual notes or groups brings nothing but scraps of melody, each of which, looked at in itself, appears in its "purest" or "oldest" reading. However, together they all produce melodies which have never existed in that form. The purely statistical method of research for the "oldest" version can thus logically turn into the other extreme, *to the denial of any tradition*.[14]

This "other extreme" constituted, of course, the other meaning of modernism—the one we associate more readily with the history of art. And it is this meaning that may serve to illuminate the contested view of "history" that ultimately brought the members of the Pontifical Commission into conflict. For Mocquereau, it was precisely such a shedding of tradition—through strict discipline—that offered the promise of a true encounter with the past. By erasing preconceived notions, the Gregorian student became a *tabula rasa* on which the past could be rewritten in all its purity.

As should be abundantly clear, this modernist approach rubbed many on the commission the wrong way. Wagner himself obviously found it untenable, the "musical asceticism" of the Solesmes research having developed, as he put it, "into a certain heroism." This is a heroism we have already encountered, a quality plainly audible in Mocquereau's speech to the Gregorian Congress, described at the end of the previous chapter. But for Wagner this heroic ethos simply made no sense in the context of a public art like Church music:

> How could one judge it otherwise, when, in all seriousness, completely archaic practices were to be imposed upon the singer of the twentieth century? Everyone else knows that at best a thing of this kind is possible only when it can be more or less hermetically sealed off from art in general. But it is not possible for those who must have a direct and living intercourse with it.[15]

Pothier certainly agreed. Throughout the committee's deliberations, he held onto a position argued in his very first book on Gregorian music, one that understood the ancient melodies, in the words of its subtitle, *d'après la tradition*. It was the act of making a connection to a distant past—*living* the tradition, as it were, through imaginative effort—that defined Pothier's concept of Gregorian restoration. Rather than cutting the cord, he worked to reattach it, restoring the umbilicus through which the chant itself had been nourished by Holy Mother Church. The Holy Father, needless to say, looked benevolently on such family values. In the end, life won.

It is of course tempting, and perhaps not altogether wrong, to read this early-twentieth-century conflict over the legitimate Gregorian text—which pitted Pothier's tradition against Mocquereau's archaeology, ear against eye—in terms of the much more recent debates in the field of American musicology over the question of chant's oral versus written transmission.[16] Indeed, in the now mostly forgotten struggle over the Vatican edition, we see just how much the idea of chant's ancient voice and the fact of its ancient script represented incompatible propositions—an observation that makes the contemporary debate over oral traditions seem a bit like history repeating itself.

Yet to view the two conflicts simply as parallel historical phenomena is to ignore the very different turf on which each was waged. The Pontifical Commission understood all tradition—oral or written—as the domain of the Church; and the Church claimed the chant tradition already restored. By relieving the Solesmes monks of their duties on the commission, the Holy See powerfully confirmed this belief, placing modern history beyond its purview. Any future discoveries about the repertory made in the name of such history would, in other words, have no bearing on what faithful Catholics might sing. The historical chant, as Mocquereau conceived it, was torn from its ritual context, an act that essentially completed the transformation discussed in chapter 4: the "secularization" of the repertory. From this point on, historical studies of chant would take place in an entirely different field.

Obviously, it is in this completely secular field (much expanded in the half century since Mocquereau's death) that the contemporary debates about the chant traditions have been played out. This fact alone suggests that the terms have changed. For scholars like Treitler or Levy or Jeffrey, the question of chant's "oral tradition" has precious little to do with what one might hear sung at next Sunday's Mass. On the contrary: in the contemporary musicological debates, the idea of oral tradition defines an important aspect of the discipline of music history itself—the very discipline that the members of the Pontifical Commission felt compelled to dismiss in 1905. If today this notion of oral tradition still appears to define an "outside" term, it is a distinction operative only *within* the context of an already well established field, a position meaningful to the music historian alone. In short, in late-twentieth-century musicology, to invoke "oral tradition" has been in effect to redraw the line between manuscripts and their interpretation, to shift the balance between the rigorous philological method and pure speculation that make up any history of antiquity. Under the authority of such *un*written tradition contemporary musicologists have sought to escape the limits of textual criticism—the practice that gave rise to our field in the first place—in the hope of finding new paths, new historical alternatives to unanswered (or unanswerable) questions. In this respect, the study of oral tradition has represented something like Gregorian history's utopian beyond, a kind of metahistory.

This "beyond" of Gregorian history was, of course, exactly what Mocquereau imagined for his own research, although he would attain it not by escaping but by embracing textual criticism, the basic analytical method of modern philology. Thus the contemporary oral transmission debate and the conflict over the Vatican edition reflect not so much parallel as ideologically opposed historical phenomena. For the Solesmes historians, the promise of philology circa 1900 lay in its potential to supersede what was already known (or even possible to know) about the Gregorian repertory. And as we have seen, it was this potential knowledge that the Vatican ultimately deemed without value, relegating all future philological studies of chant to a "free field," in order to ensure the stability of the Vatican chant. By banishing modernist musicology in this way—essentially separating Church from State-of-the-Art History—the Holy See expected to protect its traditional chant from any future infringement. But as we shall see, things did not turn out exactly as planned.

Atypical Editions

The Vatican *Kyriale* appeared within a few months, in October 1905. As specified in the letter from Merry del Val, it was indeed based on Pothier's now ten-year-old edition and thus reflected few, if any, of the melodic changes—and obviously none of the rhythmic improvements—that had distinguished Mocquereau's 1903 *Liber Usualis*. The same was to hold true for the next installment of the *Vaticana*, the *Graduale* completed early in 1908. This second book obliquely showed its allegiance to the Pothier camp by reproducing, on its opening page, the same triptych that had adorned the first Solesmes gradual: the image of Saint Gregory receiving the Church's traditional song by ear. But in the 1908 *Graduale* the drawing is slightly altered (fig. 29). In its difference, the picture relates an important lesson, for the figure of the scribe occupies an entirely different position: his head now lowered, he hunches over a desk turned purposely away from the viewer; we can no longer see the mysterious, illegible marks he inscribes. The image of subservience would seem to summarize the fate of the whole Solesmes *école*. Indeed, in this revised iconography, the most ancient notations, like the fanatical monks who studied them, were left completely out of the picture.

But the precious strokes from Saint-Gall did not, in fact, remain invisible for long. In the same month in which the Vatican brought out the first book of the series, the Desclée press, following the rules of the *Motu proprio*, published its own version, now furnished with the Solesmes rhythmic notation—a notation whose signs supposedly harked back to the neumes of the Saint-Gall manuscripts. The edition, again in accordance with procedure, was submitted to the local ordinary, the bishop of Tournai, who readily gave his imprimatur: "The present edition, which contains the rhythmical signs of the Solesmes monks, has been examined by the censors assigned for the supervision of the Gregorian Chant. It has been found to conform with the *Typical Vatican Edition*. We testify to that fact."[17] Taking extra precautions, Desclée also submitted the book to the Sacred Congregation of Rites, which before too long granted its approval, although in slightly more equivocal language than that of the Belgian bishop. The letter stated that

PROPRIUM DE TEMPORE

Dominica prima Adventus.

Introitus. VIII.

A D te le-vá-vi * á-nimam me-am: De-us me-us in te confí-do, non e-ru-bé-scam: neque ir-rí-de-ant me in-imí-ci me-i: ét-e-nim u-ni-vér-si qui te exspé-ctant, non confun-dén-tur. *Ps.* Ví-as tu-as, Dó-mi-ne, demónstra mi-hi: * et sémi-tas tu-as é-do-ce me.

Figure 29. Opening page of Vatican *Graduale* (1908), with Gregorian triptych updated from Pothier's edition of 1883.

the copy "provided with rhythmical signs by the Solesmes monks" completely agreed with the Vatican edition "in every other respect."[18] In each case, the censors recognized the book's conformity while acknowledging its exceptional status. Even the title page of the newly approved edition gave evidence of this dual personality: *Kyriale seu ordinarium missae cum cantu gregoriano ad exemplar editionis Vaticanae concinnatum et rhythmicis signis a Solesmensibus monachis diligentur ornatum* (Kyriale or ordinary of the Mass with Gregorian chant in accord with the exemplar of the Vatican edition and carefully furnished with the rhythmic signs of the monks of Solesmes).[19] Proclaiming itself in harmony with the Vatican exemplar, the book also hinted at its own improvements, having acquired a certain distinction (*ornatum*, meaning both "furnished" and "honored") through the marks of the monks' research.

On this publication, then, hangs one final tale—a few words about a few signs that accumulated, in the end, significant clout. Indeed, once it was approved, the edition created a kind of confusion no papal legislation could have foreseen, for the tiny marks they contained did not belong to Rome. When Dom Delatte turned everything over to the Vatican press, the rhythmic notation remained in the abbey's control, simply because the pope himself had decided not to use it. After the events of June 1905, however, the notation took on new symbolic importance. It came to represent the views of the Solesmes monks themselves, views that were now judged extreme, if not insubordinate. The dots and slashes of their Gregorian rhythm, which imitated (albeit with considerable poetic license) the wonderfully strange phonography of Saint-Gall, became a visible sign of the authority the Solesmes monks still maintained, even in the "free field" to which they had been banished. Just as Dom Pothier, by redesigning the face of Saint Gregory, became a veritable figure in the chant revival, the Solesmes monks emerged, in this rhythmic imprinting, as an irrepressible presence.

Not surprisingly, there were objections. Over the course of the next few months a new dispute arose over the propriety of these additional signs. Dom Pothier was among those who complained the loudest, not only questioning the historical value of the notation, but also claiming that the monks themselves had "no right to impose their special ideas on the universal practice of a typical and official edition."[20] According to Dom David, Pothier believed the signs—which he took to be Mocquereau's own invention—would mar "the integrity of the traditional notation restored in the Vatican edition."[21] Never mind that it was Pothier himself who had furnished the original design for that traditional Gregorian font. It now belonged to the Vatican, and for that reason, the question of integrity had more serious implications.

The argument eventually came to focus on the Vatican character itself. Merry del Val's fateful letter had, in fact, contained a clause reminding the Pontifical Commission that the Vatican copyright would be "guaranteed by the *type* of the publication," that is, by its distinct typographic appearance. Opponents of the rhythmic editions found one sign—the vertical *episema*—particularly offensive in this respect. It was not simply that the mark represented a dubious aspect of Mocquereau's rhythmic theory, but that, on the printed page, it touched the Vatican types. Forging a direct link, the *episema* altered the "typicality" of the Vatican notes, and therefore compromised the book's integrity (fig. 30). A ruling from the Sacred Congregation of Rites, issued in January 1906, addressed this infringement, revising the approbation previously granted to Desclée:

> The form of the notes of the chant should be integrally maintained in such fashion that all of them which have the same purpose and meaning, and which therefore in the Typical Vatican Edition always exhibit one and the same shape, should also, in any other edition—which may be approved by the Ordinary—maintain also amongst themselves an exact similarity of shape. And therefore any signs which may be introduced by permission of the Ordinary should in no way affect the shape of the notes or the way in which they are connected.[22]

This new opinion redefined the space of the Typical Edition to include not just the form of the melodies, but the shape of individual *notae*, which from this point on came to be known as Typical Notes. The integrity of tradition, in short, would be secured only by maintaining all notes in exactly the same condition. Desclée complied by altering the rhythmic notation, redesigning the typography to remove the offending strokes. But the controversy by no means ended here. Having left its mark on the Vatican books, rhythm became a presence—a distinct character—to be dealt with. During the next five years, the Sacred Congregation of Rites had to issue at least four more decrees in order to redefine the boundaries of the *Vaticana*. One of the last, from January 1911, put the case in lan-

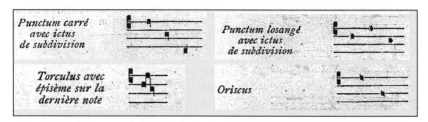

Figure 30. Examples of various Solesmes rhythmic signs as they appeared in editions published by Desclée before 1906. Courtesy of Abbaye Saint-Pierre, Solesmes, France. Authorization No. 105.

guage as plain (and as strong) as possible: "The reproductions of this typical edition containing the extra signs, known as rhythmical, are abusively called *Rhythmical Editions* and as such have not been approved but merely tolerated upon request; this toleration, under the circumstances, can no longer be admitted except for the editions already made."[23]

The abuse articulated by this text lay not so much in the printed signs themselves, which were "tolerated" for their practical value, as in the perception they eventually fostered. The Sacred Congregation of Rites saw the notation as overstepping its bounds only when it had begun to claim for itself a separate territory, a space that was to be known as *Rhythmical*. By making its way into the Vatican edition, the Solesmes notation created the unavoidable impression of an alternative practice—one that, in fact, appeared to improve on the standard praxis. The added rhythmic signs, in this way, *im*perfected the Vatican notation. The insinuation could barely be avoided by those who wished to dispel it most, as is obvious from the wording of the decree: while condemning the use of the term *Rhythmical Editions*, the officials managed nonetheless to underscore it. Like an unwanted houseguest, this unauthorized rhythm had penetrated the pristine space defined by the *typical*, and it refused to leave. The Vatican officials, ruing the day they welcomed the signs, could do nothing but assert that the *rhythmical* had no place in their edition.

Yet an interesting (and unforeseen) problem arose once this notation had been officially *un*recognized. For in disclaiming the idea of a Rhythmical Edition, the officials seemed to make the Typical Notes of the *Vaticana* "free" once again, as if releasing them from the imposition of all such uninvited characters. In other words, the action seemed to leave the unmarked space of the traditional Gregorian rhythm open to interpretation. This was apparently what Franz Haberl, director of the Caecilienverein, concluded, a fact we may infer from a letter sent to him in 1910 by Cardinal Martinelli, prefect of the Sacred Congregation of Rites:

His Holiness has learned that, particularly in Germany and among Germans of the United States, a view concerning the liturgical chant is being spread which is absolutely false in itself and very prejudicial to the uniform restoration of the said chant in the whole Church. It is insinuated that the Holy Father in publishing the aforesaid edition did not intend to embody in it a special form of rhythm, but to leave to the individual music directors the right to apply to the series of notes, taken materially, any rhythm they deem most appropriate.

How erroneous this opinion is may be deduced from a simple examination of the Vatican edition, in which the melodies are evidently arranged according to the system of the so-called free rhythm. . . . It is well known that the Pontifical Commission, charged with compiling the liturgical Gregorian books, had expressly intended from the beginning and

with the open approval of Holy See to mark the single melodies of the Vatican in that particular rhythm. . . . The approbation which the Sacred Congregation of Rites bestowed
upon the Roman Gradual by order of the Holy Father extends not only to all the particular rules by which the Vatican edition has been made up, but includes also *the rhythmical form of the melodies, which, consequently, is inseparable from the edition itself.*[24]

The new abuse addressed by Cardinal Martinelli involved the spread of men-
suralist theories of performance, in which long and short rhythmic values were
applied to the singing of the Gregorian melodies. Such theories were by no
means new: non-Benedictine chant scholars in both France and Germany had
promoted this type of performance throughout the last quarter of the nineteenth
century. But the Vatican clearly regarded the practice as illegitimate. The Holy
Father's opinion made it quite clear that the true Gregorian performance resided
within the Typical Notes themselves. The ethos, or stamp, of legitimacy, which
was guaranteed by the Vatican *stamperia*, was evidently strong enough to seal the
fate of musical performance. There *was* a legitimate Gregorian rhythm, approved
by the Holy Father himself—one that was neither arbitrary nor open to interpretation. This rhythm was, on the contrary, "free." The logic of the passage seems
to imply that when the Vatican assumed the copyright of the Benedictine chant
in 1904, it took control not only of the melodies and notation, but of the manner of performance as well—the mysteriously elusive practice known as *la méthode bénédictine*. This formerly Benedictine performance was now, like the edition itself, released from any privilege or monopoly, thus available for all to
reproduce, as it were, "freely." From the terms of Martinelli's letter, in fact, choirs
appeared to have no other choice.

· · · · ·

With this ruling, the Vatican completed the set of legislative actions by which it
officially dis-enchanted the Benedictines of Solesmes for the good of the
Church. When rhythm yielded to the letter of the law and Gregorian performance became canonical—when, in short, all unauthorized freedoms had been
accounted for—the case of the Gregorian restoration, which the pope had
deemed complete as of November 1903, was definitely closed.

Even so, one small space remained open. It was a place that the Holy Father
himself had ordained during the conflicts of the Pontifical Commission—the so-
called free field to which he had relegated the "studies of learned Gregorianists."
Here our story finally comes to an end.

Where was this field? Mocquereau did not need to ask: he had been living
there for decades; he would remain for several more. It was the very *campo aperto*
in which he had been searching for the pure Gregorian melody since 1889—a

space that escaped the Vatican stamp because it existed between the pages, between the lines, between the Typical Notes. It was, we could say, in the *blanches* of the Typical Edition that he found this last site of freedom, which involved rights the pope had not yet claimed: the right to make fresh discoveries, the freedom to await new insights. This was where the Solesmes monks now left their mark, depositing the evidence of their own performance, the very footprints of a modern discipline, in order to spell out the forward march of Gregorian history. Camping in this free field with the pope's blessing, Mocquereau and his fellow scholars left behind the signs—indeed, the considerable repercussions—of a future of musicological research, repercussions whose unauthorized movements preserve, to this day, the original traces of Gregorian enchantment.

Notes

The following abbreviations have been used throughout for frequently cited texts:

HRCG   Dom Pierre Combe, *Histoire de la restauration du chant grégorien d'après des documents inédits* (Solesmes: Abbaye de Solesmes, 1969)

MG   Dom Joseph Pothier, *Les Mélodies grégoriennes* (Tournai: Desclée, 1880)

NMG   Dom André Mocquereau, *Le Nombre musical grégorien*, 2 vols. (Tournai: Desclée, 1908, 1927)

PM   *Paléographie musicale* (Solesmes: Imprimerie de Saint-Pierre/Tournai: Société Saint-Jean l'Evangéliste, 1889–1958); 2d ser., Monumentale (Tournai: Desclée, 1900–1924)

PS   Dom André Mocquereau and Dom Paul Cagin, *Plainchant and Solesmes* (London: Burns & Oates, n.d.). The introductory note explains that the text is an adaptation of articles from the *Rassegna gregoriana*, translated "with the approval of the learned authors." The articles in question appeared in April 1904 and July 1905.

1. Restoration and Decay

1. François René Chateaubriand, *The Genius of Christianity, or the Spirit and Beauty of the Christian Religion*, trans. Charles I. White (Philadelphia: Lippincott, 1856), 50.

2. Or as Chateaubriand himself recalled, the work was a "mausoleum erected to the memory of his mother." Like so many of the nobility who perished at the hands of revolutionaries, she died in a Parisian prison, expressing as her last wish only that her infidel son one day be converted. "I wept and I believed" was the son's famous response. See Chateaubriand, *Génie du christianisme* (Paris: Mignaret, 1802), 1:2. The preface to the first edition is reprinted in Chateaubriand, *Génie*, ed. Pierre Reboul (Paris: Garnier-Flammarion, 1966), 2:397–399.

3. Dominique Poulot, "Alexandre Lenoir et les musées des monuments françaises," in *Les Lieux de mémoire*, ed. Pierre Nora, vol. 2 (2): *La Nation* (Paris: Gallimard, 1986), 497–531.

4. André Chastel, "La Notion du patrimoine," in Nora (ed.), *Lieux de mémoire*, vol. 2 (2):414. See also Louis Réau, *Histoire du vandalisme: Les Monuments détruits de l'art français* (Paris: Robert Laffont, 1994).

5. Henry James expands on Chateaubriand's sentiments in the following passage from *Italian Hours*: "To delight in the aspects of sentient ruin might appear a heartless pastime, and the pleasure, I confess, shows a note of perversity" (quoted by Rose Macaulay in *Pleasure of Ruins* [London: Weidenfeld & Nicolson, 1953], i). See also Laurence Goldstein, *Ruins and Empire: The Evolution of a Theme in Augustan and Romantic Literature* (Pittsburgh: University of Pittsburgh Press, 1977).

6. Chateaubriand, *Génie du christianisme*, 2:40; English translation in White ed., 467–468.

7. "The ruin creates the present form of a past life, not according to the contents or remnants of that life, but according to its past as such" (Georg Simmel, "The Ruin," trans. David Kettler, in *Georg Simmel, 1858–1918*, ed. Kurt H. Wolff [Columbus: Ohio State University Press, 1959], 259–266).

8. The museum remained in operation as such until 1814.

9. Chateaubriand, *Génie du christianisme*, 2:98 (n. 1); English translation adapted from White ed., 520 (my emphasis).

10. Walter Benjamin's notion of the "aura" surrounding the (authentic) work of art is constructed according to a similar logic, conceived in the moment of its apparent destruction—in this case, by mechanical reproduction. Benjamin's aura, the sign of the authentic artwork, is defined as "a unique phenomenon of distance, however close one might be." It is precisely such a distance effect, I would suggest, that Chateaubriand imagines in the ruin, an effect of remoteness that carries with it, almost by necessity, the idea of a distant past. See Benjamin, "The Work of Art in the Age of Mechanical Reproduction," in Walter Benjamin, *Illuminations*, ed. Hannah Arendt, trans. Harry Zohn (New York: Harcourt Brace, 1968), 219–253.

11. Alfred de Musset, *La Confession d'un enfant du siècle*, ed. Gerard Barrier (Paris: Gallimard, 1973), 105; quoted by Richard Terdiman in *Present Past: Modernity and the Memory Crisis* (Ithaca: Cornell University Press, 1993), 122. Terdiman offers de Musset's complaint as an early example of the shock generated by the image of a Paris *démoli*, prefiguring the even greater trauma that was to emanate from the urban renewal undertaken by Haussmann in the 1850s—trauma that became, as he argues with Benjamin and others, the very substance of Baudelairean "modernity."

12. Victor Hugo, "Guerre aux démolisseurs!" *Revue des deux mondes* 5, no. 5 (1832): 607–622. See also Montalembert's passionate response to Hugo in "Du vandalisme en France: Lettre à M. Victor Hugo," *Revue des deux mondes*, 2d ser., 1, no. 5 (1833): 477–524.

13. See Georg Germann, *Gothic Revival in Europe and Britain: Sources, Influences, and Ideas*, trans. Gerald Onn (Cambridge, Mass.: MIT Press, 1972), 46–47.

14. Laurent Theis, "Guizot et les institutions de mémoire," in Nora (ed.), *Lieux de mémoire*, 2(2):569–592. See also Pierre Nora, "Between Memory and History: *Les Lieux de*

Mémoire," trans. Marc Roudebush, *Representations* 26 (spring 1989): 7–25; and Linda Orr, *Headless History: Nineteenth-Century French Historiography of the Revolution* (Ithaca, N.Y.: Cornell University Press, 1990).

15. Vitet wrote regularly for *Le Globe* during the years 1826 (when he took over from Castil-Blaze) to 1830. See Maurice Parturier's introduction to *Lettres de Mérimée à Ludovic Vitet* (Paris: Plon, 1934); also André Fermigier, "Mérimée et l'inspection des monuments historiques," in Nora (ed.), *Lieux de mémoire*, 2(2):593–611.

16. Richard Klein traces such perils and seductions of knowledge in his chapter titled "The Devil in *Carmen*," in *Cigarettes Are Sublime* (Durham, N.C.: Duke University Press, 1993).

17. M. F. Hearn, ed., *The Architectural Theory of Viollet-le-Duc: Readings and Commentary* (Cambridge, Mass.: MIT Press, 1990); Eugène-Emmanuel Viollet-le-Duc, *The Foundations of Architecture: Selections from the "Dictionnaire Raisonné,"* trans. Kenneth D. Whitehead (New York: George Braziller, 1990). The transformation of Viollet-le-Duc from a hero to a villain of French history had its origins in the 1940s with the critical writings of the architect Achille Carlier, whose *Anciens Monuments dans la civilisation moderne* (Paris: n.p., 1945) advanced an opinion that the restorer was himself a criminal who had "vandalized" buildings from the past, an opinion that has been sustained to the present day. See Bruno Foucart, "Viollet-le-Duc et la restauration," in Nora (ed.), *Lieux de mémoire*, 2(2):615–649; also idem, "La Restauration des ruines architecturales," *Connaissance des arts*, no. 478 (December 1991): 98–105.

18. Viollet-le-Duc, *Dictionnaire raisonné de l'architecture française du XIe au XVIe siècle*, 10 vols. (Paris: A. Morel, 1854–1868), s.v. "Restauration," 8:14–34; translated in Viollet-le-Duc, *Foundations of Architecture*, 195.

19. Viollet-le-Duc, *Foundations of Architecture*, 198.

20. Ibid., 197.

21. Viollet-le-Duc, *Dictionnaire raisonné*, 8:14; translated in *Foundations of Architecture*, 195 (my emphasis).

22. Ibid., 209.

23. Prosper Guéranger, *Institutions liturgiques*, vol. 1 (Paris: Débécourt, 1840), xix.

24. Charles Louandre, "Statistique littéraire: De la production intellectuelle en France depuis quinze ans," *Revue des deux mondes* 20, no. 2 (15 October 1847): 255–286, and no. 4 (15 November 1847): 671–703; cited in Orr, *Headless History*, 17.

25. Lammenais's 1828 tract *Du progrès de la Révolution et de la guerre contre l'église* virtually prophesied the 1830 Revolution and the spiritual crisis that would follow. For an early account of the movement, see William Gibson Ashbourne, *The Abbé de Lamennais and the Liberal Catholic Movement in France* (London: Longmans, Green, 1896). See Olivier Rousseau, *Histoire du mouvement liturgique* (Paris: Editions de Cerf, 1945). R. W. Franklin's *Nineteenth-Century Churches: The History of a New Catholicism in Württemburg, England, and France* (New York: Garland, 1987) connects the French movement to its counterparts in England and Germany.

26. The work that resulted was *Les Institutions liturgiques*. See also Léon Robert, O.S.B., *L'Abbé Guéranger et la révolution de 1830* (Sablé: Les Amis de Solesmes, 1965); Dom Louis Soltner, *Solesmes et Dom Guéranger (1805–1875)* (Solesmes: Abbaye Saint-Pierre de

Solesmes, 1974); Dom Cuthbert Johnson, *Prosper Guéranger (1805–1875): A Liturgical The-*
ologian (Roma: Pontificio S. Anselmo, 1984).

27. Guéranger, *Institutions liturgiques*, xix.

28. Chateaubriand, *Genius of Christianity*, 544.

29. "The writings of the ancients, by being dispersed in the monasteries, partly
escaped the ravages of the Goths. . . . [By reproducing books] either to propagate the
faith or to confute heresy, [the monastic orders] powerfully contributed to the preservation and the revival of learning" (ibid., 676–677).

30. Montalembert, *Les Moines d'Occident depuis Saint Benoît jusqu'à Saint Bernard*
(Paris: Lecoffre, 1860), 2:1; translated in *The Monks of the West: From Saint Benedict to Saint*
Bernard (Edinburgh and London: William Blackwood, 1861), 2:3.

31. R. Franklin, *Nineteenth-Century Churches*, 394.

32. *L'Abbaye Saint-Pierre de Solesmes* (Sablé-sur-Sarthe: Abbaye Saint-Pierre, 1978),
18–25.

33. Soltner, *Solesmes et Dom Guéranger*, 43–47.

34. Hearn (ed.), *Architectural Theory of Viollet-le-Duc*, 282.

35. Soltner, *Solesmes et Dom Guéranger*, 37.

36. Combe, *HRCG*, 22. The books used during the first years had been recently published in Dijon in 1827 and 1828.

37. "Il est évident que si l'on est quelquefois en droit de croire qu'on possède la
phrase grégorienne dans sa pureté sur un morceau en particulier, c'est lorsque les exem-
plaires de plusieurs Églises éloignées s'accordent sur la même leçon" (Guéranger, *Institu-*
tions liturgiques, 306).

38. Combe reports that in 1846 Fétis traveled to Solesmes to consult Guéranger
about producing an edition of chant based on an old manuscript.

39. Danjou's discovery was anticipated by his publication of *De l'état et de l'avenir du*
chant ecclésiastique en France (Paris: P. Desbarres, 1844).

40. Lambillotte's important publications include, not counting his compositions of
sacred choral music, two theoretical works: *Clef des mélodies grégoriennes dans les antiques*
systèmes de notation et de l'unité dans les chants liturgiques (Brussels: C. J. A. Greuse, 1851) and
Esthétique, théorie et pratique du chant grégorien restauré d'après la doctrine des anciens et les sources
primitives (Paris: LeClere, 1855). According to Fétis, Nisard (the pseudonym of Abbé Théodule Normand) was both editor and writer for a number of midcentury publications on
archaeology and sacred music; see François Fétis, *Biographie universelle des musiciens*, vol. 6
(Paris: Firmin-Didot, 1870), 329–332. In the 1850s Nisard worked with d'Ortigue on the
Dictionnaire liturgique, historique et pratique du plain-chant et de musique d'église au moyen âge
et dans les temps modernes (Paris: Migne, 1853), as well as on a précis of the modern chant
restoration, *Etudes sur la restauration du chant grégorien au XIXe siècle* (Rennes: Vatar, 1856).
Some of Nisard's more important articles from the 1840s and 1850s were reprinted in a
posthumous volume titled *L'Archéologie musicale et le vrai chant grégorien* (Paris: Lethielleux,
1890). For an overview of this fertile period, see Augustin Gatard, *La Musique grégorienne*
(Paris: Laurens, 1913); also John Emerson, "Western Plainchant: Nineteenth-Century
Restoration Attempts," in *The New Grove Dictionary of Music and Musicians*, ed. Stanley
Sadie (New York: Macmillan, 1980), 14:827–830.

41. Gontier's address to the congress was later published separately in a pamphlet titled *Le Plain-chant: Son Exécution* (Le Mans: Monnoyer, 1860).

42. Combe implies that Gontier learned everything he knew at Solesmes, and from Guéranger in particular, although Gontier gives no direct indication of this in his treatise. On this point, see commentary provided by Nino Albarosa in his Italian translation of Gontier's *Méthode raisonée du plain-chant* (Le Mans: Monnoyer, 1859): *Metodo ragionato di canto piano*, Quaderni di "Studi Gregoriani," vol. 2 (Rome: Torre d'Orfeo, 1993), 18.

43. See François Furet and Jacques Ozouf, *Reading and Writing: Literacy in France from Calvin to Jules Ferry* (Cambridge: Cambridge University Press, 1982); and Maurice Agulhon, *The French Republic 1879–1992*, trans. Antonia Nevill (Oxford: Basil Blackwell, 1993).

44. Etienne Cartier, *Les Moines de Solesmes: Expulsions du 6 novembre 1880 et du 22 mars 1882* (Le Mans: Monnoyer, 1882); cited in Dom Augustin Savaton, *Dom Delatte, abbé de Solesmes* (Sablé: Abbaye de Solesmes, 1975), 71.

45. Pothier, *MG*, 9.

46. Ibid., 67. We find this same metaphor invoked again in the preface to his treatise (p. 4), when Pothier mentions the contemporary "habit of heavy hammering that had denatured and almost ruined the musical phrase."

47. Amadée Gastoué, *La Musique d'église* (Lyon: Janin, 1916), 151.

48. Guéranger's approval, which appeared in the form of a long letter at the front of the 1859 edition, ends by reminding the author that his own judgment of the treatise came from practical knowledge, issuing as it did from one "whose profession [has been], for many years, constantly to sing the gradual and the antiphoner" (reproduced in Gontier, *Méthode raisonnée de plain-chant*, xii).

49. Ibid., xv.

50. Ibid.; passage paraphrased by Pothier in *MG*, 5.

51. "Nous espérons voir [les pages suivantes] . . . accueillies avec interêt et bienveillance par les musiciens profanes eux-mêmes, par ceux surtout qui estiment que la musique moderne a besoin d'être régénérée, retrempée aux sources vives des inspirations anciennes, et que la musique du passé mieux connue . . . doit être saluée comme la vraie musique de l'avenir" (Pothier, *MG*, 6).

52. One of the visitors was the local prefect, apparently none too pleased about the manner in which the monks were flaunting their repossession of the abbey. Dom Jean Claire, the current choirmaster of Solesmes, told me the story of the day the prefect called Dom Delatte to his offices. "You're not being reasonable," the official said to the abbot. It had been possible to look the other way when the monks first moved back home, the prefect explained, but now that their blatant disregard for the law was causing such a public stir, he could no longer tolerate it. Dom Delatte listened respectfully to the reprimand while surveying the premises. The lavish offices of the prefect were in the cloister of what had formerly been the local cathedral. After a thoughtful silence he replied: "Monsieur, we are simply building the prefectory of the future." A shorter version of the story appears in Savaton, *Dom Delatte*, 181–185.

53. For a useful summary of this Catholic literary fashion, see the chapter "Religious Unease" in Jean Pierrot, *The Decadent Imagination, 1880–1900*, trans. Derek Coltman (Chicago: University of Chicago Press, 1981), 79–118.

54. Debussy is reported to have visited Solesmes in 1893; see Julia d'Almendra, *Les Modes grégoriens dans l'oeuvre de Claude Debussy* (Paris: G. Enault, 1950), 181–187.

55. Joris-Karl Huysmans, *L'Oblat*, vol. 17 (in two parts) of *Oeuvres complètes* (Paris: G. Cres, 1934); translated by Edward Perceval as *The Oblate* (New York: Dutton, 1924), 3–4

56. Camille Bellaigue, "A l'abbaye de Solesmes," *Revue des deux mondes* 150, no. 2 (15 November 1898): 342–376.

57. Joris-Karl Huysmans, *En Route*, vol. 13 (in two parts) of *Oeuvres complètes* (Paris: G. Cres, 1932); translated by C. Kegan Paul (New York: Howard Fertig, 1976), 7.

58. Bellaigue, "A l'abbaye de Solesmes," 372.

2. Bibliophilia

1. Joris-Karl Huysmans, *A rebours*, vol. 7 of *Oeuvres complètes* (Paris: G. Cres, 1929); translated by Havelock Ellis as *Against the Grain* (New York: Dover, 1969), 132.

2. Huysmans, *Against the Grain*, 133.

3. See John Southward, *Progress in Printing and the Graphic Arts* (London: Simkin, Marshall, Hamilton, Kent, 1897); Stanley Morison, *Politics and Script: Aspects of Authority and Freedom in the Development of Graeco-Latin Script from the Sixth Century b.c. to the Twentieth Century a.d.* (Oxford: Clarendon, 1972); and *Encyclopaedia Britannica*, 1966 ed., s.v. "Printing Type" by Beatrice Lamberton Warde.

4. Robin Kinross, *Modern Typography: An Essay in Critical History* (London: Hyphen, 1992).

5. Quoted by Frederic W. Goudy in *Typologia: Studies in Type Design and Type Making* (Berkeley: University of California Press, 1940), 123.

6. D. B. Updike, "A Translation of the Reports of Berlier and Sobry on Types of Gillé Fils," *Fleuron* 6 (1928): 167–183; quoted in Kinross, *Modern Typography*, 22.

7. Quoted in Kinross, *Modern Typography*, 32–34. These studies were developed at the turn of the century by typographers such as Theodore Low DeVinne.

8. Stanley Morison and Kenneth Day, *The Typographic Book, 1450–1935* (London: Ernest Benn, 1963), 4.

9. John Southward, "Typography, Practical," in *Encyclopaedia Brittanica*, 9th ed. (repr. Chicago: R. S. Peale, 1892), 23:710.

10. P. M. Handover, "British Book Typography," in *Book Typography, 1815–1965, in Europe and the United States of America*, ed. Kenneth Day (Chicago: University of Chicago Press, 1965), 139–174.

11. Recent writings on William Morris and the Kelmscott Press include William Peterson, *The Kelmscott Press: A History of William Morris's Typographical Adventure* (Berkeley: University of California Press, 1991); Duncan Robinson, *William Morris, Burne-Jones, and Kelmscott Chaucer* (London: Gordon Fraser, 1982); Colin Franklin, *Printing and the Mind of Morris: Three Paths to the Kelmscott Press* (Cambridge: Rampant Lions Press, 1986); and John Dreyfus, *Morris and the Printed Book* (London: William Morris Society, 1989).

12. Handover, "British Book Typography," 154.

13. See John Nash, "Calligraphy," in *William Morris*, ed. Linda Parry (exhibit catalog, Victoria and Albert Museum, London: Philip Wilson, 1996).

14. Discussed by Jerome McGann in *Black Riders: The Visible Language of Modernism* (Princeton: Princeton University Press, 1993), 45–75.

15. William Morris, *The Art and Craft of Printing: A Note by William Morris on His Aims in Founding the Kelmscott Press* (New Rochelle, N.Y.: Elston: 1902), 2 (note dated 11 November 1895).

16. Ibid.

17. Pothier, *MG*, 31.

18. Ibid., 56.

19. Combe, *HRCG*, pl. 5 (app.).

20. Dom Lucien David, *Dom Joseph Pothier: Abbé de St-Wandrille et la restauration grégorienne* (pamphlet, Saint-Wandrille: Abbaye Saint-Wandrille, 1943).

21. Huysmans, *Oblate*, 209–211.

22. See Fernand Baudin, "Books in Belgium," in Day (ed.), *Book Typography*, 3–36.

23. Arthur Vermeersch describes the site: "The brothers chose a picturesque site on an estate of Henri Desclée in the province of Namur, for the erection of a monastery in which to establish the monks of Beuron. The monastery of Maredsous, constructed in the purest Gothic style of the thirteenth century after the plans of Baron Béthune, is one of the finest and most remarkable masterpieces produced in Belgium by the movement for the restoration of the architectural art of the Middle Ages" (Vermeersch, "Henri Desclée," in *The Catholic Encyclopedia* [New York: Appleton, 1911], 16:32–33). See also John Emerson, "Desclée," in *Music Printing and Publishing*, ed. D. W. Krummel and Stanley Sadie (New York: Norton, 1990), 214.

24. "Donc nous allons nous y mettre et donner du Saint Grégoire le plus pur possible" (David, *Dom Joseph Pothier*, 19; my emphasis).

25. This fact is confirmed in several sources, most directly in Mocquereau and Cagin, *PS*, 5. David's posthumous biography of Pothier also relates the same story.

26. For examples of the types, see Mary Kay Duggan, "The Music Type of the Second Dated Printed Music Book, the 1477 *Graduale Romanum*," *Bibliofilia* 89 (1987): 285–307; and idem, *Italian Music Incunabula: Printers and Type* (Berkeley: University of California Press, 1992).

27. Pothier wrote in a letter (to Dom David) in 1879: "Ce que me préoccupe sérieusement, c'est de mettre à jour le travail préliminaire sur les principes, qui doit servir d'introduction au Graduel et à l'Antiphonaire, et pour lequel les caractères grégoriens sont aussi nécessaires" (quoted in David, *Dom Joseph Pothier*, 22).

28. Theodore Low De Vinne, *The Practice of Typography* (New York: Century, 1901), 182.

29. René Rancour, ed., *Correspondance de J.-K. Huysmans et de Madame Cécile Bruyère, abbesse de Sainte-Cécile de Solesmes* (Paris: Editions du Cendre, 1950); Joris-Karl Huysmans, *The Road from Decadence: From Brothel to Cloister—Selected Letters of J.-K. Huysmans*, trans. Barbara Beaument (London: Athlone, 1989).

30. Combe, *HRCG*, 191.

31. Jean Olive, "Ecriture de plain-chant," *Revue de musique religieuse et du chant grégorien* 5 (April 1896): 90.

32. A. Dabin, "Comment, à Marseille, on écrit . . . Solesmes." *Revue du chant grégorien* 6, no. 12 (15 July 1898): 194–196.

33. David, *Dom Joseph Pothier*, 24.

34. Théodore Beaudoire, *Musique pour la liturgie notée* (Paris: Beaudoire, 1895).

35. Schmidt, "La Typographie et le plain-chant," *Revue du chant grégorien* 4, no. 4 (15 Novemember 1895): 59.

36. Ibid.

37. Stanley Morison, *First Principles of Typography* (Cambridge: Cambridge University Press, 1936), 12.

38. Morison and Day, *Typographic Book*, 4.

39. William Butler Yeats, "Literature and the Living Voice," *Contemporary Review* 90 (1906): 474; cited in Linda Dowling, *Language and Decadence in the Victorian Fin de Siècle* (Princeton: Princeton University Press, 1986), 279.

40. Louis Zukovsky, *An "Objectivists" Anthology* (New York: To Publishers, 1932); quoted in McGann, *Black Riders*, 83.

3. Gregorian Hands

1. Huysmans himself had been attracted to Saint-Wandrille in 1894 after having made the acquaintance of Dom Besse, a Benedictine who apparently had aspirations similar to those of Pothier. When Dom Besse ended up at the Spanish abbey of Santo Domingo di Silos, Huysmans changed his plans, deciding in 1896 to give Solesmes a try. The monks had some hopes of keeping him there, but the indecisive Huysmans, finding the surrounding village unsuited to his tastes, departed the following year. It was during this time that he made the acquaintaince of the abbess of Sainte-Cécile, who was to remain his confessor for the next several years. See Rancour (ed.), *Correspondance de Huysmans et Bruyère*, 13; Huysmans, *Road from Decadence*, 260.

2. Maeterlinck rented the abbey in 1907 and spent his summers there with Georgette until 1919; see Maeterlinck, *Les Trésors des humbles* (Paris: Société du Mercure de France, 1904).

3. Dom Pothier was installed as abbot on 24 July 1898.

4. D. L. Guilloreau, "La stamperia di S. Petro a Solesmes," *Rassegna gregoriana* 3–4 (1906): 121.

5. Combe, *HRCG*, 134.

6. Among these was the famous essay, attributed to Dom Mocquereau, entitled "De l'influence de l'accent tonique latin et du cursus," which formed the greater part of volume 3. Although the prefaces to all the volumes were, out of monastic modesty, left unsigned, the actual attributions are known through oral tradition, as revealed in Norbert Rousseau's history of the Solesmes restoration, *L'Ecole grégorienne de Solesmes* (Tournai: Desclée, 1910).

7. The notion of a "practical school" comes from a description of Mocquereau's working methods by Mocquereau's fellow monk Dom Paul Cagin; see *PS*, 19. Although the text lists no English translator, a likely candidate would be the Reverend William Maloney, the priest from Westminster Chapel who helped organize with Dom Mocquereau a "summer school" for English-speaking Gregorianists in 1904.

8. The letters in question, originally published in Florentius Romita, *Jus Musicae Liturgicae* (Rome: Edizioni Liturgiche 1947), are reproduced in Combe, *HRCG*, 112–113.

9. Dom André Mocquereau, letter to Dom Lhoumeau, quoted in Combe, *HRCG*, 127 (emphasis in original).

10. Mocquereau, "The Origin and Classification of Different Neumatic Notations," *PM*, 1:99.

11. Ibid. (my emphasis).

12. Quoted in Combe, *HRCG*, 124.

13. Michel Foucault, "Fantasia of the Library," in *Language, Counter-Memory, Practice*, trans. and ed. Donald F. Bouchard and Sherry Simon (Ithaca, N.Y.: Cornell University Press, 1977), 90.

14. Reprinted in Nisard's posthumous *Archéologie musicale*, ii–iii. Note that I have translated Nisard's editorial pronoun "nous" as "I" throughout.

15. E. T. A. Hoffman, "The Golden Pot," in *Tales of Hoffman*, trans. and ed. Christopher Lazare (New York: Grove, 1946), 185 (my emphasis). Friedrich Kittler offers a virtuosic reading of this story in *Discourse Networks 1800/1900*, trans. Michael Metteer (Stanford: Stanford University Press, 1990), 88–108.

16. Pierre Larousse, *Grand Dictionnaire universel du XIXe siècle* (Paris: Administration de Grand Dictionnaire Universel, 1865–1890), s.v. "fac-similé."

17. Mocquereau, "Introduction générale," *PM*, 1:7.

18. Among his compositions from that period we find a motet from 1848 based on a text about the Immaculate Conception. It was a timely topic, since six years later in 1854 Pope Pius IX elevated the long-standing oral tradition of the Immaculate Conception of the Virgin to the status of dogma.

19. Louis Lambillotte, *Antiphonaire de Saint Grégoire: Facsimilé du manuscript de Saint-Gall (VIIIe siècle)* (Paris: Poussielgue, 1851; repr. Brussels: Greuse, 1867).

20. Mocquereau, "Introduction générale," *PM*, 1:11.

21. Ibid., 17.

22. Ibid., 18.

23. Ibid., 3.

24. Delisle's published work includes a huge inventory of manuscripts and early imprints housed in the Bibliothèque nationale; facsimile reproductions, such as the *Album paléographique, ou Receuil de documents relatifs à l'histoire et à la littérature nationale, reproduits en héliogravure* (Paris: Quantin, 1887); and writings on paleography, such as *Mélanges de la paléographie et de bibliographie* (Paris: Champion, 1880).

25. For a discussion of calcage, see Elizabeth Pennell in her *Lithography and Lithographers* (New York: Macmillan, 1915), 285–293.

26. Mocquereau, "Introduction générale," *PM*, 1:4.

27. Lambillotte, *Antiphonaire*, 3.

28. Ibid., 32.

29. Dom Froger, "Notice," *PM*, ser. 2, vol. 2 (1924).

30. Delisle, *Album paléographique*, quoted in Mocquereau, "Introduction générale," *PM*, 1:5.

31. Mocquereau, "Introduction générale," *PM*, 1:4.

32. A phototype (or collotype) refers to a common process of gelatin printing developed in the second half of the nineteenth century.

33. Froger, "Notice," *PM*, ser. 2, vol. 2 (1924).

34. Viollet-le-Duc, quoted in Hearn (ed.), *Architectural Theory of Viollet-le-Duc*, 282.

35. Mocquereau, "Introduction générale," *PM*, 1:28 (my emphasis).

36. Viollet-le-Duc, quoted in Hearn (ed.), *Architectural Theory of Viollet-le-Duc*, 278.

37. On the truth value of the photograph and the importance of new techniques of reproduction in the nineteenth century, see Charles Rosen and Henri Zerner, *Romanticism and Realism: The Mythology of Nineteenth-Century Art* (New York: Viking, 1984).

38. Sigmund Freud, "The 'Uncanny,'" in *Studies in Parapsychology*, ed. Philip Rieff (New York: Macmillan, 1967), 28 (my emphasis).

39. Georges Didi-Huberman, "Index of the Absent Wound (Monograph on a Stain)," trans. Thomas Repensek, in *October: The First Decade, 1976–1986*, ed. Annette Michelson et al. (Cambridge, Mass.: MIT Press, 1987), 41.

40. Ibid., 43–44.

41. Roland Barthes, *Camera Lucida: Reflections on Photography*, trans. Richard Howard (New York: Hill & Wang, 1981), 55.

42. Mocquereau, "Notation oratoire ou chironomique," *PM*, 1:109.

43. Ibid.

44. Mocquereau, "Introduction générale," *PM*, 1:24–25.

45. Walter Benjamin, "The Task of the Translator," in *Illuminations*, 76.

46. Ibid., 70.

47. Mocquereau, "Notation oratoire ou chironomique," *PM*, 1:108.

48. Mocquereau, "Introduction générale," *PM*, 1:47.

49. Benjamin, "Task of the Translator," 74.

50. Mocquereau, *PM*, 1:160 (my emphasis).

51. Benjamin, "Task of the Translator," 81.

52. Ibid., 76.

53. *A Sa Sainteté Léon XIII. Mémoire sur les études des Bénédictins de Solesmes concernant la restauration des mélodies liturgiques de l'église romaine* (Solesmes: Imprimerie de Saint-Pierre, 1901), 8. Combe reports that although the memo was signed by Dom Delatte, it was written by Mocquereau.

54. Mocquereau, "Introduction générale," *PM*, 1:17.

55. Jules Combarieu, *Etudes de philologie musicale* (Paris: Picard, 1897), 1:178.

56. Cagin, in *PS*, 25.

57. Mocquereau, "La Pensée pontificale et la restauration grégorienne," *Revue grégorienne* 6, no. 1 (1921): 9.

58. Susan Sontag, *On Photography* (New York: Farrar, Straus, Giroux, 1977), 358.

59. Mocquereau, "Introduction générale," *PM*, 1:6.

60. Alexander García Düttman, "On Translatability," *qui parle* 8, no. 1 (1994): 30 (my emphasis). See also "Roundtable on Translation," trans. Peggy Kamuf, in Jacques Derrida, *The Ear of the Other: Otobiography, Transference, Translation*, ed. Christie V. McDonald (New York: Schocken, 1985), 91–162.

61. Combe, *HRCG*, 130.

62. Mocquereau, *Examen des critiques dirigées par Dom Jeannin contre l'école de Solesmes* (Tournai: Desclée, 1926); quoted in ibid., 130n.10.

4. Writing, Reading, Singing

1. The etymology and history of the word are given in *Trésor de la langue française*, 16 vols. (Paris: Centre Nationale de la Recherche Scientifique, 1971–1994), s.v. "musicologie."

2. Pierre Aubry, *La Musicologie médiévale: Histoire et méthodes* (Paris: Welter, 1900), 87.

3. Ibid., 110.

4. Advertisement published in *Revue musicale* 1, no. 1 (January 1901).

5. On the subject of musicology as a discipline and its relation to musical performance, see my prologue to *Disciplining Music: Musicology and Its Canons*, ed. Katherine Bergeron and Philip Bohlman (Chicago: University of Chicago Press, 1992).

6. Jules Combarieu, "L'Archéologie au XIXe siècle et le problème de l'origine des neumes," in *Etudes de philologie musicale*, 115–192.

7. Mocquereau, *PM*, 1:32–33. Mocquereau is quoting from Edmond Egger's *Notions élémentaires de grammaire comparée* (Paris: Durand & Pedone-Lauriel, 1875), x. A good deal of Mocquereau's argument appears once again in Dom Delatte's *Mémoire sur les études des Bénédictines de Solesmes*.

8. Ernest Renan, "Les Sciences de la nature et les sciences historiques," *Revue des deux mondes* 47, no. 2 (15 October 1863): 761–774.

9. Adolphe Pictet, *Les Origines indo-européennes; ou, les Aryas primitifs: Essai de paléontologie linguistique* (Paris: Sandoz & Fischbacher, 1877); cited in Maurice Olender, *The Languages of Paradise: Race, Religion, and Philology in the Nineteenth Century*, trans. Arthur Goldhammer (Cambridge, Mass.: Harvard University Press, 1992), 98.

10. Friedrich Max Müller, *Lectures on the Science of Language, Delivered at the Royal Institution of Great Britain in April, May, and June 1861* (New York: Scribners, 1862); discussed in Dowling, *Language and Decadence*, 61–77.

11. Jules Combarieu, "Notre Programme," *Revue musicale* 1, no. 1 (January 1901): 2.

12. Combarieu, "Archéologie au XIXe siècle," 179; quoted in *PS*, 22n.

13. Jerome McGann, *The Textual Condition* (Princeton: Princeton University Press, 1991); and Richard Crocker, "Notes on Text Criticism for Medieval Scholarship" (photocopy, 1993). See also Crocker, "Gregorian Studies in the Twenty-first Century," *Plainsong and Medieval Music* 4 (1995): 48.

14. As Philip Brett has noted, "[This] method of restoring a text from multiple sources...is still associated with the name of Karl Lachmann (1793–1851), whose edition

of the New Testament (1831) overcame the almost divine sanction of the then received text" (Brett, "Text, Context, and the Early Music Editor," in *Authenticity and Early Music,* ed. Nicholas Kenyon [Oxford: Oxford University Press, 1988], 87). For further discussion of the history and practice, see Paul Maas, *Textual Criticism,* trans. Barbara Flower (Oxford: Clarendon, 1958); and Jacques Froger, *La Critique des textes et son automatisation* (Paris: Dunod, 1958).

15. Dom André Mocquereau, "L'Ecole grégorienne de Solesmes," *Rassegna gregoriana* 3, no. 4 (April 1904): cols. 237–238; English translation in *PS,* 30–31.

16. Ibid., cols. 316–317; English translation in *PS,* 42.

17. Friedrich Nietzsche, *The Case of Wagner,* trans. Walter Kaufman (New York: Vintage, 1967), 170.

18. Karl Marx, "Manifesto of the Communist Party," in *The Marx-Engels Reader,* ed. Robert Tucker (New York: Norton, 1978), 476; cited by Marshall Berman in *All That Is Solid Melts into Air: The Experience of Modernity* (New York: Penguin, 1988), 21.

19. Mocquereau, "Notation oratoire ou chironomique," *PM,* 1:110.

20. Pothier, *MG,* 8.

21. Kittler, *Discourse Networks,* 32 (emphasis in original).

22. Ibid., 222.

23. Julius Zeitler, "Tachistoskopische Untersuchungen über das Lesen," *Philosophische Studien* 16 (1900): 403; cited in Kittler, *Discourse Networks,* 222n.84.

24. Dom Claire intimates that Mocquereau's confusion nearly cost him his religious vocation; see "Dom Mocquereau, cinquante ans après sa mort," *Etudes grégoriennes* 19 (1980): 3.

25. Eugen Weber, *France: Fin de Siècle* (Cambridge, Mass.: Harvard University Press, 1986), 10.

26. Pothier, *MG,* 12.

27. Werner Pfister, ed., *Briefwechsel Goethe Zelter* (Munich: Artemis, 1987), 72.

28. Pothier, *MG,* 32.

29. Leo Treitler, "The Early History of Music Writing in the West," *Journal of the American Musicological Society* 35 (1982): 237–279. In a footnote to his translation of Schubinger's *Die Sängerschule St. Gallen* (1858), Nisard claimed that it was he who first made the observation in 1849—that is, before Coussemaker—although Mocquereau points out in a footnote to this footnote (*PM,* 1:102n.1) that examination of Nisard's oeuvre turns up no such evidence.

30. Leo Treitler, "Reading and Singing: On the Genesis of Occidental Music-Writing," *Early Music History* 4 (1984): 181.

31. Treitler does represent an aspect of this paradox in a sentence whose convoluted syntax mirrors the inherent confusion of the *accentus* idea: "As accent could refer to both an inflection and the sign for it . . . the concept and phenomenon of accent evidently do swim in the murky waters from which we have to fish out the components of whatever understanding we are ever going to have about the very beginnings of music writing" ("Early History of Music Writing in the West," 268).

32. Michel Foucault, *The Order of Things* (New York: Vintage, 1970), 286.

33. Pothier, *MG,* 12.

34. Ibid., 163.

35. According to Mocquereau, the theory of the arsis and thesis was adumbrated in Pothier's primer *Principes pour la bonne execution* (Solesmes, 1891) and later expanded in essays published in *Revue du chant grégorien* between 1895 and 1900.

36. Pothier, *MG*, 177.

37. Ibid.

38. Ibid., 178 (my emphasis).

39. Ibid., 179.

40. Pothier includes the passage in the body of his own text: "Aures enim vel animus aurium nuncio naturalem quemdam in se continent omniem mensionem. Itaque et longiora et breviora judicat."

41. Louis Becq de Fouquières, *Traité générale de versification française* (Paris: Charpentier, 1879), 7.

42. Larousse, *Grand dictionnaire universel du XIXe siècle*, s.v. "oreille."

43. Pothier, *MG*, 191 (my emphasis).

44. Mocquereau, *NMG*, 1:8.

45. Robert MacDougall, "The Structure of Simple Rhythmic Forms," *Harvard Psychological Studies* 1 (January 1903): 330; quoted by Mocquereau in *NMG*, 1:9n.1.

46. The "disinterested character" of aesthetic feelings, he continues, "makes them more satisfactory for experimental study than other feelings" (Hugo Munsterberg, "Preface," *Harvard Psychological Studies* 1 [January 1903]: iv).

47. Mocquereau, *NMG*, 1:20.

48. Ibid., 33.

49. Charles E. Bennett, "The Ictus in Latin Prosody," *American Journal of Philology* 19, no. 4 (1898): 363; quoted in Mocquereau, *NMG*, 1:22n.1.

50. Mocquereau, *NMG*, 1:45.

51. In his first comprehensive essay on Gregorian rhythm, Mocquereau praised Pothier for this theoretical insight: "However apparently small, it was a big step. The rhythmic principle of arsis and thesis, long practiced, took its place in theory" (Mocquereau, "L'Accent tonique latin dans l'enseignement de Solesmes," *PM*, 7:137).

52. "Le Beau est léger, dit Nietzsche; tout ce qui est divin marche sur des pieds délicats" (Mocquereau, *NMG*, 1:100). The passage, which Nietzsche called "the first principle of his aesthetics," appears at the beginning of the first section of *The Case of Wagner*. Mocquereau, however, seems to have learned it not from Nietzsche but from an essay by Combarieu published in the *Revue musicale* in 1902, which pulled the line completely out of context.

53. Mocquereau, *NMG*, 1:100.

54. Ibid., 2:669.

55. Mocquereau credits Dom Ambroise Kienle with the historical justification for this term, in an 1885 article from the *Vierteljahrsschrift für Musikwissenschaft;* see *NMG*, 1:103.

56. Mocquereau, *NMG*, 2:670.

57. Ibid., 1:44n.1.

58. First printed in *PM*, vol. 7 (1901).

59. See Michel Leiris, "Persephone," in *Scratches*, vol. 1 of *Rules of the Game*, trans. Lydia Davis (New York: Paragon, 1991), 75.

60. Mocquereau, *NMG*, 1:182–183.

61. Emile Jaques-Dalcroze, "Foreword," in *Rhythm, Music Education*, trans. Harold Rubenstein (New York: Putnam, 1921), vi.

62. Ibid., 79 (emphasis in original).

63. "Music and the Dancer," in ibid., 292.

64. Mocquereau, *NMG*, 1:101; also 2:671 (emphasis in original).

65. Justine Ward, *Gregorian Chant According to the Principles of Dom André Mocquereau* (Washington, D.C.: Catholic Education Press, 1923). See also Pierre Combe, *Justine Ward and Solesmes* (Washington, D.C.: Catholic University Press, 1987).

66. Emile Gautier, *Le Phonographe: Son Passé, son présent, son avenir* (Paris: Flammarion, 1905), 28; quoted in translation in Thomas Y. Levin, "For the Record: Adorno on Music in the Age of Its Technological Reproducibility," *October* 55 (winter 1990): 37–38. An essay by Adorno from 1934, also translated by Levin, makes a strikingly similar point. In "The Form of the Phonograph Record" (*October* 55 [winter 1990]: 56–61), Adorno describes the "delicately scribbled, utterly illegible writing" that covered the record as a form of writing: "through the curves of the needle on the phonograph record, music approaches its true character as writing."

67. Mocquereau, *NMG*, 1:14.

68. Ibid., 15 (emphasis in original).

69. Dalcroze, "Foreword," ix–x.

70. "Preface," *Chants des offices extraits du Paroissien noté de Solesmes et du Variae Preces* (Solesmes: Imprimerie Saint-Pierre, 1900), 10.

71. Cited in Anthony Rhodes, *The Power of Rome in the Twentieth Century* (New York: Franklin Watts, 1983), 202.

72. *L'Abbaye Saint-Pierre de Solesmes*, 29.

73. Dom Pierre Combe tells the complete story that led to the sale of the press, including the secret deal Pothier made with the Parisian publisher Poussielgue in 1901, in an attempt to wrest control of the books from the Solesmes monks before the communities were exiled. By turning things over to Desclée the Solesmes monks effectively absolved themsleves of further negotiations with Poussielgue. The story, which Combe reports cryptically, reveals the extent of the strain that existed between the master and his former disciple. See Combe, *HRCG*, 230–233.

74. Mocquereau, *NMG*, 1:12.

75. Quoted in A. Grospellier,"Les Fêtes et le congrès du centenaire grégorien," *Revue du chant grégorien* 12, no. 9 (15 April 1904): 156–157.

76. William Shaman, "The Vatican G & T's," in *Record Collector* 28, nos. 7–8 (1983): 147–191. My gratitude to David Hamilton for sending me a copy of this article.

77. Advertisement printed inside the back cover of *PS*.

78. Dan Leno, a popular singer, and Dame Nellie Melba and Charles Santley, operatic virtuosi, were among the Gramophone Company's most popular artists at the beginning of the twentieth century. After special concessions to the diva, Gramophone released a special "Melba" series in 1904, which sported attractive mauve labels and sold for one

guinea each, making them the most expensive Gramophone recordings on the market. Santley was a veteran baritone, with a history of performances dating back to 1857, who made recordings at Gramophone's London Studio in 1903 at the age of sixty-nine. See further Roland Gelatt, *The Fabulous Phonograph: From Tin Foil to High Fidelity* (Philadelphia: Lippincott, 1955), 118, 120; and Jerrold N. Moore, *A Voice in Time: The Gramophone of Fred Gaisberg* (London: Hamilton Hamish, 1976), 87–89.

79. Quoted in Gelatt, *Fabulous Phonograph*, 29.

80. Kittler, *Discourse Networks*, 232.

81. The lecture was titlted "Il grammophono applicato alla divulgazione ed alla tradizione del canto gregoriano"; text transcribed and translated by Mary Berry in notes to the sound recording *The Gregorian Congress of 1904*, Discant DIS 1–2. Shaman ("Vatican G & T's," 158) notes that the baron had also served under de Santi as advisor to the Pontifica Scuola Superiore and before long would be involved, with Enrico Guazzioni, in producing silent film.

82. Notes to *Gregorian Congress of 1904*.

83. A view of the startling consistency among postwar chant performances recorded by different choirmasters can be observed in the *rhythmographes* created some years later by Jean Jeanneteau. See the memorial essay by Dom Jean Claire, "Le Chanoine Jean Jeanneteau (1908–1992)," *Etudes grégoriennes* 24 (1992): 5–40.

84. See my article, "The Virtual Sacred," *New Republic*, 27 February 1995, 29–34.

85. Prou's approbation is also included in the notes to *Gregorian Congress of 1904* (my article).

86. Philippe Lacoue-Labarthe, *Typography: Mimesis, Philosophy, Politics*, ed. Christopher Fynsk (Cambridge, Mass.: Harvard University Press, 1989), 202.

87. Texts of the speeches recorded at the congress are transcribed by Mary Berry in notes to *Gregorian Congress of 1904*. The complete text of Pothier's address was published as "Le Chant grégorien est un art," *Rassegna gregoriana* 3, nos. 5–6 (May–June 1904): cols. 325ff.

88. Complete text of the address appears in Mocquereau, "Ecole grégorienne de Solesmes," cols. 234ff.

Postlude

1. By decree of 24 February 1904; see Alexandre Grospellier, "Les Livres de chant grégorien de Solesmes," *Revue du chant grégorien* 12, no. 8 (15 March 1904): 78–80.

2. Combe, *HRCG*, 296, says the document was back-dated to accommodate the Feast of Saint Mark; it was actually signed on 27 April.

3. Catholic Church, Pope, *Inter Pastoralis Officii*, in *Acta Sanctae Sedis* 36 (1904): 586–588. All subsequent passages are quoted from this source. I have also consulted the French translation of the decree published in *Revue du chant grégorien* 12, no. 9 (15 April 1904): 145–147.

4. The exception turned out to be a bit too much for the syntax to bear. In laying out the conditions under which the Vatican would approve the published editions, article (d) of the text stressed the necessity for strict conformity with the Typical Edition, unless

the nonconformity claimed "the authority of other good Gregorian codices." But note how the clause gives way under the weight of this added contingency, causing it to become ungrammatical and, indeed, to appear to say the opposite of what it intends: "The approval to be given by Us and by Our Sacred Congregation to the books of chant thus compiled and published will be of such a nature that no one will be permitted to approve liturgical books that, even in the parts that contain the chant, either do not absolutely conform to the editions published by the Vatican Press through Our auspices, or, at least, in the judgment of the Commission, they do not conform with it knowingly in such a way that the variants introduced can be demonstrated to come from the authority of other good Gregorian codices." In the attempt to provide for all possible conditions, making the law foolproof, this performative text simply breaks down, creating a condition in which it becomes impossible for the statement to "perform" at all. For an analysis of the conditions of performative language, see J. L. Austin's seminal discussion in *How to Do Things with Words* (Oxford: Clarendon, 1975).

    5. Quoted in Combe, *HRCG,* 363.

    6. *Rassegna gregoriana* 3, no. 4 (April 1904): col. 243; English translation in *PS,* 35.

    7. *PS,* 35n.

    8. Letter quoted in Combe, *HRCG,* 364–365.

    9. Ibid., 408 (emphasis mine).

    10. The letter was dated 24 June 1905. Combe states that this letter was supposed to have been secret, according to the terms of the *Motu proprio*'s "secrecy" clause, but it was almost immediately leaked to all the religious presses; see *HRCG,* 409–410. All subsequent passages are drawn from this translation.

    11. Cooperate they did. Before long a secret police would be formed at the Vatican to finger would-be offenders, and an index established for the banning of books. See M. Pernot, *La Politique de Pie X, 1906–1910* (Paris: F. Alcan, 1910).

    12. Yves Congar, *Tradition and Traditions,* trans. Michael Naseby and Thomas Rainborough (New York: Macmillan, 1967), 189.

    13. Peter Wagner, *Der Kampf gegen die Editio Vaticana* (pamphlet, Graz: Styria, 1907); published in English as "The Attack on the Vatican Edition: A Rejoinder," *Caecilia* 87 (1960): 19 (emphasis mine).

    14. Ibid., 43 (emphasis in original).

    15. Ibid., 43–44.

    16. Among the most important essays that have shaped the now twenty-year-old debate are Leo Treitler, "Homer and Gregory: The Epic Tradition and Plainchant," *Musical Quarterly* 15 (1974): 333–372; idem, "Centonate Chant: Übles Flickwerk or E pluribus unus?" *Journal of the American Musicological Society* 28 (1975): 1–23; idem, "Oral, Written, and Literate Process in the Transmission of Medieval Music," *Speculum* 56 (1981): 471–491; idem, "Reading and Singing"; Helmut Hucke, "Towards a New Historical View of Gregorian Chant," *Journal of the American Musicological Society* 33 (1980): 437–467; Kenneth Levy, "Charlemagne's Archetype of Gregorian Chant," *Journal of the American Musicological Society* 40 (1987): 1–30; and Peter Jeffrey, *Re-envisioning Past Musical Cultures: Ethnomusicology in the Study of Gregorian Chant* (Chicago: University of Chicago Press, 1992). See also Treitler's review of Jeffrey in *Journal of the American Musicological Society* 47 (1994):

137–171. For a discussion of the orality question in the larger context of twentieth-century Gregorian chant scholarship, see Crocker, "Gregorian Studies in the Twenty-first Century."

17. Robert Francis Hayburn, *Papal Legislation and Sacred Music* (Collegeville, Minn.: Liturgical Press, 1979), 291.

18. Ibid., 292.

19. Quoted by John Emerson in *The New Grove Dictionary of Music and Musicians*, ed. Stanley Sadie (New York: Macmillan, 1980), s.v. "Western plainchant, twentieth-century."

20. Letter from Pothier to Charles Widor (January 1906), published in the *Catholic Choirmaster* 35 (June 1914): 94; quoted in Hayburn, *Papal Legislation and Sacred Music*, 293–295.

21. Letter from Dom David to Caspar Koch of Pittsburgh, Penn. (October 1906); quoted in Hayburn, *Papal Legislation and Sacred Music*, 279.

22. Hayburn, *Papal Legislation and Sacred Music*, 295.

23. Ibid.

24. English translation in *The White List* (New York: Society of Saint Gregory of America, 1947), 23 (emphasis mine).

Brief Glossary of Gregorian Chant Terms

cephalicus — One of the so-called liquescent neumes. In the later manuscripts the signs looked like a modified *clivis*, the lower square having shrunk into a small "head" that hangs below the higher square.

clivis — A "sloped" two-note descent, the notation of which is read from left to right.

episema — In the editions prepared by Mocquereau's Solesmes school, a short vertical stroke attached to certain neumes or portions of neumes as a means of representing the *ictus*. In ninth- and tenth-century manuscripts the sign appeared as a horizontal stroke attached to the cursive neumes, presumably to indicate nuances of performance.

ictus — A Latin word meaning "blow" or "stroke." In the rhythmic theory of Dom Mocquereau this term designates the elusive downbeat of Gregorian chironomy, not so much a "blow" as a brief *touchement* in the continuously moving musical phrase, marked by the conductor with a subtle movement of the hand.

neume — A melodic figure consisting of one or more notes within a Gregorian melody. This voiced element, or *vox*, produced by the movement of the breath (*pneuma*), was represented in writing by a notational figure—a *nota neumarum*—designed to convey such movement; hence, the shortened form, neume.

pes, podatus — A two-note ascending figure or "foot," whose notational sign of two superimposed squares is read from bottom to top.

porrectus — A three-note figure, moving down and then up again, whose initial descent is rendered in notation with an oblique stroke "stretched" diagonally across the staff.

punctum(pl. puncta) — A single note represented by the simplest of diacritical marks: a "point." In ninth- and tenth-century manuscripts this mark was rendered as a dot; in later manuscripts it took the form of a square.

punctum morae — A dot designating a *mora vocis,* or lengthening of a certain note. The sign appeared for the first time in 1896 in modern chant books prepared at Solesmes under the direction of Dom Mocquereau.

quilisma — An ornamented neume rendered in earlier cursive notation by three loops, in later notation by a jagged, oblique square, suggestive of trilling or a shaking of the voice.

scandicus — A three-note "climbing" figure represented as a compound neume joining a *pes* with a *punctum* or *virga.*

torculus — A "little turn" figure consisting of three notes, rising then falling.

virga — A mark for a single note that, in early chant manuscripts, appeared as a slanted vertical stroke, or "rod"; in later manuscripts it was rendered as a *punctum* with a vertical tail.

Bibliography

L'Abbaye Saint-Pierre de Solesmes. Sablé-sur-Sarthe: Abbaye Saint-Pierre, 1978.

Adorno, Theodor. "The Form of the Phonograph Record." Translated by Thomas Y. Levin. *October* 55 (winter 1990): 56–61.

Agulhon, Maurice. *The French Republic, 1879–1992*. Translated by Antonia Nevill. Oxford: Basil Blackwell, 1993.

Almendra, Julia d'. *Les Modes grégoriens dans l'oeuvre de Claude Debussy*. Paris: G. Enault, 1950.

The Art of the Printed Book, 1455–1955. Boston: Godine, 1973.

Ashbourne, William Gibson. *The Abbé de Lamennais and the Liberal Catholic Movement in France*. London: Longmans, Green, 1896.

Aubry, Pierre. *La Musicologie médiévale: Histoire et méthodes*. Paris: Welter, 1900.

Austin, J. L. *How to Do Things with Words*. Oxford: Clarendon, 1975.

Barthes, Roland. *Camera Lucida*. Translated by Richard Howard. New York: Hill & Wang, 1981.

——— . *The Responsibility of Forms*. Translated by Richard Howard. New York: Hill & Wang, 1985.

Baudin, Fernand. "Books in Belgium." In *Book Typography, 1815–1965, in Europe and the United States of America*, edited by Kenneth Day, 3–36. London: Ernest Benn, 1966.

Beaudoire, Théodore. *Musique pour la liturgie notée*. Paris: Beaudoire, 1895.

Becq de Fouquières, Louis. *Traité générale de versification française*. Paris: Charpentier, 1879.

Bellaigue, Camille. "A l'abbaye de Solesmes." *Revue des deux mondes* 150, no. 2 (15 November 1898): 342–376.

Benjamin, Walter. "A Small History of Photography" (1931). Translated by Edmund Jephcott and Kingsley Shorter. In Walter Benjamin, *One Way Street and Other Writings*, 241–257. London: New Left Books, 1979.

——— . "The Task of the Translator." In Walter Benjamin, *Illuminations*, edited by Hannah Arendt, translated by Harry Zohn, 69–82. New York: Harcourt, Brace, 1968.

——— . "The Work of Art in the Age of Mechanical Reproduction." In Walter Benjamin, *Illuminations*, edited by Hannah Arendt, translated by Harry Zohn, 219–253. New York: Harcourt, Brace, 1968.

Bennett, Charles E. "The Ictus in Latin Prosody." *American Journal of Philology* 19, no. 4 (1898): 361–383.

Benveniste, Emile. "The Notion of Rhythm in Its Linguistic Expression." Translated by Mary Meek. In *Problems in General Linguistics*, 281–288. Coral Gables: University of Florida Press, 1977.

Bergeron, Katherine. "Representation, Reproduction, and the Revival of Gregorian Chant at Solesmes." Ph.D. diss., Cornell University, 1989.

———. "The Virtual Sacred." *New Republic*, 27 February 1995, 29–34.

Bergeron, Katherine, and Philip Bohlman, eds. *Disciplining Music: Musicology and Its Canons*. Chicago: University of Chicago Press, 1992.

Berman, Marshall. *All That Is Solid Melts into Air: The Experience of Modernity*. New York: Penguin, 1988.

Berry, Mary. "The Restoration of Chant and Seventy-five Years of Recording." *Early Music* 7 (1979): 197–217.

Bibliographie des Bénédictins de la Congrégation de France. Paris: Honoré Champion, 1906.

Brett, Philip. "Text, Context, and the Early Music Editor." In *Authenticity and Early Music*, edited by Nicholas Kenyon, 83–114. Oxford: Oxford University Press, 1988.

Burt, Sir Cyril. *A Psychological Study of Typography*. Cambridge: Cambridge University Press, 1959.

Cagin, Paul. "L'Oeuvre de Solesmes dans la restauration du chant grégorien." *Rassegna gregoriana* 3 (April 1904): 205–226.

Cardine, Eugène. "Solesmes." In *The New Grove Dictionary of Music and Musicians*, edited by Stanley Sadie, 17:452–454. New York: Macmillan, 1980.

Carlier, Achille. *Les Anciens Monuments dans la civilisation moderne*. Paris: n.p., 1945.

Cartier, Etienne. *Les Moines de Solesmes: Expulsions du 6 novembre 1880 et du 22 mars 1882*. Le Mans: Monnoyer, 1882.

Catholic Church. Pope. *Inter Pastoralis Officii*. In *Acta Sanctae Sedis* 36 (1904): 584–588.

"Ce que c'est que le 'Motu proprio.'" *Tribune de St. Gervais* 10 (1904): 15–26.

Chants des offices extraits du Paroissen noté de Solesmes et du Variae Preces. Solesmes: Imprimerie de Saint-Pierre, 1900.

Chastel, André. "La Notion du patrimoine." In *Les Lieux de mémoire*, vol. 2, no. 2: *La Nation*, edited by Pierre Nora, 405–450. Paris: Gallimard, 1986.

Chateaubriand, François Réné. *Génie du christianisme*. Paris: Mignaret, 1802. Reprint edited by Pierre Reboul. Paris: Garnier-Flammarion, 1966.

———. *The Genius of Christianity, or the Spirit and Beauty of the Christian Religion*. Translated by Charles I. White. Philadelphia: Lippincott, 1856.

Claire, Jean. "Le Chanoine Jean Jeanneteau (1908–1992)." *Etudes grégoriennes* 24 (1992): 5–40.

———. "Dom Mocquereau, cinquante ans après sa mort." *Etudes grégoriennes* 19 (1980): 3–23

Combarieu, Jules. *Etudes de philologie musicale*. Vol. 1. Paris: Picard, 1897.

———. "Notre Programme." *Revue musicale* 1, no. 1 (January 1901): 1–4.

Combe, Pierre. *Histoire de la restauration du chant grégorien d'après des documents inédits.* Solesmes: Abbaye de Solesmes, 1969.

———. *Justine Ward and Solesmes.* Washington, D.C.: Catholic University Press, 1987.

Congar, Yves. *Tradition and Traditions.* Translated by Michael Naseby and Thomas Rainborough. New York: Macmillan, 1967.

Coussemaker, Edmond de. *Scriptorum de Musica Medii Aevi.* 4 vols. Paris: A. Durand, 1864–1876.

Crocker, Richard. "Gregorian Studies in the Twenty-first Century." *Plainsong and Medieval Music* 4 (1995): 33–86.

———. "Notes on Text Criticism for Medieval Scholarship." Photocopy, 1993.

Dabin, A. "Comment, à Marseille, on écrit . . . Solesmes." *Revue du chant grégorien* 6, no. 12 (15 July 1898): 194–196.

Danjou, Jean Louis. *De l'état et de l'avenir du chant ecclésiastique en France.* Paris: P. Desbarres, 1844.

David, Lucien. *Dom Joseph Pothier: Abbé de St-Wandrille et la restauration grégorienne.* Pamphlet. Saint-Wandrille: Abbaye Saint-Wandrille, 1943.

Day, Kenneth, ed. *Book Typography, 1815–1965, in Europe and the United States of America.* London: Ernest Benn, 1966.

[Delatte, Paul]. *A Sa Sainteté Léon XIII. Mémoire sur les études des Bénédictins de Solesmes concernant la restauration des mélodies liturgiques de l'église romaine.* Solesmes: Imprimerie de Saint-Pierre, 1901.

Delisle, Léopold. *Album paléographique, ou Recueil de documents relatifs à l'histoire et à la littérature nationale, reproduits en héliogravure.* Paris: Quantin, 1887.

———. *Mélanges de la paléographie et de bibliographie.* Paris: Champion, 1880.

Derrida, Jacques. *The Ear of the Other: Otobiography, Transference, Translation.* Edited by Christie V. McDonald. New York: Schocken, 1985.

De Santi, Angelo. "Liturgical chant." In *The Catholic Encyclopedia*, 9:304–6. New York: Appleton, 1910.

De Vinne, Theodore Low. *The Practice of Typography.* New York: Century, 1901.

Didi-Huberman, Georges. "Index of the Absent Wound (Monograph on a Stain)." Translated by Thomas Repensek. In *October: The First Decade, 1976–1986*, edited by Annette Michelson et al., 39–57. Cambridge, Mass.: MIT Press, 1987.

Dowling, Linda. *Language and Decadence in the Victorian Fin de Siècle.* Princeton: Princeton University Press, 1986.

Dreyfus, John. *Morris and the Printed Book.* London: William Morris Society, 1989.

Duggan, Mary Kay. *Italian Music Incunabula: Printers and Type.* Berkeley: University of California Press, 1992.

———. "The Music Type of the Second Dated Printed Music Book, the 1477 *Graduale Romanum*." *Bibliofilia* 89 (1987): 285–307.

Düttman, Alexander García. "On Translatability." *qui parle* 8, no. 1 (1994): 29–44.

Egger, Edmond. *Notions élémentaires de grammaire comparée.* Paris: Durand & Pedone-Lauriel, 1875.

Eisenberg, Evan. *The Recording Angel: Explorations in Phonography*. New York: MacGraw-Hill, 1987.

Emerson, John. "Desclée." In *Music Printing and Publishing*, edited by D. W. Krummel and Stanley Sadie, 214. New York: Norton, 1990.

———. "Western Plainchant: Nineteenth-Century Restoration Attempts." In *The New Grove Dictionary of Music and Musicians*, edited by Stanley Sadie, 14:827–830. New York: Macmillan, 1980.

Fellerer, Carl Gustav. *The History of Catholic Church Music*. Translated by Francis A. Brunner. Baltimore: Helicon Press, 1961.

Fennewald, Joseph, ed. *William Morris and the Kelmscott Press*. Catalog of exhibition, University Art Gallery, University of Scranton. Scranton, PA: University of Scranton Press, 1994.

Fermigier, André. "Mérimée et l'inspection des monuments historiques." In *Les Lieux de mémoire*, vol. 2, no. 2: *La Nation*, edited by Pierre Nora, 593–611. Paris: Gallimard, 1986.

Fétis, François. "Normand, Théodule" [Théodore Nisard]. In *Biographie universelle des musiciens*, 6:329–332. Paris: Firmin-Didot, 1870.

Foucart, Bruno. "La Restauration des ruines architecturales." *Connaissance des arts*, no. 478 (December 1991): 98–105.

———. "Viollet-le-Duc et la restauration." In *Les Lieux de mémoire*, vol. 2, no. 2: *La Nation*, edited by Pierre Nora, 613–649. Paris: Gallimard, 1986.

Foucault, Michel. *Discipline and Punish: The Birth of the Prison*. Translated by Alan Sheridan. New York: Penguin, 1977.

———. "Fantasia of the Library." In *Language, Counter-Memory, Practice*, edited and translated by Donald F. Bouchard and Sherry Simon, 87–109. Ithaca, N.Y.: Cornell University Press, 1977.

———. *The Order of Things*. New York: Vintage, 1970.

Franklin, Colin. *Printing and the Mind of Morris: Three Paths to the Kelmscott Press*. Cambridge: Rampant Lions Press, 1986.

Franklin, R. W. *Nineteenth-Century Churches: The History of a New Catholicism in Württemburg, England, and France*. New York: Garland, 1987.

Freud, Sigmund. "The 'Uncanny.'" In *Studies in Parapsychology*, edited by Philip Rieff, 19–60. New York: Macmillan, 1967.

Froger, Jacques. *La Critique des textes et son automatisation*. Paris: Dunod, 1958.

Furet, François, and Jacques Ozouf. *Reading and Writing: Literacy in France from Calvin to Jules Ferry*. Cambridge: Cambridge University Press, 1982.

Gaskell, Philip. *A New Introduction to Bibliography*. Oxford: Oxford University Press, 1972.

Gastoué, Amadée. *La Musique d'église*. Lyon: Janin, 1916.

Gatard, Augustin. *La Musique grégorienne*. Paris: Laurens, 1913.

Gautier, Émile. *Le Phonographe: Son Passé, son présent, son avenir*. Paris: Flammarion, 1905.

Gelatt, Roland. *The Fabulous Phonograph: From Tin Foil to High Fidelity*. Philadelphia: Lippincott, 1955.

Germann, Georg. *Gothic Revival in Europe and Britain: Sources, Influences, and Ideas*. Translated by Gerald Onn. Cambridge, Mass.: MIT Press, 1972.

Glaister, Geoffrey A., ed. *An Encyclopedia of the Book.* Cleveland and New York: World, 1960.

Goldberg, Vicki, ed. *Photography in Print: Writings from 1816 to the Present.* New York: Simon & Schuster, 1981.

Goldstein, Laurence. *Ruins and Empire: The Evolution of a Theme in Augustan and Romantic Literature.* Pittsburgh: University of Pittsburgh Press, 1977.

Gontier, Augustin-Mathurin. *Méthode raisonnée de plain-chant.* Le Mans: Monnoyer, 1859.

———. *Metodo ragionato di canto piano.* Edited and translated by Nino Albarosa. Quaderni di "Studi Gregoriani," vol. 2. Rome: Torre d'Orfeo, 1993.

———. *Le Plain-chant: Son Exécution.* Pamphlet. Le Mans: Monnoyer, 1860.

Goudy, Frederic W. *Typologia: Studies in Type Design and Type Making.* Berkeley: University of California Press, 1940.

The Gregorian Congress of 1904. Discant DIS 1–2. (Sound recording.)

Grospellier, Alexandre. "Les Fêtes et le congrès du centenaire grégorien." *Revue du chant grégorien* 12, no. 9 (April 1904): 148–161.

———. "Les Livres de chant grégorien de Solesmes." *Revue du chant grégorien* 12, no. 8 (March 1904): 78–80.

Guéranger, Prosper. *Institutions liturgiques.* Vol. 1. Paris: Débécourt, 1840.

Guilloreau, D. L. "La stamperia di S. Petro a Solesmes." *Rassegna gregoriana* 3–4 (1906).

Handover, P. M. "British Book Typography." In *Book Typography, 1815–1965, in Europe and the United States of America,* edited by Kenneth Day, 139–174. Chicago: University of Chicago Press, 1966.

Hayburn, Robert Francis. *Papal Legislation and Sacred Music.* Collegeville, Minn.: Liturgical Press, 1979.

———. "Pope Saint Pius X and the Vatican Edition of the Chant Books." D.M.A. thesis, University of Southern California, 1964.

Hearn, M. F., ed. *The Architectual Theory of Viollet-le-Duc: Readings and Commentary.* Cambridge, Mass.: MIT Press, 1990.

Hiley, David. *Western Plainchant: A Handbook.* Oxford: Clarendon, 1993.

Hoffman, E. T. A. "The Golden Pot." In *Tales of Hoffman,* translated and edited by Christopher Lazare, 139–217. New York: A. A. Wyn, 1946.

Hucke, Helmut. "Towards a New Historical View of Gregorian Chant." *Journal of the American Musicological Society* 33 (1980): 437–467.

Huglo, Michel. "La Recherche en musicologie au XXe siècle." *Cahiers de civilization médiévale* 39 (1996): 67–84.

Hugo, Victor. "Guerre aux démolisseurs!" *Revue des deux mondes* 5, no. 5 (1832): 607–622.

Huysmans, Joris-Karl. *A rebours.* Vol. 7 of *Oeuvres complètes.* Paris: G. Cres, 1929. Translated by Havelock Ellis as *Against the Grain.* New York: Dover, 1969.

———. *En Route.* Vol. 13 (in two parts) of *Oeuvres complètes.* Paris: G. Cres, 1932. Translated by C. Kegan Paul. New York: Howard Fertig, 1976.

———. *L'Oblat.* Vol. 17 (in two parts) of *Oeuvres complètes.* Paris: G. Cres, 1934. Translated by Edward Perceval as *The Oblate.* New York: Dutton, 1924.

————. *The Road from Decadence: From Brothel to Cloister—Selected Letters of J.-K. Huysmans.* Translated by Barbara Beaument. London: Athlone, 1989.

Jaques-Dalcroze, Emile. *La Rythmique.* Lausanne: Jobin, 1918.

————. *Rhythm, Music Education.* Translated by Harold Rubenstein. New York: Putnam, 1921.

Javal, Emile. *Physiologie de la lecture et de l'écriture.* Paris: Alcan, 1906.

Jeffrey, Peter. *Re-envisioning Past Musical Cultures: Ethnomusicology in the Study of Gregorian Chant.* Chicago: University of Chicago Press, 1992.

Johnson, Cuthbert. *Prosper Guéranger (1805–1875): A Liturgical Theologian.* Roma: Pontificio S. Anselmo, 1984.

Jones, Ernest. "The Madonna's Conception Through the Ear: A Contribution to the Relation Between Aesthetics and Religion." In *Essays in Applied Psycho-analysis,* 2:266–357. London: Hogarth, 1951.

Kinross, Robin. *Modern Typography: An Essay in Critical History.* London: Hyphen, 1992.

Kittler, Friedrich. *Discourse Networks 1800/1900.* Translated by Michael Metteer. Stanford: Stanford University Press, 1990.

Klein, Richard. *Cigarettes Are Sublime.* Durham, N.C.: Duke University Press, 1993.

Lacoue-Labarthe, Philippe. *Typography: Mimesis, Philosophy, Politics.* Edited by Christopher Fynsk. Cambridge, Mass.: Harvard University Press, 1989.

Lambillotte, Louis. *Antiphonaire de Saint Grégoire: Facsimilé du manuscrit de Saint-Gall (VIIIe siècle).* Paris: Poussielgue, 1851; repr. Brussels: Greuse, 1867.

————. *Clef des mélodies grégoriennes dans les antiques systèmes de notation et de l'unité dans les chants liturgiques.* Brussels: C. J. A. Greuse, 1851.

————. *Esthétique, théorie et pratique du chant grégorien restauré d'après la doctrine des anciens et les sources primitives.* Paris: LeClere, 1855.

Lamennais, Félicité Robert de. *Des progrès de la Révolution et de la guerre contre l'église.* Paris: Belin-Mandar, 1829.

Larousse, Pierre. *Grand Dictionnaire universel du XIXe siècle.* Paris: Administration de Grand Dictionnaire Universel, 1865–1890.

Leiris, Michel. "Persephone." In *Rules of the Game,* vol. 1: *Scratches,* translated by Lydia Davis, 64–116. New York: Paragon, 1991.

Levin, Thomas Y. "For the Record: Adorno on Music in the Age of Its Technological Reproducibility." *October* 55 (winter 1990): 23–47.

Levy, Kenneth. "Charlemagne's Archetype of Gregorian Chant." *Journal of the American Musicological Society* 40 (1987): 1–30.

————. "On the Origin of Neumes." *Early Music History* 7 (1987): 59–90.

Lewis, John. *Typography: Basic Principles.* New York: Reinhold, 1964.

Liber Gradualis. Tournai: Desclée, 1883. 2d ed., Solesmes: Imprimerie de Saint-Pierre, 1895.

Liber Usualis. Solesmes: Imprimerie de Saint-Pierre, 1896. 2d ed., Tournai: Desclée, 1903.

Liebrecht, Henri, ed. *L'Histoire du livre et de l'imprimerie en Belgique des origines jusqu'à nos jours.* Vol. 3. Brussels: Musée du Livre, 1934.

Louandre, Charles. "Statistique littéraire: De la production intellectuelle en France depuis quinze ans." *Revue des deux mondes* 20, no. 2 (15 October 1847): 255–286; no. 4 (15 November 1847): 671–703.

Lussy, Matthis. *Le Rythme musicale: Son Origine, sa fonction, et son accentuation.* Paris: Fischbacher, 1884.

Maas, Paul. *Textual Criticism.* Translated by Barbara Flower. Oxford: Clarendon, 1958.

Macaulay, Rose. *Pleasure of Ruins.* London: Weidenfeld & Nicolson, 1953.

MacDougall, Robert. "The Structure of Simple Rhythmic Forms." *Harvard Psychological Studies* 1 (January 1903): 309–412.

MacErlean, A. A. "Motu Proprio." In *The Catholic Encyclopedia*, 10:602. New York: Appleton, 1911.

Maeterlinck, Maurice. *Les Trésors des humbles.* Paris: Société du Mercure de France, 1904.

McGann, Jerome. *Black Riders: The Visible Language of Modernism.* Princeton: Princeton University Press, 1993.

————. *The Textual Condition.* Princeton: Princeton University Press, 1991.

Meschonnic, Henri. *Critique du rythme.* Lagrasse: Verdier, 1982.

Mocquereau, André. "L'Ecole grégorienne de Solesmes." *Rassegna gregoriana* 3, no. 4 (April 1904): cols. 233–244; 3, nos. 5–6 (May–June 1904): cols. 313–326; 4, nos. 7–8 (July–August 1904): cols. 397–420.

————. *Examen des critiques dirigées par Dom Jeannin contre l'école de Solesmes.* Tournai: Desclée, 1926.

————. *Le Nombre musical grégorien, ou Rythmique grégorienne.* 2 vols. Rome and Tournai: Desclée, 1908–1927.

————. "La Pensée pontificale et la restauration grégorienne." *Revue grégorienne* 5 (1920): 181–189; 6 (1921): 9–18, 46–53.

Mocquereau, André, and Paul Cagin. *Plainchant and Solesmes.* London: Burns & Oates, [1905].

Montalembert, Charles. "Du vandalisme en France: Lettre à M. Victor Hugo." *Revue des deux mondes*, 2d ser., 1, no. 5 (1833): 477–524.

————. *Les Moines d'Occident depuis Saint Benoît jusqu'à Saint Bernard.* Vol. 2. Paris: Lecoffre, 1860. Published in English as *The Monks of the West: From Saint Benedict to Saint Bernard.* Edinburgh and London: William Blackwood, 1861.

Moore, Jerrold N. *A Voice in Time: The Gramophone of Fred Gaisberg.* London: Hamish Hamilton, 1976.

Morison, Stanley. *First Principles of Typography.* Cambridge: Cambridge University Press, 1936.

————. *On Type Designs Past and Present.* London: Ernest Benn, 1962.

————. *Politics and Script: Aspects of Authority and Freedom in the Development of Graeco-Latin Script from the Sixth Century b.c. to the Twentieth Century a.d.* Oxford: Clarendon, 1972.

Morison, Stanley, and Kenneth Day. *The Typographic Book, 1450–1935.* London: Ernest Benn, 1963.

Morris, William. *The Art and Craft of Printing: A Note by William Morris on His Aims in Founding the Kelmscott Press.* New Rochelle, N.Y.: Elston, 1902.

Müller, Friedrich Max. *Lectures on the Science of Language, Delivered at the Royal Institution of Great Britain in April, May, and June 1861.* New York: Scribners, 1862.

Munsterberg, Hugo. "Preface." *Harvard Psychological Studies* 1 (January 1903): i–v.

Musset, Alfred de. *La Confession d'un enfant du siècle.* Edited by Gerard Barrier. Paris: Gallimard, 1973.

Nietzsche, Friedrich. *The Case of Wagner.* Translated by Walter Kaufman. New York: Vintage, 1967.

Nisard, Théodore. *Etudes sur la restauration du chant grégorien au XIXe siècle.* Rennes: Vatar, 1856.

———. *L'Archéologie musicale et le vrai chant grégorien.* Paris: Lethielleux, 1890.

Nora, Pierre. "Between Memory and History: *Les Lieux de Mémoire.*" Translated by Marc Roudebush. *Representations* 26 (spring 1989): 7–25.

———, ed. *Les Lieux de mémoire.* 7 vols. Paris: Gallimard, 1984–1990.

"Nostro motu proprio." *Revue du chant grégorien* 12 (April 1904): 145–147.

Olender, Maurice. *The Languages of Paradise: Race, Religion, and Philology in the Nineteenth Century.* Translated by Arthur Goldhammer. Cambridge, Mass.: Harvard University Press, 1992.

Olive, Jean. "Ecriture de plain-chant." *Revue de musique religieuse et du chant grégorien* 5 (April 1896): 89–95.

Orr, Linda. *Headless History: Nineteenth-Century French Historiography of the Revolution.* Ithaca, N.Y.: Cornell University Press, 1990.

Ortigue, Joseph d'. *Dictionnaire liturgique, historique et pratique du plain-chant et de musique d'église au moyen âge et dans les temps modernes.* Paris: Migne, 1853.

Paléographie musicale. 21 vols. in 2 series. 1st ser.: Solesmes: Imprimerie de Saint-Pierre/Tournai: Société Saint-Jean l'Evangéliste, 1889–1958. 2d ser.: Tournai: Desclée, 1900–1924.

Parry, Linda, ed. *William Morris.* Exhibition catalog (Victoria and Albert Museum). London: Philip Wilson, 1996.

Parturier, Maurice, ed. *Lettres de Mérimée à Ludovic Vitet.* Paris: Plon, 1934.

Pennell, Elizabeth. *Lithography and Lithographers.* New York: Macmillan, 1915.

Pernot, Maurice. *La Politique de Pie X, 1906–1910.* Paris: F. Alcan, 1910.

Peterson, William. *The Kelmscott Press: A History of William Morris's Typographical Adventure.* Berkeley: University of California Press, 1991.

Pierrot, Jean. *The Decadent Imagination, 1880–1900.* Translated by Derek Coltman. Chicago: University of Chicago Press, 1981.

Pictet, Adolphe. *Les Origines indo-européennes; ou, les Aryas primitifs: Essai de paléontologie linguistiqe.* Paris: Sandoz & Fischbacher, 1877.

Pothier, Joseph. "Le Chant grégorien est un art." *Rassegna gregoriana* 3, nos. 5–6 (May–June 1904): cols. 325–332.

———. *Les Mélodies grégoriennes d'après la tradition.* Tournai: Desclée, 1880.

———. *Principes pour la bonne execution.* Solesmes: 1891.

Poulot, Dominique. "Alexandre Lenoir et les musées des monuments françaises." In *Les Lieux de mémoire,* vol. 2, no. 2: *La Nation,* edited by Pierre Nora, 499–531. Paris: Gallimard, 1986.

Ramstein, Matthew. *A Manual of Canon Law.* Hoboken, N.J.: Terminal, 1948.

Rancour, René, ed. *Correspondance de J.-K. Huysmans et de Madame Cécile Bruyère, abbesse de Sainte-Cécile de Solesmes.* Paris: Editions du Cendre, 1950.

Réau, Louis. *Histoire du vandalisme: Les Monuments détruits de l'art français*. Paris: Robert Laffont, 1994.

Renan, Ernest. "Les Sciences de la nature et les sciences historiques." *Revue des deux mondes* 47, no. 2 (15 October 1863): 761–774.

Rhodes, Anthony. *The Power of Rome in the Twentieth Century*. New York: Franklin Watts, 1983.

Robert, Léon. *L'Abbé Guéranger et la révolution de 1830*. Sablé: Les Amis de Solesmes, 1965.

Robinson, Duncan. *William Morris, Burne-Jones, and Kelmscott Chaucer*. London: Gordon Fraser, 1982.

Romita, Florentius. *Jus Musicae Liturgicae*. Rome: Edizioni Liturgiche, 1947.

Rosen, Charles, and Henri Zerner. *Romanticism and Realism: The Mythology of Nineteenth-Century Art*. New York: Viking, 1984.

Rousseau, Jean Jacques. *The First and Second Discourses and Essay on the Origin of Languages*. Translated by Victor Gourevitch. New York: Harper & Row, 1986.

Rousseau, Norbert. *L'Ecole grégorienne de Solesmes*. Tournai: Desclée, 1910.

Rousseau, Olivier. *Histoire du mouvement liturgique*. Paris: Editions de Cerf, 1945.

Savaton, Augustin. *Dom Delatte, abbé de Solesmes*. Sablé: Abbaye de Solesmes, 1975.

Schmidt. "La Typographie et le plain-chant." *Revue du chant grégorien* 4, no. 3 (15 October 1895): 36–39; no. 4 (15 November 1895): 59–62.

Shaman, William. "The Vatican G & T's." *Record Collector* 28, nos. 7–8 (1983): 147–191.

Simmel, Georg. "The Aesthetic Significance of the Face." Translated by Lore Furguson. In *Georg Simmel, 1858–1918*, edited by Kurt H. Wolff, 276–281. Columbus: Ohio State University Press, 1959.

———. "The Ruin." Translated by David Kettler. In *Georg Simmel, 1858–1918*, edited by Kurt H. Wolff, 259–266. Columbus: Ohio State University Press, 1959.

Society of Saint Gregory of America. *The White List*. New York: Society of Saint Gregory of America, 1947.

Soltner, Louis. *Solesmes et Dom Guéranger (1805–1875)*. Solesmes: Abbaye Saint-Pierre de Solesmes, 1974.

Sontag, Susan. *On Photography*. New York: Farrar, Straus, Giroux, 1977.

Southward, John. *Dictionary of Typography*. London: Powell, 1875.

———. *Practical Printing: A Manual of the Art of Typography*. 1882; repr. New York: Garland, 1980.

———. *Progress in Printing and the Graphic Arts*. London: Simkin, Marshall, Hamilton, Kent, 1897.

———. "Typography, Practical." In *Encyclopaedia Britannica*, 9th ed., 23:681–710. Repr. Chicago: R. S. Peale, 1892.

Spencer, Herbert. *The Visible Word*. London: Ernest Benn, 1969.

Steiner, George. *After Babel*. Oxford: Oxford University Press, 1975.

Tagg, John. *The Burden of Representation: Essays on Photographies and Histories*. Amherst, Mass.: University of Massachusetts Press, 1988.

Terdiman, Richard. *Present Past: Modernity and the Memory Crisis*. Ithaca, N.Y.: Cornell University Press, 1993.

Terry, Sir Richard. *The Music of the Roman Rite*. London: Burns, Oates & Washbourne, 1931.

Tewksbury, George E. *A Complete Manual of the Edison Phonograph.* Kent, Eng.: G. L. Frow, 1897.

Theis, Laurent. "Guizot et les institutions de mémoire." In *Les Lieux de mémoire,* vol. 2, no. 2: *La Nation,* edited by Pierre Nora, 569–592. Paris: Gallimard, 1986.

Treitler, Leo. "Centonate Chant: Übles Flickwerk or E pluribus unus?" *Journal of the American Musicological Society* 28 (1975): 1–23.

———. "The Early History of Music Writing in the West." *Journal of the American Musicological Society* 35 (1982): 237–279.

———. "From Ritual Through Language to Music." *Schweizer Jahrbuch für Musikwissenschaft* 2 (1982): 109–124.

———. "Homer and Gregory: The Epic Tradition and Plainchant." *Musical Quarterly* 15 (1974): 333–372.

———. "Oral, Written, and Literate Process in the Transmission of Medieval Music." *Speculum* 56 (1981): 471–491.

———. "Reading and Singing: On the Genesis of Occidental Music-Writing." *Early Music History* 4 (1984): 135–208.

Trésor de la langue française. 16 vols. Paris: Centre Nationale de la Recherche Scientifique, 1971–1994.

Tucker, Robert, ed. *The Marx-Engels Reader.* New York: Norton, 1978.

Updike, D. B. "A Translation of the Reports of Berlier and Sobry on Types of Gillé *Fils.*" *Fleuron* 6 (1928): 167–183.

Vermeersch, Arthur J. "Henri Desclée." In *The Catholic Encyclopedia,* 16:32–33. New York: Appleton, 1911.

Viollet-le-Duc, Eugène-Emmanuel. *Dictionnaire raisonné de l'architecture française du XIe au XVIe siècle.* 10 vols. Paris: A. Morel, 1854–1868.

———. *The Foundations of Architecture: Selections from the "Dictionnaire Raisonné."* Translated by Kenneth D. Whitehead. New York: George Braziller, 1990.

Wagner, Peter. *Der Kampf gegen die Editio Vaticana.* Pamphlet. Graz: Styria, 1907. Published in English as "The Attack on the Vatican Edition: A Rejoinder." *Caecilia* 87 (1960): 10–44.

Ward, Justine. *Gregorian Chant According to the Principles of Dom André Mocquereau.* Washington, D.C.: Catholic Education Press, 1923.

Weber, Eugen. *France: Fin de Siècle.* Cambridge, Mass.: Harvard University Press, 1986.

White, Hayden. "The Politics of Historical Interpretation: Discipline and De-sublimation." In *The Content of the Form: Narrative Discourse and Historical Representation,* 58–82. Baltimore: Johns Hopkins University Press, 1987.

Zachrisson, Bror. *Studies in the Legibility of the Printed Text.* Uppsala: Almqvist & Wiksell, 1965.

Zeitler, Julius. "Tachistoskopische Untersuchungen über das Lesen." *Philosophische Studien* 16 (1900): 380–463.

Zukovsky, Louis, ed. *An "Objectivists" Anthology.* New York: To Publishers, 1932.

Index

Moreschi, Alessandro, 133, 138

Morris, William, 31–35; compared to Pothier, 40–41, 44, 46, 48–49, 59; and photography, 77; and Emery Walker, 31

Motu proprio (Pius X), 129–30, 136, 143–46

musicology, discipine of, xiii–xiv, 92–95, 129, 142; Vatican's reaction to, 151, 155, 161

Musset, Alfred de, 4, 164n11

neumes, Gregorian: and concept of accent, 66–68, 105–7; designed by Beaudoire, 56–57, 96; designed by Pothier, 40–46, 49–50; historical importance of, 35–37, 56–57, 61–62, and memory, 81–82, 84–85; modern versions of, 37–41, 54–55; primitive, 66–72, 80–81

Nietzsche, Friedrich, 100, 115, 175n52

Nisard, Théodore, 16, 69–70, 166n40, 174n29

Nombre musical grégorien (Mocquereau), 112–19

Notker Balbulus, 123

Notre-Dame, Cathedral of, 2; nineteenth-century restoration of, 5, 7, 9, 14, 48, 76. *See also* Viollet-le-Duc

Notre-Dame de Paris (Hugo), 5

L'Oblat (Huysmans), 22–23; 44; 64

Order of Saint Benedict. *See* Benedictines

Paléographie musicale, xii, 65–69, 72–73, 79–80; compared to typographic edition, 87–91; conceived as translation, 82–85, 87; as model for musicology, 92–94, 96; Pothier's view of, 88–89, 92

Paroissien romain. See Liber Usualis

Performance, Gregorian, 16–18, 60–62, 100–105; legislation on, 130, 154, 160–61; preserved on early Gramophone recordings, 131–38. *See also* motu proprio; rhythm

philology, science of, 15, 94; and music, 93–95; and Solesmes school, 97–98; and textual criticism, 95–96; 122

photography, 65–66; 75; Morris's use of, 34; as scholarly weapon, 85–89; and the uncanny, 77–80. *See also* facsimiles; *Paléographie musicale*

Pictet, Adolphe, 94

Pius X, 129–30, 143–44, 151

Pothier, Dom Joseph, xiii–xiv; as choirmaster, 34–35, 64, 137; compared to Mocquereau, 87–89, 98–104, 111–12, 148–49; compared to Morris, 35, 40–44, 46–49, 59; compared to Viollet-le-Duc, 17–18; and Gregorian editions, 25, 35–52, 54–58, 65; *Mélodies grégoriennes,* 17–18; 46–48; preserved on Gramophone recordings, 138–40; work on Vatican edition, 146–48, 151, 153, 157

printers, 19th- and 20th-century: Babin, Dom Étienne, 53, 56, 65; Beaudoire, Théophile, 30, 44, 55–57, 96; Deman, Edmond, 45; Desclée, Henri, 45–52, 125–28, 176n73; De Vinne,

Theodore Low, 50–52; Mingardon, J., 54–56; Morison, Stanley, 29, 58–59; Morris, William, 31–35, 77; Pustet, Friedrich II, 37–39; Schmitt, Dom Antonin, 52–53, 56; Southward, John, 30; Vatar, Henri, 39–40; 50; Whittingham, Charles, 30–31

Processional monastique (Solesmes), 40–44, 71

Prou, Dom Jean, 138

Ratisbon edition (Pustet), 37–39, 65, 86, 88, 130

Renan, Ernest, 94

restoration: of Abbaye Saint-Pierre, 12–15, 20–21; defined by Commission des monuments historiques, 5–8; defined by Viollet-le-Duc, 7–9; of Gregorian chant, early history of, 15–18; Guéranger's view of, 10–11; Hugo's view of, 4–5, 9; of Notre-Dame, 5, 7, 9, 14, 48, 76. *See also* ruins

Revue de musique religieuse, 54

Revue du chant grégorien, 54–56

rhythm, Gregorian: and concept of accent, 104–8, 110, 114; and concept of arsis and thesis, 107–8, 115, 120, 175n51; freedom of, 103–4, 137, 161; Mocquereau's view on, 111–16, 118–19, 121; notation of, 116–17, 121–24, 126–29, 141, 146–47, 155–59; pedogogy of, 118–19, 120–21; Pothier's view on, 101, 107–11, 139–40; Vatican legislation of, 147, 158–60

Rolland, Romain, 95

ruins, 1; bibliographic, 24, 37, 56–58; of Catholicism, 1–3, 10–12; of chant, 17–19, 37, 56–58, 101, 123, 167n46; and concept of decay, 3–4, 8, 19, 24, 100; restoration of, 4–9, 14; as seen by Romantics, 2–3, 19, 24, 164n5. *See also* decadence; restoration

Sacred Congregation of Rites, 143, 145, 155, 158–59

Saint-Gall, monastery of. *See* manuscripts, Gregorian

Santley, Charles, 133, 176n78

Sarto, Giuseppe. *See* Pius X

Simmel, Georg, 3, 164n7

The Science of Language (Max Müller), 94

Scriptorum de Musica (Coussemaker), 40–41

Solesmes, school of, 64–65, 92–95, 97–99, 140–42, 171n7; and archaeology, 85–87, 150–53; and pedagogy of rhythm, 118–19, 137; and Vatican edition, 150–53, 161. *See also* Mocquereau

Solesmes monastery. *See* Abbaye Saint-Pierre

Solesmes monks. *See* Benedictines of Solesmes

textual criticism, 95–96, 151, 154, 173n14. *See also* philology

Tipographia Sancti Petri. *See* Abbaye Saint-Pierre, printing press in

translation: as philosophical concept, 82–85, 88

Designer: Barbara Jellow
Text: 10/13.5 Bembo
Display: Goudy Old Style
Composition, Printer, and Binder: Braun-Brumfield, Inc.